# DESIGNING INSTRUCTION FOR HUMAN FACTORS TRAINING IN AVIATION

# Designing Instruction for Human Factors Training in Aviation

Edited by
GRAHAM J.F. HUNT
*School of Aviation*
*Massey University*

Aldershot • Brookfield USA • Hong Kong • Singapore • Sydney

© Graham J.F. Hunt 1997

All rights reserved. No part of this publication may be reproduced, stored in a retrieval system, or transmitted in any form or by any means, electronic, mechanical, photocopying, recording, or otherwise without the prior permission of the publisher.

Published by
Avebury
Ashgate Publishing Limited
Gower House
Croft Road
Aldershot
Hants GU11 3HR
England

Ashgate Publishing Company
Old Post Road
Brookfield
Vermont 05036
USA

**British Library Cataloguing in Publication Data**
Hunt, Graham J.F.
    Designing instruction for human factors training in aviation
    1. Aeronautics - Human factors 2. Aeronautics - Study and teaching
    I. Title
    629.1'3252

**Library of Congress Catalog Card Number:** 96-79122

ISBN 0 291 39800 6

Printed and bound in Great Britain by
Biddles Limited, Guildford and King's Lynn

# Contents

*List of figures* vii

*List of tables* x

*List of contributors* xi

*Preface* xvi

**Instruction and evaluation** 1

1. Instruction and evaluation: Design principles in instructional design
   *Graham J. F. Hunt* 3
2. Influences on the learning process and learning outcome: Practical implications for the instructor
   *Lynn M. Hunt* 17
3. Management of instruction and assessment in aviation
   *Andrew S. Gibbons, A. F. O'Neal and Peter G. Fairweather* 28

**Simulation and computer-based learning** 45

4. Design requirements for computer-based learning systems for aircraft manufacturers
   *A.F. O'Neal* 47
5. Simulation as an instructional procedure
   *Richard Macfarlane* 59
6. Object technology and simulation life-cycle costs
   *Peter G. Fairweather* 94

| 7 | Evaluators and extended feedback models in aviation CBT  
*Andrew S. Gibbons* | 104 |

## Human factors instruction - airlines — 115

| 8 | Human factors training in airlines  
*Ross Telfer, John Bent and Norm Dowd* | 117 |
| 9 | Teaching human factors for airline operations  
*Neil Johnston* | 127 |
| 10 | The university airline internship programme: Educational entrance to professional airline employment  
*Graham J.F. Hunt* | 161 |

## Human factors instruction - air traffic control — 171

| 11 | Teaching human factors for air traffic control  
*V. David Hopkin* | 173 |
| 12 | Evaluating standards in air traffic operations and training  
*Rod Baldwin* | 205 |
| 13 | Teaching for visualizing in air traffic control  
*Anne R. Isaac* | 226 |

## Human factors instruction - aviation medicine — 237

| 14 | Teaching - aviation medicine  
*Robin Griffiths* | 239 |

## Human factors instruction - some specific applications — 255

| 15 | Training accident investigators for the human factors investigation  
*Dmitri V. Zotov* | 257 |
| 16 | Human factors in Chinese civil aviation training  
*Liu Hanhui* | 272 |
| 17 | Assessing human factors in primary aviation  
*Stanley R. Trollip* | 279 |

*Author index* — 305

*Subject Index* — 309

# List of figures

| | | |
|---|---|---|
| Figure 1.1 | Knowledge structure hierarchy | 8 |
| Figure 1.2 | Organizationally determined differentiated missions | 9 |
| Figure 1.3 | Components of a competency specification | 11 |
| Figure 1.4 | Example of a competency specification | 12 |
| Figure 1.5 | Interaction of content and information processing for test specifications | 14 |
| Figure 2.1 | The learning process | 18 |
| Figure 2.2 | A comparison of processing, learning and knowledge levels | 21 |
| Figure 3.1 | The varied structure of a system for performance support and training | 40 |
| Figure 5.1 | An example of a basic instrument trainer: The Frasca 141 | 60 |
| Figure 5.2 | The motion system hardware for Air New Zealand's DC10 simulator | 62 |
| Figure 5.3 | There's nothing like the real thing | 63 |
| Figure 5.4 | Relationship between simulator fidelity flight crew skill | 64 |
| Figure 5.5 | First year students utilizing desktop PC's at the elementary stage | 65 |
| Figure 5.6 | Third year students utilizing Boeing 737-300's simulator for their type conversion | 65 |
| Figure 5.7 | Type specific capabilities for WLG - AKL sortie | 66 |
| Figure 5.8 | Advanced training device capabilities for WLG - AKL sortie | 67 |
| Figure 5.9 | Advanced training device from Hawker De Havilland | 68 |

| | | |
|---|---|---|
| Figure 5.10 | What do you really want in a simulator? | 71 |
| Figure 5.11 | Instructor-induced motivation | 73 |
| Figure 5.12 | Is it really worth it? | 75 |
| Figure 5.13 | Let's take it from the beginning ... | 82 |
| Figure 5.14 | Horses for courses - part tasking visual approach in an ATD | 84 |
| Figure 5.15 | Engineering CBT prior to type conversion | 85 |
| Figure 5.16 | The syllabus, training and testing inter-relationship | 86 |
| Figure 5.17 | Just testing! | 88 |
| Figure 6.1 | The trip from real to simulated | 96 |
| Figure 6.2 | Encapsulation produces boundaries | 96 |
| Figure 6.3 | How encapsulation yields value | 97 |
| Figure 6.4 | Outside-in zone development | 100 |
| Figure 6.5 | Possible composition of a procedure object | 101 |
| Figure 6.6 | Abstract anatomy of a production rule and a simple example | 102 |
| Figure 9.1 | From Brown, Collins and Duguid (1989) | 137 |
| Figure 9.2 | Summary of CTA, expertise and situated learning | 141 |
| Figure 9.3 | The experiential learning cycle (from Johnston, 1993b) | 145 |
| Figure 9.4 | Training analysis, development & implementation - summary framework | 154 |
| Figure 10.1 | Way points in Airline Internship Programme | 163 |
| Figure 10.2 | Comparison of direct entry ab initio to airline pilots at 1500 hours criterion with a jet first officer rating | 167 |
| Figure 10.3 | Assessment of overall quality of B737-400 flight performance | 169 |
| Figure 12.1 | Stages involved in evaluating standards | 207 |
| Figure 12.2 | Performance checking | 210 |
| Figure 12.3 | Checking the standards of operational controllers | 213 |
| Figure 13.1 | Imagery and visualization as a PROACTIVE system | 228 |
| Figure 17.1 | Evaluation checklist for stress | 289 |
| Figure 17.2 | Evaluation checklist for workload management | 291 |
| Figure 17.3 | Evaluation checklist for situational awareness | 292 |
| Figure 17.4 | Evaluation checklist for decision making and judgement | 294 |
| Figure 17.5 | Evaluation checklist for background information | 295 |
| Figure 17.6 | Evaluation checklist for the brain | 296 |
| Figure 17.7 | Evaluation checklist for the body | 297 |
| Figure 17.8 | Evaluation checklist for the eyes | 298 |
| Figure 17.9 | Evaluation checklist for the ears | 299 |
| Figure 17.10 | Evaluation checklist for cockpit resource management | 300 |

Figure 17.11 Evaluation checklist for good flying practices
Self- assessment                                            301

# List of tables

| | | |
|---|---|---|
| Table 2.1 | Task representations | 19 |
| Table 9.1 | Comparison of CTA and traditional methods | 138 |
| Table 9.2 | Training framework | 150 |
| Table 15.1 | Elements of Human Factors training for air accident investigators | 262 |

# List of contributors

**Dr Rod Baldwin** commenced his career as an electronic and communications engineer. After some years in industry and as a University lecturer, he moved into the aviation field with International Aeradio Limited now Serco-IAL, and was for six years Principle of their ATC Training Centre, Bailbrook College. This was followed by five years as Director of the Eurocontrol Institute of Air Navigation Services. Dr Baldwin is now Managing Director of his own company, Baldwin International Services, which provides comprehensive consultancy services for civil aviation authorities, international agencies, airlines, airports, air navigation services.

**Captain John Bent** is a senior training captain and Flying Training Manager (Policy) for Cathay Pacific Airways in Hong Kong. He is the co-designer and manager of a new workshop for Air Force aircrew and three airlines. His training experience has included military flying instruction, management of a flying school in Germany, and development of a new multicultural pre-school and primary school in Hong Kong. The last half of his sixteen years with Cathy Pacific has been in the check and training department. He is now engaged in the development of future flight training programs for the airline. More recently he was responsible for developing the training programme to introduce the A330/A340 fleet to Cathay Pacific.

**Peter G. Fairweather** is the Senior Manager of education research at the IBM T.J. Watson Research Centre in Yorktown Heights, NY, USA. Dr Fairweather works in cognitive tutoring, assessment tools, and collaborative learning. Beginning with problems of machine simulation of comprehension to shed light on how people understand what they read, he moved to the development of computer-based training and simulation systems and the authoring tools needed to put them together. Along the way, he developed several courseware offerings in reading and mathematics for Science Research Associates, IBM, WICAT Systems, and Jostens Learning Corporation, where he was Vice-President for Instructional Systems Design.

**Dr Andrew S. Gibbons** designs instructional systems, computer-based instruction and simulations, and tools for instructional designers. His experience combines eighteen years of industry experience at Wicat Systems, Inc. and Courseware, Inc. in product development for both training and school use with academic interests in instructional strategy, simulations, and high-volume production of computer-based instruction. Dr. Gibbons is preparing a book for publication this year on the design of computer-based instruction. His experience includes project management for numerous large and small development projects, multimedia development, applied research, innovative design projects, and consulting with government organizations and businesses entering the computer-based instruction world.

**Dr Robin Griffiths** is a medical specialist with particular interest in aviation medicine education. He is an associate lecturer in aviation medicine at both Massey and Otago Universities, and academic co-ordinator of the Postgraduate Diploma in Aviation Medicine taught in Australasia, SE Asia and SW Pacific. He is also medical adviser to the Transport Accident Investigation Commission and Chairman of the NZ Aviation Medicine Review Board. He is also a public health/occupational medicine specialist, working as senior medical adviser to the National Health Committee. Robin was a lecturer in aviation medicine in the RAF from 1982-1984, and Chief Medical Officer of the NZ Ministry of Transport 1984- 1989.

**Dr Liu Hanhui** is an Advisor on aviation safety to CAAC and Vice President of Civil Aviation Institute of China, also a professor the Navigation Department and the director of Civil Aviation Safety Scientific Research Institute of the CAIC.

Before joining CAIC in June 1980, Dr Liu served at the Flight College of CAAC as an academic training teacher for more than twenty years. Dr Liu is a graduate of the Beijing Aeronautical Institute and received a Master Degree in Flight Mechanics. In 1984, he went to the United Kingdom and studied at Queen Mary College as a visiting scholar, and received a Doctorate Degree in philosophy from the University of London. Following his doctoral studies he began a series of research on the influences of atmosphere turbulence and low level wind shear on aircraft, and the system safety of civil aviation. Now Dr Liu is an expert on aviation safety and human factors in China.

**Professor Graham J.F. Hunt** is the Head of the School of Aviation at Massey University. After completing a Master's degree, Professor Hunt joined the Royal New Zealand Air Force as an Instructional Psychologist, involved in the research and development of new training and selection methods for air force pilots. Dr Hunt is the foundation professor of aviation at Massey University. He has extensively researched the nature of professional flight crew licences and has applied much of this knowledge to Massey University's flight crew development programme. He is a member of the International Civil Aviation Organisation's Human Factor's group, and is an editor of the International Journal of Aviation Psychology. He lecturers extensively internationally on human factors and aviation human resource development

**Dr Lynn M. Hunt,** is the Director for Reseach & International Programmes at Massey University's School of Aviation where she has taught since its inception in 1990. She has a Ph.D degree in instructional psychology from Massey University, and first and second degrees from Victoria University Wellington and Massey University. Her research interest is in the identification and application of cognitive learning strategies. She has examined these in the context of ab initio pilot training, business studies and engineering. She is currently involved in a series of research projects which include curriculum development for airline flight training in Indonesia, instructional pre-requisites for low time students in transitional full-flight simulator training and an examination of the effects of anxiety on ab initio flight training.

**Mr V. David Hopkin,** M.A., C. Psychol., F.R.I.N. Independent Human Factors Consultant. Formerly Full-time Human Factors Consultant to the United Kingdom Civil Aviation Authority, Senior Principal Psychologist at the Royal Air Force Institute of Aviation Medicine, Farnborough.
Consultancy work for ICAO, NATO, Eurocontrol, FAA, and numerous other international and national organizations and firms; lectured very

extensively, and now teaches regularly at Embry-Riddle Aeronautical University in Florida.

Over 300 referred publications. Author or editor of 8 textbooks. A recent publication is: V. David Hopkin (1995) "Human Factors in Air Traffic Control", London: Taylor and Francis.

**Dr Anne R. Isaac** is a lecturer at the School of Aviation, Massey University, New Zealand. She holds an undergraduate degree and masterate in human performance, a PhD in neuropsychology and a post-graduate qualification in ergonomics.

Anne has specialized in visual cognition and human performance and most recently has concentrated on mental imagery and situational awareness in the air traffic control (ATC) environment.

She has been instrumental in developing human factors training and research in the NZ ATC system and has been invited to investigate issues in Australian en-route centres.

**Captain Neil Johnston** is an A330 pilot with Aer Lingus. He is a Research Fellow of Trinity College Dublin and was Visiting Scientist at the E.C. Joint Research Centre in 1994. He is a former chairman of the IFALPA Medical and Human Performance Study Groups and of the IATA Human Factors Working Group.

Captain Johnston is an Associate Editor of the *International Journal of Aviation Psychology* and has published many papers and book chapters on pilot training, accident investigation, human factors, cockpit automation and allied issues. He was an Editor of *"Aviation Psychology in Practice"* and one of the authors of *"Beyond Aviation Human Factors"*.

**Mr Richard Macfarlane** is a lecturer in Navigation Systems and Human Factors at the School of Aviation, Massey University, New Zealand. He spent the first part of his professional life as a navigator in the Royal Australian Air Force and has approximately 4000 hours on both operational and training squadrons. He is also a pilot and flight instructor with some 2000 hours and his research interests encompass the application of modern navigation systems, flight instruction and testing methods, and the human factor skills associated with these two areas.

**Dr A.F. O'Neal** has been active in computer-based instruction and training since he founded and directed the Kansas City Public Schools computer-assisted instruction activity in 1966. He finished a Ph.D in instructional design while working on the NSF computer-based learning 'TICCIT' project at Brigham Young University in 1977.

He has served as Technical Director and Director of Computer Applications for Courseware, Inc., Technical Director and Director of Adult Basic Education for Wicat systems, Director of Instructional Design, Adult Basic Education Division, Jostens Learning, President of Island MultiMedia, Vice President of R&D for Performx, Inc and is currently Senior Principal Analyst for JIL Information Systems, Inc. Since 1966 he has been continually involved in innovative applications of emerging technologies to training and educational problems in military, industrial and educational settings, with special emphasis on aviation, telecommunications and medical training.

**Dr Ross Telfer** was the foundation Professor and Head of the Department of Aviation at the University of Newcastle, Australia, where Australia's first University degree in aviation is offered. He is the author/co-author of seven books, including *The Psychology of Flight Training* (Iowa State University, 1988). He was the principal researcher of the Australian study of pilot judgement training, has worked with airlines on training methods, and currently is examining how pilots learn and optimal ways of instructing them. He is now an aviation consultant.

**Dr Stanley R. Trollip** was born in South Africa and went to the United States to undertake his post graduate studies at the University of Illinois. After receiving his PhD in aviation psychology he taught at the University of Minnesota and then the University of North Dakota were he was employed as an instructional designer at that University's Aviation Spectrum programme. More recently Dr Trollip has been a principal of a consulting group in Minnesota specializing in instructional design and development of computer based delivery systems. He is the author of a number of texts in instructional design and aviation human factors. In addition, he holds a Commercial Pilot Licence and flight instructor ratings.

**Mr Dmitri V. Zotov** graduated from the Royal Air Force College, Cranwell, and served in the RAF for 18 years. He was involved with the HS Nimrod trials at Boscombe Down, and was awarded the MBE on the successful completion of those trials. He returned to a flying career in New Zealand, before becoming an Inspector of Air Accidents, and is now an associate lecturer in Air Safety Investigation at the Massey University School of Aviation.

# Preface

There is now little debate over the need for human factors training in aviation. The bi-annual *International Symposium on Aviation Psychology* convened by Dr Richard Jensen at the Ohio State University since 1981 and the *three ICAO Global Flight Safety and Human Factors Symposia* (1990 (Leningrad); 1993 (Washington, D.C.); and 1996 (Auckland)) organized by Captain Daniel Maurino have significantly contributed to a universal recognition that human factors is a critical component in flight, air traffic, maintenance, engineering and organizational safety in aviation. Justifying human factors is not at issue.

The seminal issue of this book is not *whether* to teach human factors, but *how* to teach it. The objective of the project was to develop an instructional resource for people who had responsibilities for designing, teaching or evaluating human factor issues in aviation training and educational programs. With the mandated requirement by most regulatory authorities for human factors in flight crew licensing, an increasing concern of those who a required to deliver this content is how to maximize the effectiveness of human factors training to enhance safety. This book brings together a range of insights and experiences structured to follow the instructional process from the initial design principles and underlying theories, through the use of technology for teaching, the specific needs of groups such as air traffic controllers and air accident investigators to assessment procedures.

Despite the diverse backgrounds of the contributors a number of recurring themes flow through the book. The first of these is the need for competency-based skills that have practical value in the workplace. The first chapter discusses a methodology for competency identification using proven needs assessment tools. David Hopkins continues the theme by specifying crucial or difficult to teach human factor skills for air traffic controllers, and suggesting ways in which these might be conveyed during training. At a more specific level of application, Anne Isaac stresses the importance of visualizing by air traffic controllers and describes the manner in which this skill might be inculcated in trainees. Finally, Rob Griffiths delineates the boundaries of responsibility between various specialists in aviation medicine. He suggests that each specialization would benefit from a slightly different emphasis and focus in their medical training depending on their ultimate purpose.

A second clearly identifiable theme relates to the importance of context to training effectiveness. Lynn Hunt in a previous study confirmed an increasingly recognized finding that the nature of the task should influence the manner in which instruction should be modified in order to achieve task related competency. In her chapter she applies this finding by describing the effect of the learning task context on the student's approach to learning and upon the eventual quality of the learning outcome. The importance of context is picked up by Gibbons, O'Neal and Fairweather who promote techniques to situate learning in the context in which it will be used. The Johnston chapter continues the theme in a discussion on the limitations of traditional teaching. Neil Johnston overviews the current state of educational psychology and draws together several threads to underpin his HARI model of training in aviation, the heart of which is situated learning. A practical working example of situated learning is described in Graham Hunt's chapter on his airline internship programme. This chapter describes the process of setting up such a venture and the benefits that accrue to all the stakeholders involved. Finally, Stan Trollip proposes a series of checklists to assess human factor knowledge and skills in the context in which they are used, that is as a regular part of their flying activities.

A third theme can be found in the rising importance of technology as a powerful tool for implementing the new ideas emerging from instructional psychology. Fred O'Neal, Griffiths and Peter Fairweather describe the difficulties and advances in the development of software for creating computer learning environments capable of replicating operational contexts but, with the added bonus of tracking and profiling student performance. These applications provide instructional staff with more detailed and diagnostic information than ever before. Richard Macfarlane draws out the important distinction between instructional fidelity versus task (aircraft) fidelity in flight simulation. His argument that regulators and simulator manufacturers may have emphasized the latter to the expense of the former holds important consequences for the acquisition of new skills, particularly for students with low time operational experience.

When human factors was first identified as an issue the focus of attention was Western flight crews. An excellent example of a programme in this more traditional application is described in the chapter by Telfer, Bent and Dowd. However, a fourth identifiable theme in this book is the spread of human factors training to other aviation domains. Baldwin addresses human factors in air traffic control. Zotov describes how human factors training might be made more acceptable to experienced accident investigators with no prior training in this field; and Lui Hanhui describes how the Republic of China seeks to adapt a Western concept of human factors to suit an Eastern culture.

Historically, this book may be viewed as one of the first texts which began the process of examining ways of structuring instructional methods and conditions conducive to inculcating human factor behaviors in operational personnel. Although it has to be conceded that that the state of our knowledge in the instructional design, delivery and evaluation of human factors remains essentially an arts-based practice, the goal of acquiring scientifically determined principles in human factors instruction must be preeminent. This book is a first step in that direction.

Finally, I would like to declare my indebtedness to many people for bringing this project to its fruition. Firstly, to the 15 contributors without whom there would not have been a book. Secondly, to the editorial assistance I have had from Lynn Hunt in working with many of the contributors and their papers. However, any mistakes or misinterpretations that may have found their way into the book are mine and not hers. Thirdly, to Janet Lowe who has tirelessly word processed the material and put off delivering her baby until the project was complete! Last, but not the least, to John Hindley of Ashgate who never gave up on the project when lesser mortals might well have. To all these people, and others, thank you.

Graham J.F. Hunt
Palmerston North
September, 1996

# Instruction and evaluation

# 1 Instruction and evaluation: Design principles in instructional design

*Graham J.F. Hunt*

**Introduction**

Human factors education and training has become a major concern in aviation, especially since the International Civil Aviation Organization (ICAO) adopted resolution A26-9 on Flight Safety and Human Factors at its 1989 Assembly. As a follow-up to the resolution the Air Navigation Commission formulated the following objective for the task

> To improve the safety in aviation by making States more aware and responsive to the importance of human factors in civil aviation operations through the provision of practical human factors material and measures developed on the basis of experience in States. (ICAO, 1989).

The ICAO has described human factors as a concept of people in their living and working situations; about their relationship with machines, with procedures and with the environment about them; and also about their relationships with other people. In aviation, human factors involves a set of personal, medical and biological considerations for optimal aircraft and air traffic control operations (ICAO,1989). McCormick and Sanders (1983) have attempted to define human factors more generically by means of suggesting a set of three interrelated dimensions which they have labelled the 'focus', 'objectives' and 'approach' of human factors.

- *Focus* relates to the: (1) design and creation of human-made objects, products, equipment, facilities and environments that people use; (2) the development of procedures for carrying out tasks and work; (3) the provision of services to people; and (4) the evaluation of the things people use in terms of their suitability for people.

- The *objectives* of human factors relates to two functions: (1) enhancing the effectiveness and efficiency with which work and other activities is carried out by people; (2) maintaining and enhancing certain desirable human values such as safety, health, aesthetic value, etc.

- The main *approach* of human factors is the systematic application of relevant information about human abilities, characteristics, behaviour (psycho-social) and motivation, and communication patterns in the execution of work and social interactions.

There is a growing library of written material on the nature of human factors. Most of it relates to the interface of human factor issues with flight crew performance. Slowly, more material is becoming available about human factor applications to air traffic systems management, and still all too sparingly, its application to aviation maintenance engineering and corporate management. This book does not seek to replicate the literature that already exists. Its primary focus is on *how* the knowledge and skills extent about human factors can be communicated through education and training to the trainers and trainees in the various contexts of the aviation system. That does not mean to say that the book will not address human factor issues *per se*, it will. But the primary focus will be on how this important dimension of behaviour can be more effectively inculcated in the operational and training environments of aviation.

Instruction is defined as the critical process of *creating learning*. Traditionally, the term, has meant different things to different people. In the context of this book, we use it to mean the design and use of conditions and strategies which are prerequisite to the effective creation of learning in students. These conditions and strategies are part of the discipline now known as *instructional psychology*. Students are defined as individuals or groups of people brought together for the specific purpose of acquiring predefined competencies. These variables are examined from the standpoint of the question, 'how can I better teach these principles (eg., skills to enhance better crew coordination) in *this* particular training context' (eg., *ab initio* flight crew development)? In order to answer the question, there are a number of sub-questions which implicitly, or explicitly need to be in the mind of the instructional developer. They include:

- understanding the *instructional conditions* involved in the delivery of the instruction;
- improving *methods* for delivering the instruction;
- *implementing* the instruction in a training or educational context; and
- *evaluating* the effectiveness that *the outcomes* of instruction have had on individual and group performance.

Let's comment briefly on these terms. Instructional 'conditions' are defined as those factors which influence the effectiveness of an instructional method. In some situations conditions may refer to constraints imposed on the 'resources' for delivering the instruction (limited visual displays in a part task training device). In another situation conditions may refer to a 'learner characteristic' which might directly influence the way in which learning is likely to occur (eg., high state anxiety in the context of pre-solo flight training). Instructional 'methods' are the different ways in which learning outcomes can be achieved (eg., computer-based learning). Implementing instruction refers to the way in which the instructional resources are managed, including the human resources, physical resources, and time-based resources. 'Outcomes' refer to the ultimate demonstrable performances, capable of measurement and from which inferences may be drawn as to the qualitative effects the methods and conditions have had.

In designing an instructional programme, one does not simply apply a learning theory (such as behavioural learning) to an instructional situation. Instead, one must *formulate* a theory of instruction which is as Bruner (1966) has said is 'congruent with those theories of learning and development to which it subscribes'. Unlike theories of learning, which merely *describe* what happened after the learning event, theories of instruction must not only describe, but *prescribe* the methods and strategies for individuals so that learning outcomes can be guaranteed. How this might be done is still subject to debate and understanding. As early as 1966 Bruner believed that instructional theory should specify:

- Ways of encouraging the student to learn.
- Ways of structuring knowledge to enhance student learning.

- Ways of sequencing instructional material in order to reduce learning difficulty.

- Ways of providing reinforcement or punishment in the process of instructing.

This information for instructional systems development is quite different from the kind of knowledge which underlies an understanding of a learning theory. This knowledge is primarily concerned with *diagnosing* and *prescribing* the best way for a student to represent a problem in a given situation and the techniques or methods that can be used to help him or her represent the problem in the most appropriate manner. To achieve this, instructional design issues can be translated into three decision making requirements:

- The goal or purpose of instruction (not to be confused with instructional objectives). Decisions relating to this requirement may include an analysis of the specific competencies to be taught (we will examine this in a moment when we look at the *knowledge hierarchy* model of instructional design); the identification of requisite learner characteristics (eg., anxiety, achievement motivation, cognitive style, etc.); and particular elaborative instructional strategies which may need to be developed in order to address the characteristics.

- The situation as it presently exists - including the way in which a student currently demonstrates his or her understanding of the knowledge to be learned; the available instructional resources; and the wider social dynamics of the situation.

- The alternatives available for creating learning - especially the relationship between instructional characteristics (eg., the nature of a graphic presentation, colour) and the psychological processes (eg., attending, perceiving, decision making).

## A model of instruction - knowledge structures hierarchy

Analyses of requisite pilot performance have traditionally been derived from observations of flying skills ('stick and rudder') and the individual's knowledge of flight rules and procedures. When these dimensions have been translated into predictive indices, no more than about 25 percent of the variance of performance at advanced stages of competency have been accounted for (Roscoe and North, 1980). However, as these researchers noted, despite the prediction problem, flight crew were able to identify 'abilities' such as *estimating* probable outcomes for different courses of action, or *attending* to *resolving* an emergency without losing control of the on going routine procedures. The trick in developing a map of pilot competency is to be able to relate these types of requisite abilities to contextual applications. For instance, consider the abilities involved in executing a landing. At least two are critical: 'assessing' the relative position of the aircraft in relation to the ground; and 'perceiving' the changes in the shape of the runway in relation to reducing height. A description of this interactive process of *ability* and *context* might be provided in an instruction to a trainee pilot such as:

> You will recognize the flare height when the runway appears to expand rapidly outwards. Use this view as the cue for assessing the moment at which you need to flare.

In this example, the identification of each 'ability' assumes a larger, more integrative knowledge base from which it has been derived. In a knowledge structures hierarchy model of instruction for pilot competency, this assumption is structured in a top down, three-level knowledge structure hierarchy (figure 1) of increasingly specific capacities to process knowledge. This method developed by Hunt (1986), provides a procedure for mapping abilities in a manner in which interactive specifications of human competency can be prescribed for instruction and evaluation purposes.

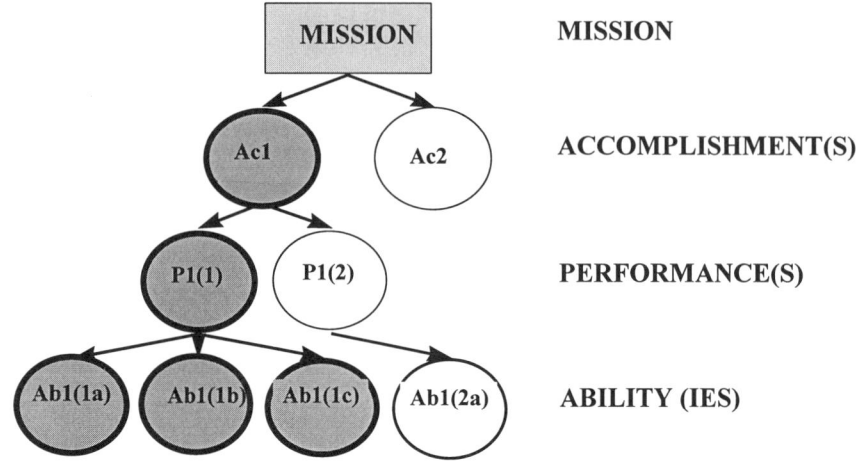

**Figure 1.1  Knowledge structure hierarchy**

At the apex of the hierarchy is what might be described as the 'macro' mission or overriding goal (figure 2) for the endeavours. This is the purpose to which all the accumulating activities are directed. The macro mission statement claims its validity from the degree to which all participants within the mission's purview can agree to its value and usefulness in providing direction and purpose. In civil aviation an acceptable mission might be the 'safe and effective operation of civil air transportation'. Macro mission statements such as this can be further defined by more 'micro' mission statements to reflect the specific goals and purposes of the increasingly differentiated organizational entities within the system. For example, in civil aviation an airline might define its micro mission as 'managing and operating an air services company, both nationally and internationally, in a manner which maximizes safety, efficiency and profitability and achieves a level of market share which is acceptable to the majority shareholders'. These micro mission statements provide goal directed purpose for identifiable sectors within the industry; aviation regulators; air traffic controllers, airline operators; aircraft manufacturers; travel and tourist operators; airport managers and administrators; flight crews; cabin crews; aircraft maintenance engineers; and passenger service personnel. Each of these groups must in turn translate the macro based statement into sector mission statements giving specific focus and direction. For an airline's flight operations, its micro mission might be 'to operate and maintain scheduled aircraft services which maximize safety and efficiency and enhances passenger and customer satisfaction.' In this statement implicit reference is being made to a number of pre-requisite capabilities. Such a micro mission could not be achieved without the prior attainment of the organization's ability to be 'accomplished' or highly competent in the complex behaviours which make up the knowledge and skills which underlie flight standards and flight operations management, command, and the management of other technical sub systems.

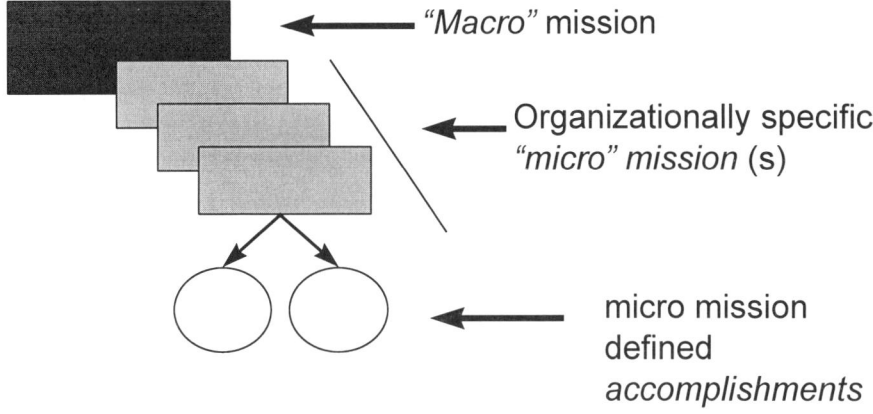

**Figure 1.2  Organizationally determined differentiated missions**

The level beneath the mission provides individual elaborations of the goal's directives. These elaborations or 'accomplishments' are the broad functional capabilities which contribute to personal expertise. They can be defined as a job-related knowledge base. The knowledge base is stored in, and retrieved from, long-term memory. For example, the flight crew accomplishment of 'command' defines a capacity to exercise formal, legal power and authority over aircraft crew and passengers, and to establish and maintain the effective and efficient management of crew performance.

Each accomplishment is in turn defined by two or more 'performances'. A performance is a procedurally based group of intellectual skills which summarize 'knowing how' to do a major aspect of the job as identified by the accomplishment. This entity is an application of the concept developed by Newall and Simon (1972) who propounded the notion of a cognitive entity as a *production,* which entered into more complex *production systems.* Such an entity comprised a rule of procedural knowledge composed of a *condition* and *action* (Gagné & Glaser, 1987). In this knowledge structures hierarchy model, performances provide the intellectual skill definitions related to individual accomplishments. One performance (for example 'making in-flight adjustments') may, with other performances, provide the particular characteristic of a given accomplishment (say, 'aircraft performance management'). That performance, in a different constellation of performances, will provide the construct for another accomplishment (for example, 'navigation management'). Competency analyses of flight crew behaviour (Crook & Hunt, 1988) have identified that the 'command' accomplishment can be defined by six performances, each one providing a subordinate contribution to its dependent accomplishment. These performances have been identified as 'captain supervising', 'pilot managing', 'managing critical incidents', and 'managing crew interactions'.

The base of the hierarchy is provided by the specific *abilities* which define each of their superordinate performances. These abilities are the individual cognitive, affective (attitude), attribute (personality and motivation) or practical skills which can be taught or shaped through learning and education. For example, from the accomplishment of 'command management' and its performance, 'crew interacting', specific cognitive abilities may include included 'assessing', 'monitoring' and 'decision making', with an affective ability of an 'accepting attitude', and an attributional ability of a 'high need to achieve'.

**Competency specification**

In instructional design a competency specification provides the planning structure for analyzing the specific interactions of an accomplishment, performance and abilities within the context of a specific job (figure 3). In a competency specification, the analyzed knowledge structure is seen as fixed or 'constant' to which unlimited task-related exemplars may be generated. Each knowledge structure is derived through needs assessment processes involving the analyses of expert performances. They are the job's generic knowledge base. On the other hand, the *specific task context* in which the knowledge or attitudes are to be applied are quite variable. Change the aircraft type, or the technical system and the way in which the previously learnt knowledge will be used will be different. The generic nature of the knowledge, or attitude will however, remain unchanged.

Instruction and Evaluation: Design Principles in Instructional Design

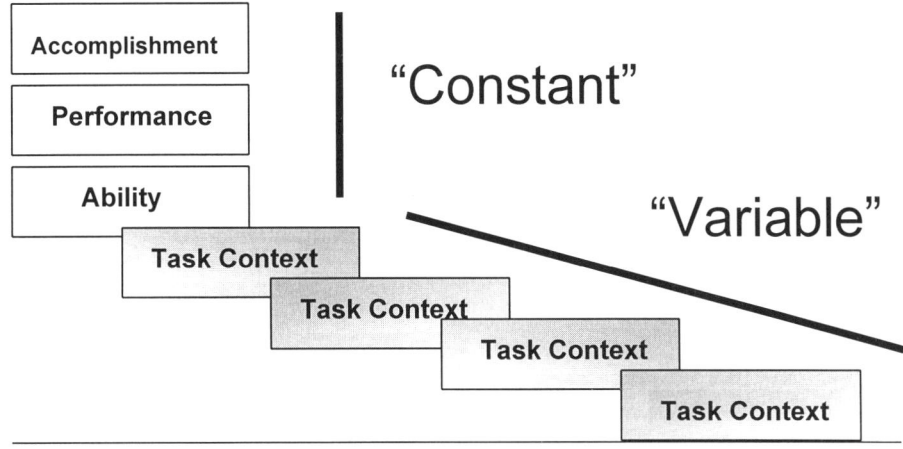

**Figure 1.3  Components of a competency specification**

The value of this model for instructional design is considerable. It provides educators, trainers and licensing examiners with an objective means of defining, prioritizing, instructing and evaluating individual and group competencies. For example (figure 3), in a flight crew competency specification which focuses on the accomplishment 'command management', and the performance 'pilot managing', an instructional assessment of a particular crew resource training application might be:

Given busy radio/telephone traffic, including the issuance of amended descent profiles, the First Officer is required to brief the air crew on arrival and approach procedures in accordance with the airlines standard operating procedures. The Captain will assess the appropriateness of the plan and the alternatives which have been suggested to cope with a shortened visual approach or emergency. The Captain will decide on which strategy is best.

## Competency Specification

| Accomplishment | Command |
|---|---|
| Performance | Pilot Managing |
| Abilities | Oral Communicating;  Active listening<br>Assessing;  Decision Making |

**Task Context**

Given busy radio/telephone traffic, including the issuance of amended descent profiles, the FO is required to brief air crew on arrival and approach procedures in accordance with airline's SOP's. The Captain assesses appropriateness of plan and alternatives which have been suggested to cope with shortened visual approach or emergency. The Captain will decide on which strategy is best.

**Figure 1.4   Example of a competency specification**

In this example, the performance of pilot managing is being examined through the interactive application of the abilities of such as 'speaking' (oral communicating), 'active listening' (being able to critically listen for relevant information) 'assessing' (determining relevant environmental and interpersonal conditions), and 'decision making' (choosing the best of competing alternatives). Cognitive and affective skills are embedded in the overall mastery of the accomplishment.

## What is the relationship between instruction and evaluation?

- In this chapter we have been using the term 'instruction' to mean any intentional activity that an instructor (academic lecturer, ground instructor, flight or simulator instructor, etc.) consciously uses in order to move students towards the attainment of specified goals (instructional objectives, flight standards, etc.). As Gronlund and Linn (1990) state, in order to achieve these goals there are a number of instructional decisions which require some type of measurement data if they are to be resolved. In aviation training, answers to the following types of questions are particularly important.

- How realistic is this course of training for this candidate? (Pilot aptitude tests in relation to *ab initio* training; command readiness in relation to command training, etc).

- What content areas are already known by the candidate, and therefore do not require further teaching? For example, what tests should be used or developed to measure previously learned or acquired knowledge, attitudes, attributes, and skills which already exists in the students repertoire of behaviour?

- What are the minimum knowledge, skills, attributes or attitudes which must be known before the candidate can proceed to the next stage of learning? (mastery or progress tests).

- What kinds of learning difficulties is the candidate experiencing? (diagnostic tests, learning strategy tests, observations tests).

- What are effective measures of final competency for the candidate? (achievement tests, attitude tests attribute tests, performance-based observation tests, etc).

- How can instructors improve the quality and effectiveness of their instruction? (achievement tests, students' ratings, supervisors' ratings).

**Instructional tests**

The ultimate purpose of developing instructional interventions is to affect human behaviour. We do this by designing courses and developing delivery methods (computer-based instruction; interactive internet systems, etc.) which enable learners to master the competencies identified. However, only when some assessment has been made of that behaviour will quantitative and qualitative conclusions be able to be made about the interventions.

The basic rationale behind instructional tests is that the instructional designer's mission is to make beneficial changes in the learners ability to become accomplished in some identifiable area of human endeavour. This entails providing a learning environment through which the student may demonstrate mastery (through the application of remembering skills, using skills, or problem-solving skills) over the specific content knowledge (facts, concepts, rules or cognitive and flight procedures) which underlie the performance he or she wishes to become competent in (figure 5). The process for achieving this is:

- Identify the performance and abilities which contribute to the desired accomplishment. These competency specifications provide the basis for achieving test item *validity*.

- Examine each ability and determine what *content type* (facts, concepts, rules, and cognitive or flight procedures) the ability represents.

- Select the most appropriate *test type* for measuring that content.

- *Design the test* items.

- Pilot the test to determine *item reliability* (that is, the degree to which each item is consistent in measuring a criterion ability from one test administration to the next.

- Implement the test as either a *formative* (monitoring student and instructional effectiveness through the course of instruction) or *summative* (evaluating final mastery of learning at the end of the course) assessment instrument.

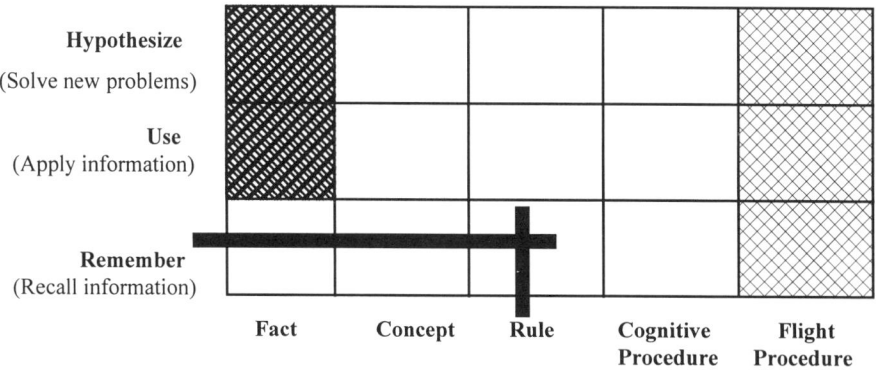

**Figure 1.5   Interaction of content and information processing for test specifications**

This model of instruction assessment hypothesizes that learning outcomes can be measured through the interactive effect of at least two interacting conditions; *content* and *information processing* (Figure 5). The degree to which an item matches the expected knowledge or content type with the level of information processing is a major component of the items validity. A more detailed examination of this model is provided in Hunt and Hunt (1993).

## Conclusion

This chapter proposes that professional competency in aviation requires the systematic identification of knowledge which can be tested for its utility in achieving pre-determined behavioural outcomes. A model is posited to achieve this end. Its underlying notion is that knowledge bases are stable constructs which should be used as the primary focus for instructional interventions. The task context provides the means for demonstrating meaningful applications of that knowledge and defining the conditions and standards under which acceptable evidence of that knowledge might be measured. Such a model may contribute to a re-definition of 'professional aviation competency' and suggest means by which it might be more scientifically assessed for licensing and operational performance purposes.

## References

Bruner, J.S. (1966) *Toward a Theory of Instruction.* Cambridge, Massachussetts: Harvard University Press.
Crook, C., & Hunt, G.J.F. (1988) *Competent flight crew licensing II: the terms of reference for the Hurda Programme.* Palmerston North: Instructional Systems Programme, Massey University.
Gagné, R.M. & Glaser, R. (1987) 'Foundations in learning research'. In R.M. Gagné (Ed.), *Instructional Technology: Foundations* (pp .49-83). Hillsdale, NJ: Lawrence Erlbaum Associates.
Gronlund, N. E., and Linn, R. L. (1990) *Measurement and Evaluation in Teaching (6th Edition).* New York: Macmillan Publishing Company.
Hunt, G.J.F. (1986) 'Needs assessment in adult education: tactical and strategic considerations'. *Instructional Science*, 15, 287-296.

Hunt, G.J.F., and Hunt, L.M. (1993) 'Computer-based testing in flight crew licensing'. In R.A. Telfer (Ed.), *Aviation instruction and training.* Aldershot, Hants: Ashgate Publishing Limited.

Hunt, G.J.F. (1990) 'An abilities based approach to pilot competency and decision making'. In *ICAO Human Factors Digest* No. 4 (pp. A302-A309). Montreal, Canada: ICAO.

Hunt, G.J.F., and Hunt, L.M. (1986) 'Computer-based training'. *Interface,* December, 50-51.

ICAO, (1989) 'Human factors digest no. 1'. *Fundamental Human Factors Concepts.* Montreal: ICAO.

McCormick, E.J., & Sanders, M.S. (1983) *Human Factors in Engineering and Design,* (5th Ed.). Singapore: McGraw-Hill, International Student Edition.

Merrill, M.D. (1983) 'Component display theory'. In C.M. Reigeluth (Ed.), *Instructional design theories and models: an overview of their current status.* Hillsdale, NJ: Lawrence Erlbaum Associates.

Newell, A.A., and Simon, H.A. (1972) *Human Problem Solving.* Inglewood Cliffs, NJ: Prentice Hall.

Roscoe, S.N. and North, A.A. (1980) 'Prediction of pilot performance'. In S.N. Roscoe (Ed.) *Aviation Psychology.* Ames, Iowa: The Iowa University Press.

# 2 Influences on the learning process and learning outcome: Practical implications for the instructor

*Lynn M. Hunt*

**Introduction**

Traditionally, teaching and learning have been conceived as the process of transferring knowledge from instructor to student with the instructor being the more active agent. More recently attention has focused on a *constructivist* view of learning in which the learner is seen as an active agent in the construction of his or her knowledge (Pines & West, 1986). Here the student takes new information and interprets it in light of his or her existing knowledges and experiences. The process of interpretation may result in a knowledge base that looks significantly different to the original information. As Shuell (1986) says; 'It is helpful to remember that what the student does is actually more important in determining what is learned than what the teacher does' (p. 429). Recent research into the role of the student in the learning transaction may provide insights to improving the instructors effectiveness (Hunt, 1995). This chapter examines the process of student learning and then identifies those components of the process which offer the most scope for instructor improvement.

**The process of learning**

Learning proceeds in three stages. In the first stage the student appraises the learning task; a kind of situation assessment. From this appraisal the student determines how they will approach the task. They activate prior knowledge that they perceive to be relevant and use specific learning strategies in the context of their study management skills. The appropriateness of these activities to the learning task determines the quality of the learning outcome.

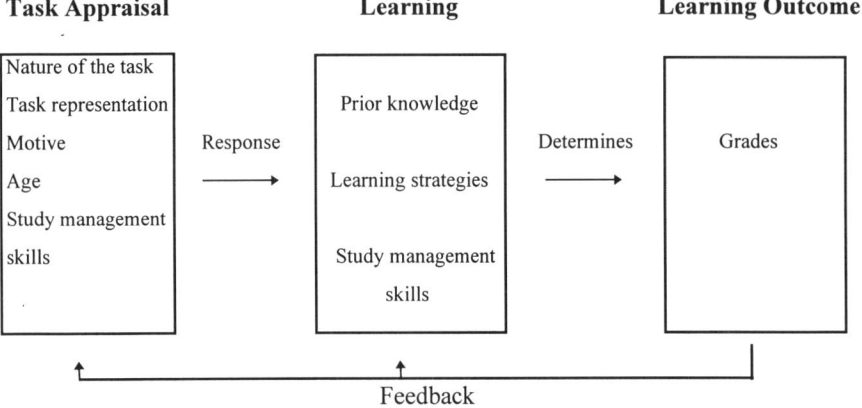

**Figure 2.1 The learning process**

**The appraisal process**

Students appraise the learning task and its context to determine an appropriate response. This appraisal appears to be a *perceptual* process rather than an objective assessment, and is therefore highly individual. The process is shaped by the particular combination of context variables that are important or relevant to any given student. These variables, which include the nature of the task, the student's representation of the task, motive for studying, age and study management skills, seem to guide the student towards selecting specific learning strategies. For example, if the student sees the task as being highly fragmented, then learning strategies to facilitate an integration of the fragmented components are likely to be chosen. Similarly, students faced with an essay task respond with background reading strategies.

Of all the influences on learning strategy selection, task representation is the most powerful and pervasive. Task representation describes the manner in which the student mentally represents the task. The student in effect defines the task in light of his or her knowledge or understanding of it. This definition acts as a cognitive framework for the task from which the student determines what must be done to achieve a successful outcome. To date four different task representations have been identified. These are shown in table 1.

**Table 2.1 Task representations**

| Component | Description |
|---|---|
| Declarative | Task requires student to be able to explain or describe the information, but not use or apply it. |
| Investigative | Students must find much of the information for themselves |
| Contained | Task structure and assessment requirements clearly understood |
| Fragmented | Task perceived to be made up of many fragmented, unrelated components. |

Some students represent tasks in quite different ways to teachers and instructional designers. The knowledgeable student with a contained task representation sees the task in terms of the interconnections between task components. This is probably quite close to that of the instructor. The novice student, who may have a fragmented representation, is faced with many unrelated components, rather like a jigsaw before its assembled. This student must make sense of these components before he or she can successfully finish the task. An investigative task representation is similar to a fragmented representation in that the student must tackle a preliminary task, finding the relevant information, before the actual task can be completed. A declarative task representation interprets the task in terms of the processing level at which it must be performed. Students with different task representations, given the same objective task, may in fact be faced with quite different learning tasks.

The student's state of knowledge would seem to play a large part in defining the task. It is likely that a student who is low in prior knowledge would have difficulty accurately representing the task and is more likely to see it as a series of unrelated, fragmented components. A student who has already achieved some competence in the task is more likely to understand the task parameters, see the interrelationships between components and be clear about the assessment criteria. His or her representation is likely to be a more complete and coherent definition of the task. In this sense task representation is very similar to the concept of problem representation that has been widely used in the field of problem solving. The problem solver represents the problem on the basis of his or her domain-related knowledge, in particular the organization of that knowledge. The quality of the internal representations determines the effectiveness and efficiency of the solving process (Glaser, 1987). Novices classify problems on the basis of literal, surface features of the problem, according to the physical properties of the situation. Experts categorize problems in terms of relevant underlying principles.

Task representation differs from problem representation in one significant way. Novice problem solvers represent problems in a manner that generally inhibits successful solution. They tend to be influenced by surface characteristics and irrelevant detail such that they often misrepresent the problem and so fail to reach a solution (Larkin, McDermott, Simon & Simon, 1980; Chi Feltovich & Glaser, 1981). Learners represent tasks in a personal way that defines what they need to do to accomplish the task. For example, novice students may recognize a task as being confusing, fragmented and full of irrelevant detail. This is not a misrepresentation of the task; resolving this state is the first step to achieving the task. When they respond with strategies that reduce the confusion, clarify relationships and identify important information they are in a much better position to successfully complete the whole task. However, should they use inappropriate coping mechanisms such as remember strategies on their own, they are likely to be as unsuccessful as the novice problem solver. The important point seems to be that the student represents the task in a framework that is valid for that particular student. This may mean that students faced with the same objective task, say an essay, are dealing with quite different tasks according to the representations by which they have defined the task. These differences require different responses to achieve the same final end.

The importance of task representation lies in the influence it exerts on the student's approach to learning as a result of this initial act of definition. Task representation strongly predicts the learning strategy selection process. These strategies then affect the learning outcome. In this way, the influence of task representation flows through the whole learning process.

Other contextual variables are also considered by the student. Many of these variables are a reflection of the relationship between the task and the student rather than being inherent in the task. For example, older students may see *relevance* in a task that is not apparent to younger students. Older students are able to relate the new task to previous experiences or situations and recognize how they can use the new knowledge or skills in the future. Students who are intrinsically interested in a topic find *value* in completing a task that is not shared by a student who dislikes a subject. These variables also influence the student's response to the learning task.

**The learning response**

In the second stage of the learning process, students respond to their task appraisal by deploying learning strategies that they believe match the functional needs of the task.

Learning strategies seem to arrange themselves into seven hierarchical functions, from memorizing (remember and grouping strategies) at the simplest level of cognitive complexity to hypothesizing (projecting/predicting strategies) at the highest level (see figure 2.2). These strategy groups appear to operationalise the descriptions of levels of cognitive processing that have been described by others (taxonomy of objectives- Bloom, Englehart, Furst, Hill & Krathwohl, 1956; categories of learning outcome- Gagné & Briggs, 1979; Component Display Theory- Merrill, 1983). Each level subsumes lower levels, but a strict linear progression through the seven levels is not envisaged. As students move to a higher level it is probable that they keep feeding back into lower levels and developing the support foundation that these lower levels provide for more sophisticated levels of learning. So, for example, the student working at skill development (proceduralising) will also continue to build his or her declarative knowledge using comprehension strategies.

| Bloom et al (1956) | Gagné & Briggs (1979) | D. Merrill (1983) | Learning Strategies | Types of Learning | Knowledge Structures |
|---|---|---|---|---|---|
| Knowledge | Verbal knowledge | Remember verbatim | Remember Grouping | Memorize | |
| Comprehension | | Remember paraphrase | Key ideas Relating Background | Comprehension | Declarative |
| Application | Intellectual skills | Use | Practice | Procedural | |
| Analysis Synthesis | | Find | Projecting/ predicting | Hypothesize | Procedural |

**Figure 2.2  A comparison of processing, learning and knowledge levels**

Prior knowledge also has an important role to play in this part of the process. It is thought to work by providing a context or framework in which new material can be more readily understood or remembered (Montague, 1972; Wittrock, 1974; 1978; Bellezza, 1981; 1982). Information-to-be-learnt is received into the working memory and matched with knowledge structures held in the long term memory. When a perfect match is found, the new content has been previously learned and no changes are made to the knowledge structures. When no match can be found the learner is unable to comprehend the new material and again no learning is likely to take place. Learning is optimized when a partial match is made with knowledge structures in the long term memory (Biggs, 1969; Siegler & Klahr, 1982).

Learning strategies seem to work by integrating the new content with the existing content, resulting in new knowledge structures that are not just quantitatively increased but are more complex and sophisticated. The type of learning strategy used influences the sophistication of the hybrid knowledge structures (Entwistle & Ramsden, 1983; Biggs, 1987; Jansweijer, Elshout, & Wielinga, 1990). For example, if rote rehearsal strategies (from the 'remember' strategy group) are used, the new and existing knowledge are linked relatively superficially. That is, similarities between surface characteristics, such as names, become the basis for the relationships. Strategies which encourage the student to process the information at a more meaningful level, such as relating strategies, integrate prior knowledge and new information to create a new structure in which the seams between old and new are no longer discernible.

The learning process may be further enhanced or diminished by the student's study management skills, that is, the conditions under which it takes place. For example, good planning ensures that students maximize their opportunities for receiving information, have a wider range of learning strategies available to them (some strategies are more time consuming than others) and have the time to effectively use learning strategies. However, an overemphasis on neat, organized study notes may act as a crutch to the student, and detract from his or her ability to understand or remember information.

**The learning outcome**

*Generic influences*

How do the patterns of learning identified influence learning outcome? In a generic context, prior knowledge is the most important predictor of learning success. This finding is already well documented in the literature (Alexander

& Judy, 1988). Students who already have some background knowledge in a subject area are able to understand and remember information better than those who do not. While the importance of prior knowledge to learning outcome is clear, its relative importance varies from task to task and is dependent upon specific task characteristics.

Procrastination and an over-concern with neat, complete study notes are both associated with a poor learning outcome. Across tasks, the high procrastinator tends to perform poorly. This accords with the findings of Entwistle & Ramsden (1983) who found 'disorganized study methods' were associated with a surface approach and a poor learning outcome. This result is not surprising. The student who delays learning until the last possible moment is probably relying on the anxiety generated by an imminent event such as a examination as the motivation to commence work. As Fransson (1977) and others (Naveh-Benjamin, McKeachie, & Lin, 1987) have found, increases in anxiety result in much of the working memory's limited capacity being distracted by fear of failure and negative self thoughts. The student's capacity to learn is effectively reduced. In addition to the problems created by anxiety, the student is faced with a lack of adequate time to complete the learning task. A lower learning outcome usually eventuates.

At first sight, the finding that neat and complete study materials are associated with a poor learning outcome seems contradictory. We would expect that students who have carefully assembled and organized their notes would have improved their chances of a good learning outcome. However, study management skills are only *conditions* which may facilitate effective learning. They are unlikely, in the absence of other effort, to create learning. Students who rate very highly on this skill may be expending too much effort on the form and appearance of study materials and too little effort on the learning itself. This conclusion echoes Spring's (1985) finding that some students rely too heavily on 'study' strategies such as underlining ideas instead of strategies that would aid understanding. In both cases students seem to be using these behaviours as a coping mechanism instead of more appropriate learning strategies.

Learning strategies do not *generically* influence learning outcome. Learning strategies are appropriate to specific tasks. A learning strategy that facilitates learning in one context may hinder effective learning in another. The influence of learning strategies on learning outcome emerges when they are examined in the context of specific tasks.

*Specific influences*

When learning outcome is examined in the *context of specific learning tasks*, particular learning strategies emerge as influencing learning outcome. For example, students preparing for an essay task who used relating and remembering strategies experienced a successful learning outcome. The use of practice or grouping strategies for this task predicted a poor learning outcome (Hunt, 1995).

Successful learning then depends on both *generic factors* such as prior knowledge, non-procrastination and not being overly concerned with neat, complete study notes and *context specific variables* such as appropriately matching the task with learning strategies.

Learning outcome eventually becomes prior knowledge for the next learning task and this aids new learning (shown in the feedback loop in figure 2.1). Prior knowledge also feeds back to influence the manner in which students interpret and understand (represent) new learning tasks.

**Strategies for the instructor**

*Task representation should be used by both students and teachers*

Task representation showed such a strong influence on learning strategy selection it seems clear that students would benefit from having adequate skills to develop accurate mental representations of the learning task. If, as Glaser (1988) and others have suggested in the related area of problem representation, high prior knowledge is a significant advantage in the initial representation of a task, then providing students with either a task representation (from the instructor) or the skills to develop their own representations may lessen the disadvantage of low prior knowledge. Given the dominance of prior knowledge on learning outcome, the overall effect could be quite large. This information could be provided in two ways.

First, it is suggested that students should be actively taught task analysis skills so that they can determine for themselves an appropriate learning response. Wherever possible students should be given the tools to control their own learning. Equally, instructors who commence a lesson by providing students with a useful task representation may enhance the learning that ensues. Since the early 1960s instructional objectives have been widely used. It may be that the effectiveness of these objectives relates to the extent that they provide students with a useful representation of the task. Such instructional objectives may provide a clearer task representation if they indicate the processing level at which students must perform, for example, memorize or apply information; the evaluation format, for example, multiple choice questions or practical activities; clear assessment criteria and a diagrammatic representation of the task.

*Learning strategies should match the type of learning task*

All learning strategies are not equally effective for all tasks. For example, students who use practice strategies for an essay task will probably have a poor learning outcome. Students should be taught how to match task and strategy. This could be done in a learning skills course, but should also be reinforced by instructors of specific subjects.

*Students should be taught study management skills*

Students are not necessarily good managers of their learning environment. These skills impact on learning effectiveness and should therefore be taught just as reading and writing skills are.

*Students should be taught a range of learning strategies*

There is no systematic attempt to teach learning strategies in the New Zealand education system. The development of these skills seems to depend largely on chance. If students are to learn 'how to do for themselves what teachers typically do for them in the classroom' (Wendon, 1985: p.7) then they must be given the tools to do the job. In the training context instructors might most effectively achieve this by sharing with students the learning strategies that they used in the same context. This provides the students with a model of learning behaviour that may be different to their own and has the immediacy and relevance of a task at hand.

**Conclusions**

Training has traditionally followed pedagogical principals so that trainers are perceived of as being the fountain of knowledge and decision-maker, and the student is seen as being dependent on the trainer for information about what to know and how to learn it. The challenge for the nineteen nineties and twenty-first century is to develop instructional practices and procedures that seek to pass the responsibility for learning from trainer to student. The focus should move from merely transmitting knowledge, to fostering the management and development of cognitive skills that will enable the student to build, modify and manipulate their own knowledge bases in informal learning environments.

Learning eventuates as a result of decisions made by students. To the extent that students can be helped to make better decisions, it may be possible to improve the effectiveness of the learning process.

**References**

Alexander, P.A. & Judy, J.E. (1988) 'The interaction of domain-specific and strategic knowledge in academic performance'. *Review of Educational Research.* 58, 4, 405-437.

Bellezza, F.S. (1981) 'Mnemonic devices: classification, characteristics and criteria'. *Review of Educational Research*, 51, 247-275.

Bellezza, F.S. (1982) 'Updating memory using mnemonic devices'. *Cognitive Psychology,* 14, 301-327.

Biggs, J.B. (1969) 'Coding and cognitive behaviour'. *British Journal Educational Psychology.* 60, 3, 287-305.

Biggs, J.B. (1987) *Student Approaches to Learning and Studying.* Melbourne: Australian Council for Educational Research.

Bloom, B.S., Englehart, M.D., Furst, E.J., Hill, W.H. & Krathwohl, D.R. (1956) *Taxonomy of educational objectives. Handbook 1: Cognitive domain.* New York: Longmans, Green

Chi, M.T.H., Feltovich, P.J. & Glaser, R. (1981) 'Categorization and representation of physics problems'. *Cognitive Science.* 5, 121-152.

Entwistle, N. & Ramsden, P. (1983) *Understanding Student Learning.* Beckenham, Kent: Croom Helm.

Fransson, A.. (1977) 'On qualitative differences in learning IV:Effects of intrinsic motivation and extrinsic test anxiety on process and outcome.' *British Journal of Educational Psychology.* 47, 244-257.

Gagné, R.M. & Briggs, L.J. (1979) *Principles of Instructional Design.* New York: Holt, Rinehart and Winston.

Glaser, R. (1987) 'Thoughts on expertise'. In C. Schooler & W. Schaie (Eds), *Cognitive Functioning and Social Structure over the Life Course.* Norwood, NJ: Ablex Publishing Corp.

Glaser, R. (1988) 'The reemergence of learning theory within instructional research'. American Psychological Association's Distinguished

Scientific Award for the Applications of Psychology Address. August 15, 1988, Atlanta, Georgia.

Hunt, L.M. (1995) *Approaches to Learning: The Selection and Use of Learning Strategies.* Unpublished PhD Thesis. Palmerston North: Massey University.

Jansweijer, W. Elshout, J.J. & Wielinga, B.J. (1990) 'On the multiplicity of learning to solve problems'. In H. Mandl, E. de Corte, N. Bennet, & H.F. Friedrich (eds), *Learning and Instruction. Vol 2.1 Social and Cognitive Aspects of Learning and Instruction.* Oxford: Pergamon Press.

Larkin, J., McDermott, J., Simon, D.P., & Simon, H.A. (1980) 'Expert and novice performance in solving physics problems'. *Science.* 208, 1335-1342.

Merrill, M.D. (1983) 'Component display theory'. In C.M. Reigeluth's (Ed), *Instructional-design Theories and Models: An Overview of their Current Status.* Hillsdale, NJ: Lawerence Erlbaum.

Montague, W.E. (1972) 'Elaborative strategies in verbal learning and memory'. In G.H. Bower's (ed) *The Psychology of Learning and Motivation* (Vol 6). New York: Academic Press.

Naveh-Benjamin, M., McKeachie, W., & Lin, Y. (1987) 'Two types of test-anxious students: Support for an information processing model'. *Journal of Educational Psychology.* 79, 2, 131-136.

Pines, A.L. and West, L.H.T. (1986) 'Conceptual understanding and science learning: An interpretation of research within a sources-of-knowledge framework'. *Science Education*, 70, 583-604.

Shuell, T.J. (1986) 'Cognitive conceptions of learning'. *Review of Educational Research*, 56, 411-436.

Siegler, R.S. & Klahr, D. (1982) 'When do children learn? The relationship between existing knowledge and the acquisition of new knowledge'. In R. Glaser (ed) *Advances in Instructional Psychology* Vol 2. Hillsdale, NJ: Lawerence Erlbaum.

Spring, C. (1985) 'Comprehension and study strategies reported by university freshmen who are good and poor readers'. *Instructional Science.* 14, 157-167.

Wendon, A (1985) 'Learner strategies'. *TESOL Quarterly.* 19, 5, 1-7.

Wittrock, M.C. (1974) 'Learning as a generative process'. *Educational Psychology.* 11, 87-95.

Wittrock, M.C. (1978) 'The cognitive movement in psychology'. *Educational Psychology.* 13, 15-29.

# 3 Management of instruction and assessment in aviation

*Andrew S. Gibbons, A. F. O'Neal and Peter G. Fairweather*

**Introduction**

The management of training is changing because training itself is changing. The chapters of this volume describe how new theories of learning and instruction, research on the effects of instruction, and new technologies for instructing - both hard and soft - are changing our practices as we respond to demands for products of greater precision and power. Management of instruction, rather than being a sideline player in this transformation, will be a central figure, drawn increasingly toward the center of the action, becoming finally the very moderator of training, administering a spectrum of automated and non-automated technologies for the benefit of the individual learner.

The purpose of this chapter is to describe current management metaphors and to project the future of instructional management as we see it.

**The instructional past**

Three historical forces have shaped the use of computer-based instruction (CBI) and therefore of computer-managed instruction (CMI):

1. The instructional metaphor chosen for CBI. The systematic approach to instructional design. The transfer of training functions to the

classroom setting. The current state of the art in the management of computer-based instruction is dominated by the metaphor which designers chose to impose on this new instructional medium during its formative period. Computer-based instruction in its early years mimicked the older media already in use - the lecture, the book, the film, the video, the narrated slide show. This is the pattern for every new medium: early films were no more than a recorded lecture. In the earliest days of CBI it was easy to tell the previous media experience of a designer merely by looking at his or her CBI products, because the old metaphor and the old mindset about instruction were almost always reflected there.

2   Multimedia has not changed this pattern of mimicry. The designer can now more easily than ever ape the effects of the video and the narrated slide show in CBI products.

3   The systematic approach to instructional design influenced this practice of copying the old forms, but it did not release us from it. Instructional focus improved as designers began to target instruction to specific instructional objectives, and effectiveness improved as designers employed effective instructional strategies matched with objective types. But the analytic practices of task analysis and objectives analysis, without a balancing synthetic process, resulted in a fragmentation of instruction, and knowledge began to be dispensed in smaller packages. These packages, designed under the old metaphors of instruction, did not change the pattern of instruction. The one long lecture was simply broken into many small lectures, each having essentially the same structure as the original lecture.

4   Yet a third trend influenced the practice of instructional design: the transfer of the training enterprise from the field or workshop to the classroom.

5   Traditional forms of training relied heavily on learning within the workplace in an apprenticing relationship. As the content of training became more technical and precise, and as a greater proportion of the population sought education, education became more costly, and for largely economic reasons, instruction moved to the classroom.

6	The result of these historical trends (mimicry of older media forms, systematic design approaches, and classroom-based learning) is a style of instruction fragmented into parcels or boxes of instruction, each putatively self-contained and independently deliverable through individualized delivery systems. Computer-based instruction, the ultimate delivery system and the ultimate in individualization capability, not unexpectedly fell into this pattern. The general pattern of instruction has been 'teach-then-practice,' but unfortunately the teaching and the practice have for practical reasons fallen to the verbal level, and we are now caught in what has been called the 'lexical loop' (see Bunderson, Gibbons, Olsen, and Kearsley, 1981):

The students are expected to translate the verbal abstractions back into the skills/knowledge of the expert. They are expected to create a model of the performance of the expert from verbal abstractions. This is the lexical loop (p. 207).

## The management past

As we would expect, computer-based management systems have conformed to and supported this packaged, fragmented, and verbal view of instruction. And since packages of instruction are designed to be self-contained, with strategy and message pre-planned and complete, there are no management functions internal to the instruction that management can perform. Consequently, the functions assigned to the computer-based management system are what might be called high-level administrative functions: selection of the next package, presentation of the next package, recording of results (scores, etc.), and reporting of summarized results. Some of the more flexible management systems (Schnitz and Azbell, 1991) allow the designer or instructor to specify sequences of instructional packages for individual students, but involvement stops at the boundary of the instructional package, and the management system has become like the dockside crane - simply a loading mechanism which unstores packages and places them before the student. When instruction is finished, it returns the packages to storage.

Computer-based management has come to mean computer-based administration. As currently defined, computer-based management systems are not expected to participate in the instructional process itself. Management is typically viewed as an adjunct or an afterthought to the main activity of instruction. In a sense, the management system of today stands apart from the instructional battle, viewing its dust and the fires from a distance.

**Back to our roots**

It is surprising to most CBI designers to find that this view of management's role in computer-based instruction was not the one held by the pioneers of the CBI field. Note this description of CBI's envisioned function from Stolurow (1968):

> It should also be possible to vary the decision rule at each branch point, depending on whether the student's performance did, or did not, fall within certain bounds of accuracy and/or latency. This would make it possible to change any rule, or set of rules, during the course of instruction depending on the student's response history.

Early instructional management systems worked closer to the heart of the instructional decision making process than today's systems. Atkinson (1969) experimented with management systems that attempted to maximize or minimize certain class achievement variables by manipulating the amount of time each student worked on the system. Suppes (1966) designed a management mechanism which dealt with students as individuals, adjusting instruction to individual needs and prescribing future instruction based on past performance. Though the papers of the pioneers in the CBI field are rooted in the behaviorist notions of their day, a vision still shines through them which transcends psychological doctrine and defines the basic function of management as integral to rather than peripheral to instruction. This is a vision we seem to have lost.

**Changing conceptions of instruction**

Returning to the original conception of management's role in instruction is possible, but it may now entail meeting some interesting new challenges, because our view of instruction - computerized and non-computerized - is changing. Consider some important trends.

## The 'always' learner

It is becoming apparent to instructional designers that their task is not to get students to learn, because students are always learning. The task of the designer is to create learning environments which can influence and direct learning in ways that: (1) ensure learning will be complete, correct, and free of gaps, (2) reduce the amount of time required to learn, (3) influence the long-term retention of learning, (4) increase the likelihood of future learning, and (5) support learning in a form readily usable by the student.

## Situated learning and apprenticeship

To promote knowledge which is ready to use in real applications, designers are using techniques that situate learning within the context where it will be used. The use of the classroom as a retreat from the real world is being recognized, and techniques for moving learning into more realistic contexts are becoming the new standard. Aviation was a pioneer in this trend, moving instruction from the aircraft to realistic aircraft simulators - a trend which has accelerated in the recent past and promises to transform the long-standing concept of ground school into something much more interesting to instructor and student alike.

## Performance support

The barrier between the workplace and the learning place is dissolving. Training is being administered increasingly on a 'just-in-time' basis, rather than at times far removed from use. Training is also moving physically closer to the work, often re-entering the workplace it vacated years ago, as the classroom became the dominant place of training. Performance support systems of many types are being designed with capabilities and implementation profiles tailored to the tasks they support, and to some extent their use is replacing the need for training. In other cases these support systems are being used as extensions of the learning coach (Gibbons & Fairweather, in press), a support system for learning, into the workplace.

## Apprenticeship

The role of the learner as a participant rather than as an observer is becoming established. It is ironic that one of the most powerful advances in instructional theory in this decade has been the rediscovery of the apprenticeship method used for millennia to instruct crafts, trades, and basic life-sustaining skills. Now, under the title of Cognitive Apprenticeship (Collins, Brown & Newman, 1987) this ancient method is proving its ability to instruct complex cognitive performance as well in ways that integrate the learner into the social, intellectual, and economic community in which the learning will be used.

The key principles in the cognitive apprenticeship approach include observation of models by the student, coaching and scaffolding of practice which fades over time, student articulation of knowledge gained through problem-solving, reflection to encourage integration of knowledge and increased self-assessment, and some degree of exploration and experimentation rather than strict channeling of experience. Cognitive apprenticeship also takes into account four levels of learning rather than one. Learning how to learn is given special value, and a student is made much more responsible for learning. Finally, cognitive apprenticeship gives special attention to the manner in which instructional tasks are scoped or bounded and then given to the student in a sequence which increases the level of challenge as the student is capable. The following account from the training of a surgeon illustrates scaffolding as well as this incrementality with which practice advances:

> The surgical microscope might serve as a paradigm for what contemporary neurosurgery has become: high-tech, polished, versatile. It rolls quietly on casters, balanced with a counterweight the size of a watermelon, and contains not just the optical system that allows the surgeon to see, but a duplicate set of eyepieces - the teaching scope - that allows a second person to see exactly what the surgeon does. Generally, the attending surgeon will watch the resident's work through this until the resident reaches the limit of his experience; then they switch responsibilities, and the attending surgeon operates while the resident watches and learns. The process is accretive; no resident suddenly performs an operation from start to finish, but rather does a little bit more each time. 'I remember vividly the first time I did a case all the way through,' says Dr. Mark Dias, a senior resident on the neurological service. 'I was going right along, just concentrating on what I was going to do next, and I realized that I was doing it without anyone telling me what to do. The attending physician was just sitting there very quietly at the side of the microscope, not saying anything, and I thought, "That was it; I'm

there." It's an eerie feeling the first time to recognize that you've just done an entire operation without any help.'

Dr. Don Marion, another senior neurological resident, agrees. 'Most of what you're thinking when you're operating is that "It's important not to make any mistakes; I'm not going to do anything that I'm not absolutely sure about." But gradually you're sure of more and more; all the things you're worrying about are coming later and later in the procedure, and eventually you're thinking of the operation as a whole, not only as a series of steps. Then you're getting close.' (Shelton, 1990).

A training problem encountered by a large corporation recently further illustrates the application of apprenticeship and situated learning principles in a corporate rather than medical setting. Faced with the need to train a large team of programmers who had supported their company's rapid growth, a software firm realized that they still could not afford to release programmers from work duties for the time required to train them. An apprenticing system was designed in which job tasks were assigned by supervisors with the realization that the performer would often be learning new techniques while carrying out the assignment. Each job task was matched with a set of resources that could help the performer learn the new techniques, and senior programmers expert in the new technique were assigned as mentors and sources of help as during learning. In effect, the programmers were turned into apprentices, given expert performer support, sources of knowledge and help, and a task on which to learn under the review of both supervisor and practicing expert.

This example not only illustrates the solution of a training problem through apprenticeship methods but the accomplishment of cultural change by the same means. Relationships between workers, supervisors, and experts become closer in this type of system, and at the same time competence increases, a community of practice is knit more closely together, and learning and improvement become the goal of rather than an adjunct to the culture of the organization.

*Less direct didactic, problem- and model-centered instruction*

In training applications like this one the focus is less on direct and isolated instruction and more on instruction integrated into the fabric of daily practice. Instruction thus becomes more problem-centered. A student learns what needs to be learned in order to complete an assigned (but carefully-selected) task. Often the student must learn through a variety of means, including exploration; use of canned media presentations; attempts at solution reviewed by peers, supervisors, and experts; observation of the work of advanced peers and experts; use of performance support systems (job aids) of several kinds; and experimentation.

*Proficiency-basing*

Despite the change in instructional method, format, and location, the trends described thus far still require that training be proficiency-based. Not only must performance be monitored and recorded following training, but a determination must be made whether standards of performance have been met and whether a person can be certified to work under lower levels of expert oversight and review. A record must be kept of the qualifications and areas of expertise of the individual worker, and that record is relevant to not only performance evaluation but to the lifetime training career for the individual. It is more properly seen as a possession of the trainee than of the training organization, and it approximates the idea of a college degree but is specific to certification in proficiencies expressed at a somewhat more detailed and specific level. In medicine, once a person is certified on a proficiency basis as a generalist, it is possible to obtain additional training and experience (through a type of apprenticeship called 'residency') to become certified as a specialist. Neither this system of training nor the concept of certification is new. What we see happening as the use of apprenticeship principles increases may simply be the rest of the world catching up to practices which have been common within exclusive training preserves for decades.

**The management response**

Our designs for management must evolve with our conceptions of instruction. The trends described above place heavy demands on the management system. In an earlier article (Gibbons, Fairweather, & O'Neal, 1993), we identified five main functional areas of a computer-based management system required: (1) to meet the needs generated by new training approaches and (2) to assert management into the heart of the instructional process:

The ability to track a student's performance at an individual response level and to note both correct and erroneous behavior sequences. (Monitor Function)

The ability to adjust the degree of influence and control by the manager--the locus of initiative--at the time of instruction. (Locus of Initiative Function)

The ability to compute a family of indices at the time of performance upon which to base real-time decisions. (Statistics Function)

The ability to combine indices over several problems for each task of a set of tasks being learned in order to monitor and influence progress toward task proficiency in isolation, in the presence of other tasks, and in the face of contrary conditions. (Strategy Function)

The ability to make management decisions as a 'weighted negotiation' between various levels of performance requirement ranging from the need to fulfill a local, short term objective to the more global requirements of multiple interacting objectives at the lesson, course, curriculum and job/career certification levels. (Tailoring Function).

Only with these functions can a management system influence the instructional moment, and with these functions management not only participates but becomes the main force behind instruction: either retaining control to itself or sharing initiatives with the student, but above all, providing each student with a tailored succession of instructional tasks optimized to the student.

The work of M. D. Merrill in Instructional Transaction Theory (Merrill, Li, & Jones, 1991; Merrill, Li, & Jones, 1992a; Merrill, Li, & Jones, 1992b; Zhang, Gibbons, & Merrill, in press) is, among other things, an attempt to reposition the management function within instruction. Merrill, a student of Stolurow, is pursuing the vision of Stolurow which we have described. Doing so has required that he abandon the preplanned and presequenced message typical of virtually all instruction today and break the instructional interaction and its communications into constituent elements. This goal of Merrill's work is clearly demonstrated in Zhang, Gibbons, and Merrill (in press). Moreover, in pursuit of the self-generation of instructional message and interaction content, Merrill is attempting to define the structure of learnable knowledge and to create knowledge bases independent of the instructional transaction, rendering the transaction shell reusable. Merrill's early papers, already referenced, outline an approach for doing this for static knowledge bases, and papers by Gibbons and Anderson (1995a, 1995b) outline a method for creating dynamic knowledge from simulations, one of several approaches which are currently being explored.

**The future of management**

With the role of management defined as a more immediate instructional function in this way, it is possible to project the necessary evolution of management systems over the near-term and to speculate on what they might evolve into in the more distant future. We predict that management will become: A data base of competence on tasks. Management will change because the basic focus of instruction will change from the traditional 'lesson' to the task or task grouping. The things that are counted during tests will change from answers on multiple choice tests to performance successes. This change has begun in many areas of training, and aviation leads the parade. Certification in aviation has for years required a performance, not just a written test, and simulated practice environments haven multiplied and grown in sophistication in aviation as in few other areas.

For a long time aviation has focused not on the lesson but on the competence in instruction. When a pilot or maintenance person completes training, there is a certification which is competency-based. Competency-basing of this final hurdle has resulted in a backwards pressure on training to include hands-on, realistic practice and an incremental approach toward higher levels of practice. Skills are first learned in relatively uncomplicated performance settings. The settings then become more difficult as conditions are deliberately varied to be increasingly adverse and difficult.

The backward pressure for realistic practice and testing prior to the final certification has continued over many years, resulting in the use of increasingly sophisticated simulation devices which not only cost less to use but train better because they can simulate a wider range of adverse conditions and can integrate emergency training with normal procedures. The pressure for realistic practice has only intensified with the appearance of the glass cockpit and the cockpit management concept, so part-task simulation and hands-on training are increasingly evident in a once lecture-based ground school. This trend will persist because economic and certification pressures will continue to be forcing factors.

But the transformation of aviation training is not complete. Even aviation training has yet to accept the inevitable management consequence by changing also the way in which it marks and tracks progress in competence during training. Aviation training does not keep track of performance data for individual tasks during training, nor does it use data on performance to carry out the functions of instructional management. A data base of tasks and task complexes. To track performance for individual tasks, there must be an inventory of tasks. Our technology for inventorying tasks in aviation has been much used, but our linkage of the task analysis to training has been disappointing. Perhaps this is because we lack some key technologies for making linkages. We learned this lesson ourselves while attempting to design syllabi for aviation training, and it led us to devise some new techniques.

We discovered the problem of linking the task analysis and the syllabus as we tried to be systematic in our construction of syllabi from the raw materials of the task and objectives analysis. We found that it had to be a mapping procedure: tasks had to map onto syllabus events, but it was not a straightforward one-to-one mapping for several reasons. Tasks had to be learned individually at first, but then they had to be practiced in many integrated combinations and under a variety of conditions. This meant that one task had to map onto numerous instructional events. It also meant that performance data had to be recorded for not just the task (during early stages of training) but the various task clusters (during later stages).

Many tasks had to be practiced multiple times before they were performed at desired proficiency levels.

Many tasks had to be practiced in a succession of simulated or real environments, meaning that the task had to be practiced under increasingly real conditions.

We were anxious to create a system that would determine how much practice each task needed and ensure that the amount was given. We wanted a system that was sensitive to feedback from training showing that students were getting too much or too little practice for a particular task or combination. We wanted to create a system that could expand the amount of practice for specific tasks not yet mastered. And finally, we needed a system which could track progress not on just tasks but on task clusters, because we realized that some simple tasks become difficult in combination with other tasks or under certain conditions.

We created a mapping technology called the 'work model' which solved our problem (Bunderson, Gibbons, Olsen, & Kearsley, 1981; Gibbons, Bunderson, Olsen, & Robertson, in press). A work model consists of one or more tasks (and objectives) which are to be practiced together under a specified set of conditions and to a specified standard of performance. Whereas tasks represent the terminal goals of instruction, work models define intermediate steps toward the goals: steps which include the multiple practice opportunities and patterns of integration into larger task complexes.

We found that this approach, though requiring more detail, gave us the basis for managing instruction (and the syllabus itself) at a much higher level of resolution and with more precision. We found that as we invented the work model we also destroyed the traditional notion of the 'lesson' as the basic unit of instruction. We found that the management of hands-on forms of training entails different requirements for recording, analysis, and storage of data than the typical ground school lecture, because in a performance-oriented training system, the focus is on the performances themselves, not on packages of information.

The lecture, one of the 'boxes' of instruction we described early in this chapter, is not performance-based, so the data which results is either a completion score or a quiz score. The data resulting from a hands-on exercise based on a work model describes the performance of a specific task or complex of tasks under a given set of circumstances. This data is interpretable much differently from a lesson score and is much more useful in assessing a student's momentary trajectory in training, the student's momentary needs, and the best prescription for the next instructional event. At the moment of performance, both successful and unsuccessful attempts yield valuable data. Unsuccessful attempts are unsuccessful for a reason. Often the data from the attempt will point to the reason so that it can be corrected through feedback or focused practice. A successful attempt means that the student has performed the task successfully within a particular task complex and under specified conditions. This data, accumulating over time can certify performance ability better than single tests, but aviation training regularly discards this data by not recording it and not using it.

There are several reasons for not recording and using this data, not the least of which is the pilot's fear that the data may be misused in a legal action to demonstrate a pattern of incompetence leading to an accident. This is a definite possibility which must be avoided. However, this fear is founded only if the data kept is a historical record rather than a compiled competence profile. Whereas a historical record does record errors as well as successes, a competence profile records only successes and patterns of success. During training, an empty cell in the profile points to areas which need additional practice before they can be certified, but profile data does not reflect the training history of the performer and would not be usable in legal actions.

The point that we are trying to make is that as aviation's training has become increasingly hands-on and competency-based, but its management systems have not kept pace. Now, in the face of sustained pressures for accountability and flexibility in the management of training we believe the means is available to improve both. A data base of resources related to each task. In order to make prescriptions for instruction, a management system will not only need to know the tasks and task complexes to be mastered and the status of individual students with respect to them, but it must know the resources available for the training and support of each task. This can include an enormous range of resources such as instructional materials, practice events, organizational documentation, reference materials, and the names of experts and peers to be consulted. Only with this information can a passive recording scheme be turned into an active, prescriptive management system. Figure 3.1 illustrates a structure of resources from all parts of an organization which can support the student-worker in this fashion.

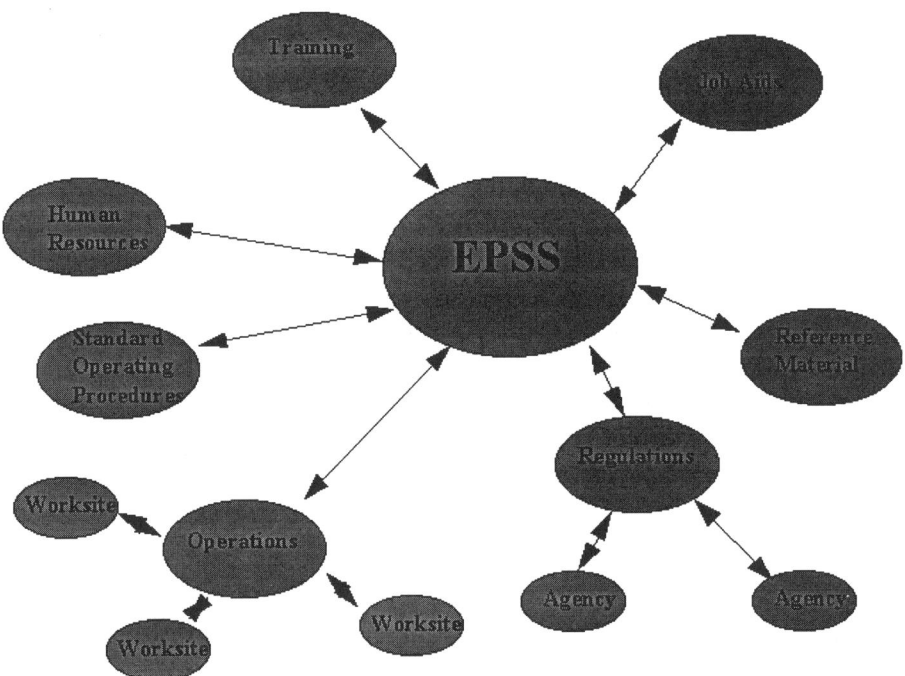

Figure 3.1   The varied structure of a system for performance support and training

Once this new concept of management (and training) is accepted, it opens the way to provide support and prescription not only during training but at the workplace as well. Note the similarities between the system we are describing now and the situation of the software developer related in an earlier section. The management concept we are describing now (whether automated or not) is an important part of the solution for their (increasingly common) training problem.

The management system as a tool appears to be headed away from an exclusively training function. It is evolving toward a support function for both training and the workplace. It is the key element that makes the just-in-time training idea work, for without management as it is described here - capable of bringing the student-worker timely and task-focused resources - the just-in-time concept has neither form nor content. With such management, just-in-time training becomes a new tool in the workplace. An active scheduling agent. With these resources, the management system is poised to become much more than the passive factotum we have created through current practice. The management system's vision is to become an active manager and scheduler of training - from the highest level of scheduling, certification, and retraining down to the scheduling of individual exercises for the advancing student-worker. The management system's scheduling ability gives it several very useful functions:

*Prescriber of resources of all kinds*

Not only training materials but work support documentation of all kinds can be supplied by the management system. This includes organizational documentation, regulations, and standard operating procedures. If resources can be supplied to student-workers through the management system, then they can be updated and kept current by the same system. Rather than spending enormous amounts on the reproduction of documentation, organizations can supply it electronically in a single package geared to the support of the worker. Moreover, as documentation changes, a system which knows the current status of every worker's knowledge can flag the change to those who are affected, announcing the need for the individual to perform self- directed retraining in the short term and noting the cumulative need for group retraining in the longer term.

*Tracker of training/recertification cycles*

In aviation, as in many fields, original certifications expire, and re-education or re-testing are prescribed methods for maintaining one's standing as a legal practitioner. A management system is the natural choice for tracking needs for certification or periodic re-training.

*Automatic scheduler*

The manager can also be the scheduler for these cycles of training and recertification. It can flag in advance training or retraining needs and schedule the needed programs to the user at an organizational level.

*Administrator for on-line training*

As the functions of the management system expand outward to include wider areas of responsibility, they also expand downward, into the heart of on-line instructional events. A system which knows about a student's momentary knowledge can adjust the course of instruction moment-by-moment at several levels to meet individual needs in the manner originally envisioned by Stolurow. This system can prescribe exercise problems and adjust their dimensions to meet the most critical momentary needs of the student.

**The far horizon**

On the more distant horizon, we feel there are even more important features for management systems which make them more powerful in meeting individual worker and organizational needs:

*Agents*

The technology of programmed 'agents' makes it possible for a management to be personalized to the individual. An agent is a type of programmed servant which moves about a computer network, performing mundane tasks, gathering information, summarizing, and creating reports. Agents can also negotiate in behalf of and stand in line for their owner. An important addition to the management system of the future will be personal agents capable of exploring the network of resources, seeking opportunities for training and support of their owners, the student-worker.

*Career manager*

Organizations are becoming aware that the progress and improvement of their work force relates directly to the progress of the organization. Moreover, workers value more highly and are more loyal to employers who provide better career enhancement opportunities. For this reason, many companies will find it good business to provide career management systems, which will be an extension of the management concept we are describing here.

## Conclusion

Management, which has always been the less-visible side of automated instruction has now begun to take center stage, becoming not only a companion to our automated systems but a controller of instruction, of information and support resources, and of the growth of learning within an organization. These new views are clearly evident in trends which are helping organizations manage and school their workforce for improved performance.

## References

Atkinson, R.C. (1969) 'Computerized instruction and the learning process'. In R.C. Atkinson and H. A. Wilson (Eds,), *Computer-Assisted Instruction: A Book of Readings,* New York: Academic Press.

Bunderson, C.V., Gibbons, A.S., Olsen, J.B., and Kearsley, G.P. (1981) 'Work models: Beyond instructional objectives'. *Instructional Science*, 10:205-215.

Gibbons, A.S. and Anderson, T.A. (1995a) *Functional Description for the Design of Automated Authoring for Tutorial-based Simulations.* Apple's East/West Authoring Tools Group CD-ROM. Apple Computer, Inc., Advanced Technology Group, Authoring Tools Program, Cupertino, CA.

Gibbons, A.S. and Anderson, T.A. (1995b) *Automated Authoring of Knowledge-based Simulations.* Apple's East/West Authoring Tools Group CD-ROM. Apple Computer, Inc., Advanced Technology Group, Authoring Tools Program, Cupertino, CA.

Gibbons, A.S., Bunderson, C.V., Olsen, J.B., and Robertson, J. (in press) *Work Models: Still Beyond Instructional Objectives.*

Gibbons, A.S., Fairweather, P.G., and O'Neal, A.F. (1993) 'The future of computer-managed instruction,' *Educational Technology*, 33(5), 7-11.

Merrill, M.D. (1992) 'Instructional transaction theory: Knowledge relationships among processes, entities, and activities'. ID2 Research

Team Technical Report, Department of Instructional Technology, Utah State University, September, 1992.

Merrill, M.D., Li, Z., and Jones, M.K. (1991) 'Instructional transaction theory: An introduction'. *Educational Technology.* 31(6), 7-12.

Merrill, M.D., Li, Z., and Jones, M.K. (1992a) 'Instructional transaction theory: classes of transactions'. *Educational Technology*, 32(6), 12-26.

Merrill, M.D., Li, Z., and Jones, M.K. (1992b) 'Instructional transaction shells: responsibilities, methods, and parameters'. *Educational Technology*, 32(2), 5-27.

Schnitz, J.E. and Azbell, J.W. (1991) 'Training for third-generation management systems effecting integrator implementation models'. Paper presented at the 9th Annual Conference on Interactive Instructional Delivery, Society of Applied Learning Technology, Orlando.

Shelton, M. (1990) *Working in a Very Small Place.* New York: Vintage Books.

Stolurow, L.M. (1969) 'Some factors in the design of systems for computer-assisted instruction'. In R. C. Atkinson and H. A. Wilson (Eds,), *Computer-Assisted Instruction: A Book of Readings*, New York: Academic Press.

Suppes, P. (1966) 'The uses of computers in education'. *Scientific American*, 215:206-221.

Zhang, J., Gibbons, A.S. and Merrill, M.D. (in press) 'Automating the design of adaptive and self-improving instruction'. In C.R. Dills and A.J. Romiszowski (Eds), *Instructional Development: State of the Art.* Englewood Cliffs, NJ: Instructional Technology Publications.

# Simulation and computer-based learning

# 4 Design requirements for computer-based learning systems for aircraft manufacturers

*A.F. O'Neal*

**Introduction**

Designing instructional systems (including computer-based learning systems) for aircraft manufacturers is especially challenging. Instructional Systems Design (ISD) is often misunderstood and its potential is constrained by the conventional preferences of subject-matter experts and client crew members. Instructional strategy is often mistakenly construed to mean little more than media selection, and the need for differential instructional strategies for different types of learning outcomes is largely unrecognized, as is the need for particular schedules of practice for skill development and maintenance. Though learners are being provided with increased control over learning, especially in sophisticated interactive courseware and simulated environments, greater attention should be given to enhancing the effectiveness of high-fidelity simulators as instructional systems. The cost-effectiveness of computer-based learning systems is being increased through the use of templates and transaction shells. Performance support tools are blurring the distinction between training programs and on-the-job support systems and are focusing attention on resolving performance problems rather than merely providing training interventions. The instructional effectiveness of computer-based learning systems can be improved significantly through the judicious application of a number of recommendations that are presented.

Designing instructional systems (including computer-based learning systems) for aircraft manufacturers is especially challenging. In an increasingly competitive business climate manufacturers must be responsive to wide ranging, often contradictory sets of client and market pressures. Their use of computer-based learning systems must accommodate internal and client training needs, provide added value for marketing support, and present an image of technological leadership and state-of-the-art technical innovation. Concurrently, hardware and software technologies involved in computer based training are evolving at an ever increasing rate.

The challenge of keeping up-to-date and responding to rapid advancements in instructional technology becomes immensely more complicated in a manufacturing environment where innovation faces an entrenched corporate culture, and more to the point, an entrenched training culture, buttressed by organizational and personnel structures that have evolved to meet historical corporate and client needs. Thus, innovation may be stymied by everything from union contracts, internal competition for personnel and resources, legacy classroom and audio-visual training systems, and established client expectations, to the ever formidable philosophical position that 'we've always done it this way'.

In recent years aircraft manufacturers have been transitioning from a heavy dependence upon traditional lecture and audio-visual training methodologies to increasing use of computer-based technologies, but the state of this transition across organizations is uneven. This chapter discusses the largely unleashed potential of instructional systems design within the context of computer-based learning systems in aviation training. We recommend ways of realizing more fully the potential of sophisticated instructional design technologies to increase the efficiency and effectiveness of training. These ideas are derived from our experience of working with aircraft manufacturing training organizations.

For purposes of clarity, we begin with a discussion of what we consider to be important aspects of a computer-based learning system within the broader context of formal instructional systems design.

**Computer-based learning systems**

Computer-based learning systems are that subset of instructional systems which harness the impressive capabilities of computers to develop, deliver and manage instruction. As such, any discussion of computer-based learning systems should include at least a cursory exploration of the major technologies involved, these being instructional design, training delivery systems, and software application programs for producing, delivering, and managing training.

*Instructional systems design*

A significant barrier to designing a computer-based learning system in aircraft manufacturing environments as an instance of a true instructional system is that 'instructional systems' as a comprehensive concept has historically been accepted only superficially. To some, instructional system is synonymous with delivery systems, for example, CBT versus standup lecture and/or traditional audio-visual presentation. To others, the term instructional system evokes images of administrative tracking systems used to manage development and delivery of training. To some, it is synonymous with the corporate organization responsible training. Even when a more meaningful interpretation of instructional systems prevails, instructional design expertise is often seen as subordinate to what has historically been considered to be the real source of training expertise, the content expert.

We use the term instructional systems design to refer to a systematic, rigorous and well documented process that integrates analysis, design, development, implementation and evaluation activities to achieve verifiable learning outcomes. Associated with each phase of this process is a set of defined products. Of particular importance is the emphasis the data-based evaluation and quality assurance, and the concerted effort to use evaluation results to identify desirable revisions to both product and process. Historically, this approach has come into conflict with the subject-matter expert centered approach dominant in the aircraft manufacturing community. A notable exception has been on military aviation projects where stringent instructional design standards have been set by military commands (ref. Interservice ISD Procedures). Recent events in the regulatory climate of the United States are providing an impetus for equally stringent training development standards in civil aviation, through emerging initiatives such as the FAA Advanced Qualification Program (AQP).

The uneven, often a low level of general understanding of and commitment to rigorous models of instructional design in aircraft manufacturer training organizations that persists does not derive from a lack of expertise with the training team. For the most part, ISD expertise and experience is typically well represented within aviation training organizations. Nevertheless, the potential contribution of these instructional design specialists is often diluted by the egos and predilections of two primary stakeholders of aviation training practice, the manufacturer's subject matter-experts and the client airline's senior crew members. In any debate about alternative instructional design strategies between the instructional designers and subject matter experts, the views of the subject matter experts, usually being more senior and embodying the proud tradition of developing successful training in the past, almost always prevail. Likewise, the expectations and views of client senior crew decision-makers, who after all are the raison d'étre for the training organization, have far more influence on course design than instructional designers. In such an environment, the real power of instructional design is minimized to incremental changes in practice at best. To some extent, subject-matter experts and crew-members are innovation proof, especially those who have considerable experience of preparing and presenting classroom courses. They seem to find it difficult to conceptualize alternative ways of helping learners achieve mastery. There is a tendency to try to force fit old ways of teaching within the context of new presentation technologies, rather then undertaking a total revamping of the overall approach to helping learners learn. Thus, the opportunity to take a fresh look at how the training is designed as the transition from conventional training approaches to computer-based instruction is thwarted. In short, the real power of instructional systems design can be realized only when all of the parties engaged in course design are willing to radically change both the design and the presentation of instructional content.

*Instructional strategy*

A cornerstone of instructional systems design is that careful consideration should be given to the types of learning objectives to be mastered and the instructional strategies selected to achieve those outcomes. The notion that different types of learning require different types of instructional strategies is widely accepted by instructional designers, and it disheartening for designers to see instructional strategy being equated often with instructional media in aviation training. We have observed that media delivery systems tend to be selected for economic or logistical reasons rather than for their potential to provide learners with the sights, sounds, and interactions required by the learning task. Minimal attention, if any, is given to identifying those media attributes that are essential or highly desirable for the learner to achieve particular learning outcomes. As a consequence, the instructional designer's flexibility is reduced to designing within a particular medium, with all of its inherent limitations. The designers' problems are further compounded when they are required to weave multiple objectives representing different types of learning into lessons or, using a sort of generic, one-size-fits-all strategy. The rationale for this approach, as often as not, is that the learner will exercise all these skills in concert on-the-job. In summary, the idea that instruction should be focused and differentially structured to meet the needs of different types of learning tasks is still not widely implemented.

*Practice strategies*

Other fundamental instructional principles that are often inadequately applied in aviation training concern the complexity and schedule of practice. Much of aviation training involves the application of procedures and rules that must be performed and applied in complex situations and contexts. In sound instructional design, the cognitive skills that need to be acquired by the target learning population are identified through a rigorous analysis of desired terminal and enabling learning objectives. These cognitive skills are then optimally sequenced based upon hypothesized hierarchical relationships, and are presented to learners using a variety of instructional strategies. Of critical importance, is the nature and frequency of practice. Within the training program itself, skills are ideally practiced in isolation until mastered, and then practiced in increasingly complex combinations until the real world context within which they will be performed is approximated. Of equal importance is the effort expended by learners to maintain competence after the training intervention. If skills are not practiced periodically, they are likely to decay. In our experience, we have seen this graduated approach applied somewhat haphazardly and performance maintenance is primarily based on regulatory and resource constraints, rather than on periodic competency assessment. Though the advantage of distributed over massed practice in skill development and maintenance is well known, recurring training is administered on a regular calendar basis for all trainees rather than on an assessment of individual performance.

It is still all too often the case that coverage is more important than competence for many skills.

*Learner control*

One area of instructional design in which considerable progress has been made is in accommodating a wide range of learner backgrounds and learning goals through implementation of relatively rich learner control structures. If one were to analyze the branching complexity and control structure of computer-based aviation courseware extant in 10 years ago, one would find that they rarely exceeded an average branching level of 4 to 6 branches per frame. More recent examples of aviation courseware provide coefficients of branching complexity above 20 branches per frame. Learners now have considerable flexibility and degrees of freedom in navigating through the instructional content. Increased learner control means that a training program can be used effectively and efficiently in a variety of instructional contexts, including initial instruction, transition courses, and refresher/review training. When high levels of branching and content control are incorporated, courseware can be used to review individual procedures, thus functioning as a performance support tool rather than pure instruction. Overall, significant advances are been made in the area of learner control.

*Instructional simulations*

The aviation industry has been a major contributor to the development of simulators and simulation techniques. Advances in visual systems, software sophistication, proprioceptive cues and performance recording have been impressive. The cost-effectiveness of simulators has been reduced considerably by the introduction of 2-D and 3-D part-task training systems on low-cost computer equipment. High fidelity simulators provide rich feedback, especially in terms of contextual cues and immediate feedback to learner actions, and some critically important training can be done safely only on the simulator. Full-flight simulators permit pilots to practice from take-off to docking in an environment which is both safe and highly motivational. However, simulated environments can be confusing to learners because of their complex and often confusing stimulus context. In addition, in the real-time, all at once context of student-simulator activity, it is often difficult for learners to discriminate which of their actions elicited which set of contextual cues.

Sophistication of simulators, therefore, does not necessarily translate into more effective instruction. On the contrary, we would propose that the more complex and multifunctional the systems being simulated, the less effective a high-fidelity simulator is likely to be as an instructional device. Of course, simulators make very powerful practice and certification devices, but they are very inefficient and expensive instructional devices, especially as currently designed. It is usually much more effective to provide instruction on knowledge (name, location, function, for example) and individual procedures in environments other than the simulator. As component skills are mastered in less complex environment, simulations can be used effectively to integrate practice and certify skill mastery.

As hardware costs continue to tumble and as the nature of the systems being simulated continue to evolve into increasingly automated computer applications, the costs of using simulators within training will decrease. However, we need to ensure that cost reductions are accompanied by increases in instructional effectiveness. The instructional power of simulators could be significantly enhanced by incorporating intelligent performance tracking and evaluation capabilities. These would permit the isolation and identification of performance problems and trends, and would provide specific and focused feedback to learners. Tomorrow's intelligent simulators will become more powerful instructional (as opposed to practice and certification) tools when they can interrupt the learning activity, freeze the action, deliver expert instructional feedback and provide the opportunity for some part-task training, before resuming the integrated activity.

*Authoring software and curriculum development tools*

As the size and complexity of computer-based curricula increase, the emphasis is shifting from 'authoring' courseware to 'manufacturing' courseware. Authoring systems (O'Neal, A.F. and Fairweather, P.G., 1984a; 1984b; O'Neal, A.F., and Jennings, J., 1989; Walker, R.A., O'Neal, A.F., and Campbell, J.O., 1989) are growing in sophistication and power, but the most impressive advances are being made in the way authoring and software tools are being used on large scale courseware development projects. Increasingly, we are seeing the use of instructional templates that prescribe in considerable detail the 'look and feel' of courseware. These templates constrain somewhat the instructional designer's degrees of freedom; they significantly improve instructional design productivity, consistency, and quality. Lesson generators such as those used by Boeing and McDonnell Douglas are evolving over time into true transaction shells (Baer and O'Neal, 1988; Merrill, Li and Jones, 1992; Li and Merrill, 1990).

Templates enable development teams to be much more productive because the nature of the instructional task is carefully analyzed and then classified into a limited set of learning outcomes and associated instructional and presentation strategies. Templates are created which represent effective strategies for each type of learning outcome (for example, concepts, rules, procedures). The scripting of individual lessons is highly leveraged because once you have classified an instructional objective in terms of the strategy template to be employed, there is little time wasted on scripting activities directed at creatively solving the instructional problem. In a highly templated environment, the scriptwriter who would aspire to poetry is limited to a well structured form, in terms of both content and structure. This leads to considerable gains in productivity in script production and content definition.

Using standard authoring tools logic and lesson integration can consume 25-40% of the development budget on complex courseware projects. With a well crafted transaction shell, this can be reduced to less than 5%. Since a mature transaction shell completely defines instructional strategy logic and lesson behaviour, this component is almost completely eliminated as a cost. Once scripting and content definition is complete, the lesson runs immediately, without further logic definition or integration activity. Minor adjustments to logic parameters are possible, but are minimally necessary or advisable.

Templates also beneficially impact lesson testing and quality control. In a transaction shell, since the branching logic is built into the tool and generated automatically according to global rules, once each strategy template has been thoroughly tested, further lesson testing need focus only on content accuracy. The elimination of logic testing on a lesson by lesson basis is elimination of a major development cost, especially in courseware where learner control is high.

Another advantage of templates and transaction shells is that the major investment of the development project, that is content analysis and courseware development, is recoverable, independent of the authoring software environment. This means that a shift to an alternative software platform or operating system requires only that the template logics be duplicated in that environment. The database of content then becomes completely runnable without further authoring, since the template environment handles lesson integration and branching logic. This idea of lesson definition above the authoring system level is growing in importance in the deliberations of forums such as those held by AICC.

*Training management and scheduling*

One of the most exciting developments in industry has been the evolution of Electronic Performance Support Systems (EPSS). This has been accompanied by a redefinition of the relationship between training and on-the-job performance. The chronological and organizational separation of training and job performance is yielding to a more integrated approach. In corporate training the emphasis is moving away from simply providing training to resolving real performance problems. Renewed interest in performance analysis is leading to careful consideration of both training and non-training solutions such as modifying operational procedures, restructuring processes, and providing performance support tools.

Managers of training functions require performance support systems that will help them match the skills, qualifications, availability and location of personnel to job requirements, while operating within regulatory requirements. Balancing these needs against tracking and scheduling needed requalification and certification activities and the scheduling of adjunct resources adds complexity. There is great value in closing the loop with systems that empower the line manager by providing him with the personnel, training, and skills/qualifications information he needs, in the context of job requirements and regulatory constraints. At the same time the system should be collecting information and providing inputs which will lead to modifications to both the training and to operational practice.

When a regulatory requirement, a piece of equipment (and its related tasks and skills), or a procedure changes, the system will identify all related documentation, training materials and/or job aids or references that must be updated. In addition the skill/qualification profile of all personnel affected will be modified to reflect their new status in terms of the new requirements, and both them and their supervisors will be notified of the change in status. Since these personnel and other databases will be widely distributed geographically, communications capability (such as TCP/IP capability) will be extremely important.

In this distributed, dynamic and highly interrelated information environment perturbations in any element of the system will ripple through the entire system until action is taken to resolve the resulting dissonance. Managers, supervisors, and personnel will know their exact status at any time, and they will be able to view their alternatives in changing that status on any dimension. The company will be better protected through assurance and documentation that tasks and procedures are carried out correctly, and by fully qualified personnel.

Both the design of the training materials and the assessment and reporting systems will be significantly different for this distributed training environment, when compared to the existing, up front training design approach.

## Recommendations

This chapter has identified several important design factors and trends that should be considered when designing computer-based learning systems for aviation. This is a fluid and rapidly evolving arena, where the principal technologies and the interactions among them will continue to change at an increasing rate. The nature of the computer based learning systems that will emerge is hard to predict; however, the following recommendations can be offered with reasonable confidence:

*Apply instructional systems design techniques and procedures*

Today's analytic-prescriptive design models offer significant advantages over the empirical and artistic-intuitive models of the past. For maximum impact, these design models must be applied systematically and comprehensively. Superficial lip service will not improve practice or training quality.

*Use appropriate instructional strategies for each type of learning outcome*

The instructional strategy for each class of objective should be appropriate for that type of instructional outcome. There is no single optimal strategy for all types of instructional problems.

*Teach each instructional objective separately*

Mixing different types of objectives in a hybrid instructional strategy is less effective and efficient than using strategies appropriate for each type of objective. One size does not fit all in instructional design.

*Design modularly and provide high levels of learner control*

Well designed modular lessons provide instructional opportunities for different types of learners and allow the materials to be used for a variety of purposes such as including initial training, review, job aiding and referencing.

*Integrate and distribute practice*

Having taught different types of objectives separately, multiple objectives should be integrated in successive levels of practice and skills building, until the full required performance context is achieved. Performance levels should be maintained by distributed practice or measured on-the-job performance.

*Simulate instructionally*

Design simulations and simulators so that they are effective instructional environment as well as integrated practice and certification devices.

*Use instructional templates and transaction shells*

Design and produce lessons using instructional templates and transaction shells to improve design and development productivity and consistency facilitate migration to new platforms and operating systems.

*Use performance support systems to assess/deliver instruction and performance support continuously*

Reconsider the artificial separation of training and on-the-job performance. Reduce reliance on up-front training by using performance support tools that incorporate easy-to-access instructional content, organized in such a way as to maximize learner control.

**References**

Baer, L.H. and O'Neal, A.F. (March 1988) 'Very large scale production of CBI for military training', *Technology in Training and Education* (TITE) conference paper and proceedings, Biloxi, Miss.

Fairweather, P.G. and O'Neal, A.F. (Summer 1984) 'The Impact of Advanced Authoring Systems on CAI Productivity'. *Journal of Computer Based Instruction.*

Li, Z., and Merrill, M. D. (1990) 'Transaction shells: A new approach to courseware authoring'. *Journal of Research on Computing in Education,* 23(10, 72-86).

Merrill, M.D., and Li, Z., and Jones, M.K. (1992) 'Instructional transaction shells: responsibilities, methods, and parameters'. *Educational Technology*, 32(2), 5-27.

O'Neal, A.F. and Fairweather, P.G. (December 1984) 'The evaluation and selection of computer-based training authoring systems'. *CALICO Journal*.

O'Neal, A.F., and Jennings, J. (1989) 'Automatic lesson generation: productivity and instructional rigor,' *Defence Systems International: The Annual Review of Air Systems,* Sterling Publishing Group, London.

Walker, R.A., O'Neal, A.F., and Campbell, J.O. (1989) 'Automated lesson generation for high volume computer based instruction - Phase II,' SALT Conference on Interactive Instruction Delivery, Orlando, Fla.

# 5 Simulation as an instructional procedure

*Richard Macfarlane*

**Introduction**

Simulation and simulator based training have been an important part of the aviation industry for many years now. They have proven to be a most effective and efficient means of transferring critical flight task methodology from one pilot to another as well as a safe and reliable platform for the practise of flight skills. In many cases, industry has come to rely on these devices and indeed flight crews expect and accept simulator sorties as part of their professional routine.

The concept of simulation however, covers a broad range of ideas and ideals and in general terms there is often discrepancy on just what simulators are and are not capable of achieving. History has recorded some very successful simulators that found a niche in the flight training and practise of their day, but the evolution of flight simulation, as a realistic representation of flight parameters, has often overshadowed the practical value of simulators and led to a number of false assumptions about their training value. Technological advances within the industry have outpaced educational practise and a general misunderstanding of the value of specific training techniques has had some less than positive ramifications in the areas of training effectiveness, training efficiency and in particular training costs.

Direct savings in operating costs have been the traditional justification for the purchase of flight simulators in the commercial world and their relative cost effectiveness has been well documented by the sales and marketing

*Designing Instruction for Human Factors Training in Aviation*

people. Adding the commensurate improvement in safety and crew competence under adverse conditions, makes the research dollars that have been directed at the more sophisticated end of the aviation industry readily understandable. Tacit recognition of the technological advances at this level has been made with the designation and approval of zero flight time (ZFT) simulators in which the entire aircraft type-training can be conducted.

In contrast, the benefits for ab initio flight training have been less spectacular with far fewer research dollars being invested and an accordant level of research interest and regulatory acceptability. This is understandable in that the concepts of skill acquisition and skill maintenance are more often misunderstood and misdirected than not. Reasons for this are varied but argument suggests that most syllabi do not reflect the range of skills flight crew need to do their job and that the more commonly used

**Figure 5.1 An example of a basic instrument trainer: The Frasca 141**

training methods don't focus on those requirements. Add to this the mismeasurement generated by the fallacy that flight time equates to competency and the demand for a new system of training and evaluation begins to emerge.

Presently the regulatory authorities in most countries will credit up to ten percent of the flight training requirements in terms of hours to ground based simulators. Those hours are designated for the procedural Instrument Flight Rules (IFR) category only. The value of simulation at this level has been well documented (Lintern and Kennedy, 1984; Lintern, 1988) and transfer benefits have been found to be quite high (Flexman, Roscoe, Williams and Williges, 1972; Jacobs, 1976; Povenmire and Roscoe, 1971; ibid, 1973). This has led to more research in the determination of optimum simulator hours for training transfer to the cockpit and ergo, cost effective training (Lintern, Sheppard, Parker, Yates and Nolan, 1989) but this seems to have escaped the regulatory authorities.

Recognition of the training value of simulation as with other aspects of flight training particularly at the ab initio level has remained stagnant despite evidence (Prophet and Boyd, 1970 cited in Caro, 1988; Povenmire and Roscoe, 1973; Roscoe, 1980) that even low cost basic ground trainers can significantly reduce the number of flight hours it takes to train pilots to fly aeroplanes. More recently, a longitudinal study by Ross (1989) demonstrated a transfer effectiveness of the skills required for first solo flight of thirty two percent using a basic Novasim FT-1 with little or no instructor training on the use of the device. The recognition problem has been further exacerbated by authority inspectors who evaluate training devices for realism rather than training effectiveness. This is evidenced by the demand for motion to be simulated to obtain credits in level I plus simulators despite overwhelming documentation (Caro, 1979; Jacobs and Roscoe, 1980; Lintern, 1987; Kennedy and Fowlkes, 1992) that complex cockpit motion has so little effect on training transfer that its contribution is difficult to measure at all and on balance is more likely to be slightly detrimental rather than beneficial.

This book is dedicated to designing human factors training in aviation as stated in the title. This chapter will explore simulation in general, look at the perceptions and needs of flight training and the syllabus requirements associated with those needs, consider the methodology to integrate the two successfully and discuss the potential advantages, disadvantages and future directions for the implementation of such a training system. In the context of this book it will consider the understanding of instructional conditions, improving methods for delivering instruction, the management of that instruction in the training / education environment and the evaluation of its effectiveness.

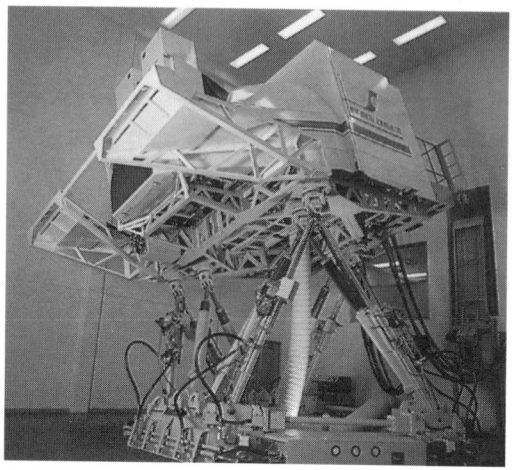

**Figure 5.2   The motion system hardware for Air New Zealand's DC10 simulator**

**The tools of the trade**

*What should a simulator do ?*

The purpose of most simulators is to educate student pilots in the basic principles underlying safe flight while teaching the specific knowledge, skills and doctrine that define the professional pilot. Doctrine, knowledge and skills are first learned and practised in the simulator before being attempted in the aircraft. Flying the aircraft then becomes a test of what has just been learned, a reward for learning it well and a chance to apply, polish and explore. For simplicity, references to simulators in this chapter means the type specific devices, which may include either or both visual and motion systems. Edward Stark (1989) in his excellent overview of simulation favoured a broad definition and described a simulator as a 'surrogate for a real system'. In many senses this is so but it does leave out the concept of fidelity. Simulator fidelity is most often regarded and assessed in terms of psychological fidelity and physical fidelity. The physical aspects embrace equipment and environmental fidelity and the psychological aspects embrace the perceived realism of those physical features. Hays and Singer (1989) take this concept further with the following definition:

*Simulation as an Instructional Procedure*

**Figure 5.3 There's nothing like the real thing**

> Simulation fidelity is the degree of similarity between the training situation and the operational situation which is simulated. It is a two dimensional measurement of this similarity in terms of: (1) the physical characteristics, for example, visual, spatial, kinaesthetic, etc.; and (2) the functional characteristic, for example, the informational, and stimulus and response options of the training situation.

Flight training requirements however show a need for an analysis that focus on the training level. That is to distinguish those simulators that are designed as an aid to skill acquisition from those focusing on skill maintenance. Fidelity in this respect could be analyzed on two ends of a continuum differentiated as task fidelity and instructional fidelity (see figure 5.4). Task fidelity is the degree to which the simulator is able to recreate the actual parameters and realism of a mission. Its specific application is in terms of practise or recurrency training. The skills necessary to complete the mission have already been learned and need to be maintained at an acceptable level or require practise until a higher level of mission accomplishment is achieved. For example, a pilot may have learned to fly an instrument approach but needs to practise approaches in a specific aircraft type over and over to improve his or her accuracy and/or maintain a level of currency that will allow the compulsory biannual flight tests to be passed easily and well within the regulatory tolerances. Specifically, task fidelity is associated with skill maintenance, and simulator missions can be designed to maintain handling skills, procedural skills and decision making skills. An example encompassing all three parameters might be flying a procedural ILS approach within a half scale deflection and carrying out the missed approach following the onset of windshear on late finals.

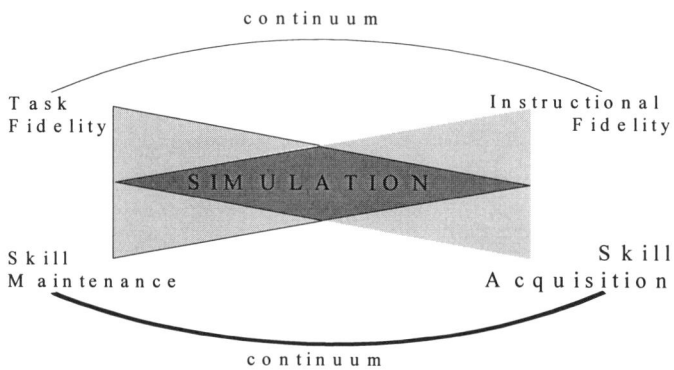

**Figure 5.4 Relationship between simulator fidelity flight crew skill**

At the other end of the continuum, it needs to be determined whether a given level of fidelity for a simulator is appropriate to the learning of a specific task or tasks. Instructional fidelity is the degree to which the instruction or the instructional system is able to effectively transfer new skills to the pilot. In other words, it is specifically associated with skill acquisition within the training context. For example, a pilot learning to use a new piece of navigation equipment such as a Global Positioning System (GPS) will have better results by initially part tasking the requirements and learning to use it as a stand alone system and then gradually integrating it into his or her full cockpit environment. As with skill maintenance, skill acquisition can equally be defined in terms of handling skills, procedural skills and decision making skills such that simulators (more realistically described as part task trainers in this role) exhibiting high levels of instructional fidelity would also have a high transfer effectiveness in each of these categories.

*Simulation as an Instructional Procedure*

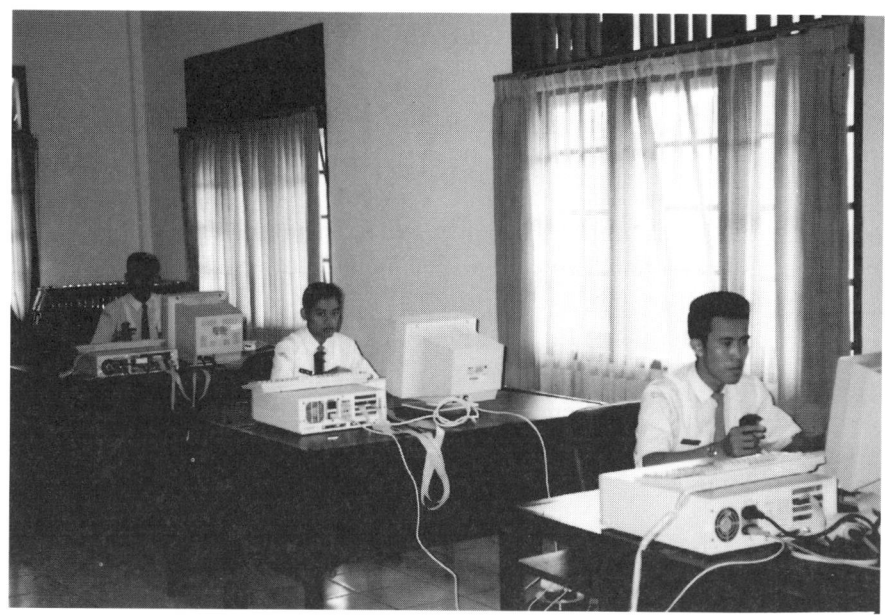

**Figure 5.5** First year students utilizing desktop PC's at the elementary stage

**Figure 5.6** Third year students utilizing Boeing 737-300's simulator for their type conversion

*Designing Instruction for Human Factors Training in Aviation*

The past suggests a fairly average record in terms of building the correct simulator for the task at hand and while many of these were brought about by a misunderstanding of what flight crews actually do, the concept of task fidelity would appear to have been paramount. Indeed, even now, many well respected pilots who purport to be in the training business, will initially judge a simulator by its level of task fidelity rather than question its potential training capability. Presently available in the market place is a quite large and reasonable selection of simulator offerings that cover the broad range of the task fidelity/instructional fidelity continuum. At one end of the scale we see widespread use of cockpit mockups, procedural trainers, and role playing scenarios which are directed towards specific training objectives and at the other end, a testament to the technological advances made in recent years with ZFT offerings which are barely distinguishable from the real thing.

The well worn adage of 'horses for courses' is as relevant to effective simulator training as it is for aircraft selection. The needs of the task will determine the appropriate level of simulation. For example, the skills needed to fly a twin turboprop aircraft from Wellington to Auckland can be well demonstrated, taught and practised in a simulator. The most appropriate simulator however would depend on why the skills were being demonstrated, taught or practised. A student learning concepts prior to professional licensing will initially aquire more skills from a desktop PC

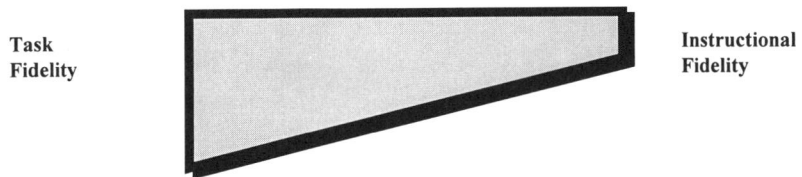

**Figure 5.7** **Type specific capabilities for WLG - AKL sortie**

based simulator than from a generic twin simulator, which would be equally more effective than a 3-axes motion type specific simulator.

*Simulation as an Instructional Procedure*

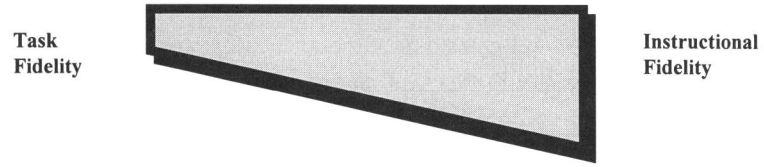

**Figure 5.8   Advanced training device capabilities for WLG - AKL sortie**

Equally, the reverse would be true for an experienced pilot maintaining both route and type currency. He or she would be much better served by the high task fidelity type specific simulators than the generic twin and so on. (See figure 5.7 and 5.8)

In the light of these claims, simulator acquisition poses a significant problem and in most cases, compromise is more cost effective then dedication. Any organization that requires simulation for both the skill acquisition and the skill maintenance roles can rarely afford the progression of simulator types to cover all requirements and a rational compromise usually based on available capital is made. This point brings the most number of acquisition mistakes. What a simulator is capable of doing and what it is most likely to do for you are very different things. Simulator acquisition is still at a stage where the people making the decision are not those at the coal face doing the job. A good salesperson in this role will always sell an organization what it can afford rather than what it needs. This condition reflects a need to have the 'best' simulator and present buying trends reflect this condition. The quality of some of the sales pitches and demonstrations are quite remarkable but an analogy exists with movie trailers. Sometimes the best bits in the entire film make up the two minute trailer.

The secret to successful acquisition relies on an in depth, needs analysis for the organization. Concepts of essential requirements, nice to haves, future needs and operational standards for approval must be addressed both at policy making and delivery level. While syllabus requirements are often the catalyst for acquisition, the more esoteric needs such as recruiting capability, prestige at management level and research capacity can all be addressed in their proper perspective if the analysis is done properly. The sales initiative of 'what a simulator *can* do for an organization' is then replaced with a set of realistic search criteria that incorporate the essential elements that cannot be compromised, those that can be can be accepted or rejected on a cost benefit basis and those that would be a bonus if included. As suggested earlier, buying trends currently reflect too many of the bonus issues and not enough of the essential elements.

**Figure 5.9   Advanced training device from Hawker De Havilland**

A pitch here should also be made for compromise at management level for commercial gain.  The concept of simulator centres even utilized by competing organizations is a sensible one which also promotes efficient usage and a better spread of capabilities with the same capital expenditure. While initial lobbying can be time consuming the resultant capability for an organization or group of organizations is quite profound. Visual, auditory and kinaesthetic discrimination issues are necessarily addressed more objectively, the perennial issue of motion as a selection criteria can be looked on as a student motivational tool rather than a regulation for credits and perhaps more importantly, use and misuse is more carefully monitored in a multi-user environment.

The attitude of the local aviation authority to simulators must also be taken into account. While there have been some concessions made over the years resulting in credits against flight time for General Aviation, there appears to be very little interest, recognition or acceptance of generic trainers in gaining flight time credits. The only common standard in General Aviation appears to be associated with procedural training for instrument rating training and renewals. More recently, in some parts of the world, recognition has been give to cheap PC programmes which do much the same thing as larger more expensive equipment. As these appear to have the same effect on training, there is no valid reason not to use them. No surprises in this result; researchers have been advocating this for many years.

Authorities cannot seem to reach agreement on standards to be applied to approve procedural trainers, simulators or ATD's or the purpose for which they should be certified. Currently instrument trainers of the Frasca or AST category are more or less accepted throughout the Western world and parts of Asia. However, there is still plenty of argument between countries as to what is required. Mostly this is brought about by zealous personnel in the Authority who want to compare it with a specific aircraft type in flight characteristics, performance, feel and motion. What the device is supposed to do is often of secondary consideration.

It is interesting to observe experienced pilots fly these devices, including CAA licensing personnel. Cockpit checks are overlooked with the expected results, e.g. gear retracted until the warning system is activated, park brake left on, out of fuel on one side and full on the other. Although generic, these devices should respond in a similar manner to the aircraft and need to be treated accordingly. Many experienced people will try an approach but let airspeed remain at cruise setting and then wonder why it all went wrong.

The most common criticism of these devices is feel. While this has some validity in type specific devices, it has little value in generic devices. The range of aircraft used in training is wide. The difference in 'feel' is also wide. If trainees are taught to use feel in preference to what the flight instruments or visual system is displaying, then negative transfer could well result.

While these conditions prevail, there will be little advancement in development of more sophisticated devices. This is unfortunate, as the cost of this type of computer equipment reduces almost by the day. A proper study into these aspects of training needs to be undertaken so manufacturers have some guidelines for product development. If such a study were to be implemented, Aviation Authorities must heed the findings and act accordingly, otherwise the effort is not worth while.

We have sufficient research results over many years which indicate the benefits to be obtained from different training strategies and techniques. Aviation Authorities need to induct into their workforce, persons who understand these and encourage progressive introduction of these methods. As Stan Roscoe (1980) points out:

Many changes in regulations are expedients designed to solve a problem that has already developed. Often solutions to existing problems create new problems, which in turn are 'solved' by new regulations.

Regulations can ensure minimum standards, but in the same process (in this industry) guarantee mediocrity. The cost of training is high, therefore any attempt to raise standards beyond that required is to the GA operator a recipe for financial disaster. On the other hand, if safety is to be improved, then training methods and standards must be improved. Perhaps it may be timely to introduce a different approach. As an example, if insurers were to take a deeper interest in training results in terms of claim pay outs, then it would be possible to regulate the training standards in proportion to its dollar value.

Other commercial considerations also need to be taken into account. Commercial aviation always has the desire to cut overheads in pursuit of better business and profitability. In many cases these cuts can be in areas which can compromise safety. For example, a reduction in training effort can impact directly on the accident rate in any airborne operation. Civil Aviation Authorities (CAA's) world wide are constantly plagued with requests for concessions, or changes to regulations for economic purposes. In some cases these changes are justified where they in fact retain or improve the operational safety and cut cost. In other cases, CAAs' incur considerable criticism when trying to implement changes which affect costs, which they believe will improve safety.

More often than not, training is carried out to the statutory minimum requirement. Because of the fierce competition between operators for the training dollar, additional costs not associated with the accrual of flight time are too hard to justify. The decision to invest in any training devices is normally driven by either regulations, cost reduction, or is justified by credits against flight time resulting in savings. The student does not have the choice, (or the knowledge or encouragement) to expand the training syllabus to include those elements which contribute to safer flight.

Essentially, the economic problems seen by GA operators are the capital cost of equipment (unnecessary in the eyes of many who stand true to the traditional method of training) and the general lack of appreciation of the concepts. The remainder of this chapter is aimed at reviewing that appreciation.

*Simulation as an Instructional Procedure*

**Figure 5.10 What do you really want in a simulator?**

In choosing a simulator, some items are essential and others are flexible to allow for off-the-shelf choices. In the essential category are:

- Reliability
- Warranty
- Maintenance
- Support
- Training

Of a more flexible nature are:

- Tactile Fidelity
- Networking
- Authority Approval

Determining the specific function of a simulator will likely result in a request for at least four different models. Once again, the art of compromise is imperative because there will always be areas of commonality where functions overlap. Issues here include:

- Configuration
- Representative a/c types
- Instruments and avionics
- Database
- Plotters
- Systems failures
- Freeze capability
- Visual and/or motion capability

**Perceptions and perspectives**

*Understanding instructional conditions*

A 747 line pilot undertaking his or her six monthly proficiency check in the interests of maintaining safety standards has a number of significantly different parameters associated with the simulator sortie than they do on an operational trip. In most cases the route for the checkride will have been well studied prior to the check, the expectation of particular emergencies will have been addressed and the human factor concerns of the actual trip, such as sleep loss, fatigue, circadian disrhythmia, communication breakdown with ESL controllers, among a myriad of possibilities, will not exist. Expectations are associated with the sortie and exercise mentality sets in. Equally, the support pilot brings an exercise mentality to the sortie though the parameters are quite different. The stress associated with a personal checkride doesn't exist, crashing the simulator has far less connotations than the real thing and 'get-home-itis' has already been taken care of, to name a few. Understanding these instructional conditions is the unenviable task of the simulator supervisor.

*Simulation as an Instructional Procedure*

*"Oh stop suspecting sir ... It's only a simulator"*

**Figure 5.11 Instructor-induced motivation**

The essence of success in this task is in the maintenance of the aim of the exercise. Simulation should not be undertaken for simulation's sake but rather for some predetermined purpose and it is this purpose that reflects both the art and the science of simulation. Instructor induced system faults in simulator exercises are the norm but oft quoted anecdotes of overloading to the point of crashing are a symptom of mismanagement and are guaranteed to cause more harm than good. Crashing is not the aim of any exercise in routine flight training and evaluation. Equally, poor performance needs to be addressed. Anecdotes of Captains crashing during 'V1 CUT' exercises in the simulator do nothing to inspire confidence in the First Officers on the line and a marked reluctance by them even to leave the seat for a nature break during normal operations. Poor simulator performance needs to be addressed, and needs to be seen to be addressed, or its purpose is nullified and the aim of the exercise unfulfilled. Unfortunately, this aspect is regularly disregarded to the detriment of organizations. An understanding of this simple criterion can make a marked difference to the instructional conditions being experienced. The aim places the whole sortie into perspective and promotes an overall understanding for everyone concerned with the exercise.

The aim of an exercise can also affect perceptions of a simulators 'worth'. While initial judgements are generally based on the level of task fidelity, one of the key factors to the acceptance of simulation comes from their acceptance by the regulatory authorities. If the simulator hours can be logged then they must be good and an absence of regulatory acceptance renders them useless. While this might appear remarkable to many, the condition exists in both instructors and students at most levels of aviation. For the younger generation, the scramble for logged hours, which is erroneously associated with competence in our industry at present, makes the time spent in non-approved simulators redundant and at the more senior levels, measures of achievement in aviation terms do not include unlogged hours. The conservative inertia of the aviation authorities on a global basis have implications in this area for unused capacity in terms of training effectiveness, training efficiency and in particular the reduction in training costs. The most definitive research in the world is useless unless it is utilized to some good. The proof of simulator worth is a misnomer if it is not used by the instructors or their students, the testing officers or their candidates but merely remains a research tool of the altruistic.

Full flight simulators would be a bonus in every organization they can be supported in but the intrinsic value of any exercise is rarely found in the fidelity of the simulation itself. In fact, the issue only arises when there is a mismatch between simulator capability and expectation. In this there is as much variability in the students as there is in the instructors. At the instructional level, the simulator should bring the classroom into the cockpit. There are, in fact, many simulator designs that have the capability to bring up lift / drag ratios, vector resolution and flight path displays. All of which are useless unless correctly utilized. The education of both instructors and students in the capability of the simulator is imperative. To conduct training in the simulator the same way as the aircraft is to misuse the device. Most simulators come with a pause or freeze capability that enables an extraordinary amount of teaching and learning during a sortie that is just not available in the aircraft itself. Examples of students who have been labelled as 'no good' and then produce excellent rides as a result of some dedicated simulator time are commonplace in the training industry and yet the persistence in not using the capability for 'normal' students almost amounts to negligence and really does need to be addressed. Here again, the emphasis on horses for courses must be considered.

Most devices, which have some form of flight controls and instruments, placed in typical aircraft configuration, are loosely called simulators in the aviation world. Interestingly, the original 'blue box' was called a link trainer by all and sundry. It's successor, the GAT (General Aviation Trainer) is labelled a trainer, but referred to as a simulator. The computer age has provided the opportunity to introduce devices which can address some of the foregoing issues. While essentially these are referred to as simulators, they are generic in nature, and in some cases, intentionally do not replicate the aircraft exactly. A better description of these is an ATD (Advanced Training Device).

When introducing any training device into a programme, care must be exercised to ensure the device will meet all the requirements of the exercise

*Simulation as an Instructional Procedure*

being undertaken. There are a number of issues that should be explored with any training device before introduction to the training programme. For example, there is no point in a visual system being used that does not meet the criterion for visual transfer. Similarly, devices that place knobs and switches in positions of convenience which are unusual, are known to create transfer problems. The psychological fidelity of the device is of particular importance if the training expectations are to be realized.

**Figure 5.12 Is it really worth it?**

The final group of perspectives associated with simulation that need to be understood to effectively use the devices, relate to the concepts of airmanship and computer phobia which are somewhat interrelated in the aviation industry. Simulatormanship does not exist as a term but it readily evokes the same well respected attributes of pilots exhibiting sound basic skills backed up with good common sense, (CDF in the old airforce terminology). The instillation of these qualities in a student or instructor is an organizational variable which must exist at management level and become part of the culture and climate of the organization. Fear of technology, especially computer based equipment, leads to distrust and an underutilization of capacity. Not in itself a dangerous thing but rather a symptom of the poor airmanship malaise which can and does have disastrous consequences. Human factors has not replaced airmanship in the computer age but excessive trust or distrust in available systems is causing misuse and inappropriate use. This condition needs to be appraised.

## Part tasking the pilots job

*Implementation of Instruction in the training/education context*

Identification of the training need is the first task and it must be considered in the light of the local licensing structure. Traditionally, pilot licenses have been segregated into three levels:

- Private (PPL)
- Commercial (CPL)
- Air Transport (ATPL)

While there are variations in legislation between countries, for a variety of valid reasons, they fundamentally remain intact in all cases. Concessions against flight time for the use of simulators are available in most countries, however, this does not in any way reduce the skill or knowledge requirement for licence issue. It is merely placing a value on this type of training. Similarly, properly constructed training courses delivered in an environment which is accountable also receive recognition by a reduction in flight time. The granting of concessions in these instances is based on the premise that the level of conceptual understanding of the elements involved, together with the skill required to fly the aircraft in accordance with the syllabus requirement, have been demonstrated by the student. The puzzling aspect of this assumption is why do some people pass theory examination well yet can not apply that knowledge to the control of the aircraft or integration of the subject matter into the aircraft operation? In the reverse sense, why can many people fly the aircraft to the required level of competency, yet fail the theory? There appears to be a missing link which is vague to say the least. In the first instance, the person may not see the relevance of the information provided to the practical application. In the other instance, it may be a case of 'monkey see, monkey do'. On the other hand, it may be a case of inappropriate rather than inadequate instruction for that particular person.

In terms of the handling skills development, there are fundamental manoeuvres associated with flight which can be easily identified as they are fundamental to aircraft control in all circumstances. These are defined in most countries' regulations in some form or another. Theory aside, there are supporting requirements without which properly controlled flight with adequate safety precautions cannot occur which are ill-defined. Examples of both applicable to private pilots are listed below.

## Simulation as an Instructional Procedure

| Defined Items | Ill-Defined Items |
|---|---|

### Handling Skills:

Defined Items:
- Effects of controls
- Further effects of controls
- Straight and level
- Gentle turns
- Medium turns
- Advanced (steep) turn
- Climbing
- Climbing turns
- Descending
- Descending turns
- Stalling
- Take off
- Landing
- Cross wind landings
- Drift Recognition
- Emergencies

Ill-Defined Items:
- Radio procedures
- Operating the complex radio equipment required to fly in controlled airspace
- Operating procedures
- Airport procedures, surface movement and traffic patterns
- Pre-flight inspection
- Check lists
- Fuel and oil checks
- Fuel Management
- Weight and balance considerations
- Engineering serviceability
- Paper work entries
- Regulatory constraints

| Defined Items | Ill-Defined Items |
|---|---|

### Procedures:

Defined Items:
- Altimetry
- Pressure height
- Density height
- Map reading
- Compass errors, variation and deviation
- Track and heading
- Drift and drift angles
- Calculating wind velocity
- Time and distance
- Dead reckoning
- Closing angles
- Diversions

Ill-Defined Items:
- Navigation management
- Route planning
- Power management
- Fuel management
- Time management
- Risk management
- Airways procedures
- Cockpit management, flight log, monitoring, clearances etc.
- Regulatory constraints
- Cockpit organization, maps, charts, flight plans etc.

Some may choose to categorize some of these ill defined items as airmanship considerations. Others will classify them as learned through experience. Whatever they may be called, they are real and must be mastered. In the majority of cases they are ill defined as a syllabus item, and neither are they specifically allocated time for the learning process - they more or less 'happen'. At the higher end of the licensing structure, however, some of these undefined concepts are treated with more respect. For example, decision making with respect to aircraft systems is largely enhanced during on the job training, but in fact includes some dedicated time to learn the systems. Systems include:

- Aircraft environmental systems
- Anti-icing / de-icing systems
- Communication systems
- Electrical fire detection
- Flight control systems
- Flight management systems
- Fuel systems
- Lift control systems
- Centre of gravity management
- Glass cockpit displays

These human factor areas have gathered considerable strength over the last 20 years due to the incidents and accidents attributed to this factor. It is a stated fact that 80% of all accidents have some human factor contribution (Phelan, 1994). In fact, the primary cause of some notable accidents have been identified as specifically human factors related. Tragically, it takes accidents to cause change, even though learned men and women working in this field have predicted similar events. For example, the L1011 in the Everglades accelerated the introduction of CRM (cockpit resource management) in airline training programmes.

While we talk about critical in-flight events from the very outset of flight training, what can be demonstrated remains limited by the risk involved. Over the years, human factors have taught us to be very wary of such things as stopping healthy engines and feathering propellers to train pilots for engine-out takeoffs or approach and landing. It is often said that there have been more accidents resulting from training people in these emergency procedures than have occurred through engine malfunction. However, the need is not diminished and it is more a question of how far this can be simulated in the aircraft within safety limitations. The basic control elements of flight are well documented and practised. If these can be learned in a device other than an aircraft with a high rate of transfer at a lesser cost and in complete safety, then there is every reason to pursue these aspects of training in such devices.

Procedural skills have, for almost half a century, been learned and practised in some form of procedural training device ranging from the original 'blue box' Link trainer, to the modern day equivalent, the Frasca. This type of training is widely accepted as satisfactory in the learning stage of instrument flight process. It is further accepted that it is cheaper, has a high rate of transfer and provides a better elementary instructional environment. It is ironical that devices that can do much the same things in elementary flight training are available, yet are not (as yet) accepted as instructional tools.

With respect to decision making skills, the mountain of research into the cause of accidents over the last two decades has highlighted the importance of human factors in the cockpit and clearly indicates the value of specific human factors training for flight crew. One of the most effective methods of training in this regard is being able to generate LOFT scenarios. Simulation, which facilitates the ability to put the crew into the real environment, is a vital component. Unfortunately the perception of LOFT by a wide section of the aviation industry, is that it is attached only to airline flying. A possible reason for this is that it is normally associated with multi crew operations, whereas in the general aviation sector, most operations are single pilot. Another reason could well be that there has been no general training available due to the prohibitive cost of sophisticated devices available to carry out these training exercises. This reason needs to be qualified. The features required to carry out LOFT are usually only available in expensive type specific simulators. There is now appearing on the market, generic ATD's with these capabilities. It may be some time however, before this training is generally available, as the industry has first to understand it and consider it's value.

In essence, LOFT does two things:

1. It allows the pilot or crew to understand the importance of, and make better use of, human factors training, and

2. It adds real life experiences to the existing knowledge store of the participants, i.e. it attempts to put a 3000 hour head onto a 300 hour body. All experienced pilots can relate situations that they have been involved in where they survived either through good luck or good management, but in retrospect would have handled the situation much differently. The programmable potential of modern simulators allows the students to relive these situations and make their own decisions. Solutions may then reasonably be analyzed.

The emergency training need is readily identifiable from the emergencies covered in the syllabus in use. Unfortunately, many of these are proceduralized and do not take into account compounding critical situations which often develop when operating in the full aviation system. Accident investigators and researchers tell us that the major proportion of accidents result from poor judgement skills (Jensen, 1989). This then indicates the special value of LOFT in developing judgmental skills and gaining valuable experience which in turn will enhance overall operational ability.

Why then part tasking? What is not recognized by many instructors, or considered in syllabus design, is the mental diversion these attendant tasks create, the effect on attention priorities and capacity to cope. Research into pilot errors as a source of workload (Hart and Bortolussi, 1984) concluded that 'Errors were rated as a significant source of workload, stress, and performance, suggesting that errors could be conceptualized is a cause of workload rather than as a symptom'. The syllabus allocation of time is normally based on the average time taken for the average student in the aircraft operated by the school.

Given the three levels of skill acquisition - cognitive, fixative and autonomous - it is not difficult to imagine that students in the elementary phase of flight training will reach the autonomous stage in individual tasks in less time when they are spared the need to attend to other events of equal or higher priority with which they may be unfamiliar, occurring simultaneously.

It is generally agreed that the worst classroom in the world is an aircraft cockpit as factors contributing to diversion of attention are prolific and ever-changing. This factor, when coupled with the fixative stage of learning, will cause errors. The research of Hart et al (1984) indicates that this factor may retard skill acquisition more than was previously thought. At the end of the day, this must be transposed into a training variable.

The issue of part tasking is fairly complex but generally accepted (Kraemer, 1984; Roscoe, 1980) in the flight training environment. Kraemer (1984) suggests in a comprehensive report on this issue that 'the application of part-task training concepts and methodology shows that simulation has a great potential to address pilot training research design issues.' Wightman and Lintern (1985) further identified three general types of part-task manipulation schemes in the psychological literature which might be applied to flight training. They were:

- Simplification; e.g. turbulence level adjustment in the simulator;

- Fractionation; independent practice of subtasks that are executed simultaneously for the whole task, e.g. pitch and roll control, and;

- Segmentation; which partitions a whole task either spatially or temporally e.g. take-off, climb, cruise, descent and landing.

These in turn could be implemented using three different methods:

- Pure-Part-Training which employs isolated practise of parts before whole task practise.

- Repetitive-Part-Training in which one part is practised, a second part is added and both are practised together before another part is added, and;

- Progressive-Part-Training which uses isolated practise of new parts before they were added in repetitive fashion.

The study by Wightman and Lintern (1985) uncovered some interesting correlations while focusing on the instruction of tracking skills for manual control. For tasks with high component complexity and high component interdependence, fractional progressive part-task training has been less effective than whole task training. However, fractional progressive part-tasking for high component complexity but low component interaction showed positive differential transfer of greater than 100%, i.e. totally superior to whole-tasking training. Another result from their study, which may not surprise many trainers, was that the segmentation reintegration termed backward chaining, where the terminal segment is practised first, was successful for both pure-part and progressive-part reintegration.

*Designing Instruction for Human Factors Training in Aviation*

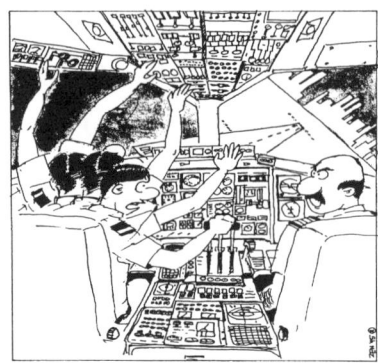

*"Now Beauregard, power + attitude = performance"*

**Figure 5.13 Let's take it from the beginning ...**

Another key design factor for enhancing and achieving instruction fidelity is the reduction and removal of distractions. For example, to achieve the parameters of straight and level flight, that is, maintaining the aircraft at a constant speed in a constant direction at a constant altitude in balanced flight, the student must comprehend the fact that POWER + ATTITUDE = PERFORMANCE. In a light aircraft there are many distractions such as turbulence, radio calls, scenery, other aircraft, engine instruments, etc. whereas a part task trainer may use something as simple as one tachometer or manifold air pressure gauge to indicate the POWER, a line on a blackboard (Stark, 1989) as the ATTITUDE indication, and the basic set of 6 flight instruments to measure PERFORMANCE for the student to gain a working comprehension of the concept.

The design of flight simulators to take advantage of part-task training principles at the ab initio level introduces issues of visual cue requirements. Roscoe and Eisele (1980) and Lintern and Roscoe (1980) concluded that 'the display could be made even more effective for landing training if it were augmented with cues that provide guidance information not present in the real-world visual scene.' i.e. taking the next step in part-tasking and augmenting the natural cues with learning facilitators would prove more effective at the skill acquisition stage. Further studies by Hays, Jacobs, Prince and Salas (1992a), Hays and Singer (1989), Jacobs, Prince, Hays and Salas (1990), Lintern (1980) and Westra, Lintern, Sheppard, Thomley, Mauk, Wightman and Chambers (1986) have all demonstrated the value of supplementary visual cues on various concepts of skill acquisition.

Particular reference in most of the papers is also made of the detrimental effect of these same supplementary visual cues for skill maintenance. Lintern and Koonce (1992) experimenting with augmented visual cues concluded that 'There is strong support here for the hypothesis that visual augmentation of both guidance and predictive forms can enhance the acquisition of visually supported skills.' The lack of research in this area however has meant that visually supported skills is a subjective determination. Hays et al (1992a) went so far as to say that 'Detailed descriptions of skills needed to perform tasks within a given training program are available, yet these descriptions have not led to a valid taxonomy for grouping aviation tasks. Research programmes in this area would benefit greatly if task categories (taxonomies) could be developed and validated. This would allow generalization of results from single tasks to task groupings.'.

The issue of separating the part-task training to a suitable level is effectively the problem facing organizations at the instructional design stage. The prediction of skill acquisition put forward by Fleishman and Quaintance (1984) suggests that if only one skill is learned in a more complex task that change should be measurable within the task itself. Lintern and Koonce (1992) effectively did this and the advice of Hays et al (1992b) and Jacobs et al (1990) suggests that proof of this concept would reasonably set up a part tasking principle for simulator training. The evidence to date however has been centred around psychomotor (practical) skills rather than cognitive (thinking) or affective (attitude) skills.

From a practical point of view the approach should be to designate the abilities defined by the performance requirements of the accomplishment to be learned. These can be grouped into handling, procedures and decision making abilities as stated earlier. By definition though, these must come from a needs analysis of the task. The syllabus then comes out of that definition. Reality however, has most organizations determining the accomplishments in terms of the syllabuses already in place or those determined by the aviation authorities which have their roots in the Smith-Barry syllabus of almost a century ago. Whether this is the case or a proper needs analysis has been done, implementation of the learning/teaching of these abilities as defined by the performance requirements becomes a relatively simple operation. For this reason, syllabus designers have little trouble with the transfer at the coal face. The decision on what key points actually make up the abilities is left to the designers who must also designate which of those points may be effectively learned in the simulators available and which should be left to the actual aircraft.

*Designing Instruction for Human Factors Training in Aviation*

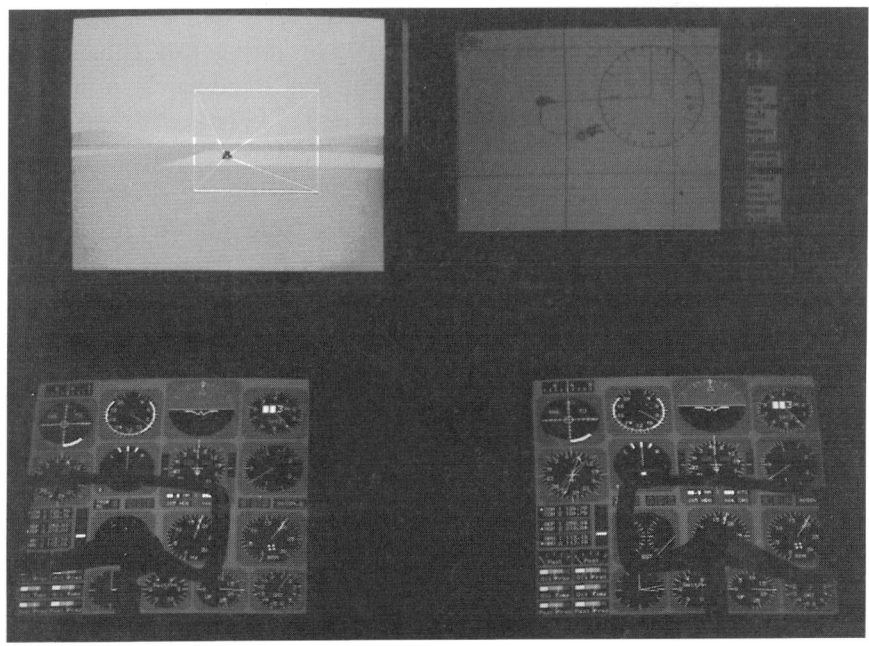

**Figure 5.14 Horses for courses - part tasking visual approach in an ATD**

A low level circuit is a good example of this. The handling aspects such as straight and level, medium bank level turns, finals profile and landing can and most probably will have been taught prior to the introduction of this type of circuit which is generally associated with poor weather flying. Even the procedural aspects of correct altitude, proper radio calls and checklist actioning can be reasonably established, but the decision making associated with the base turn point requires a wrap around visual display at the least and would ideally require variable weather conditions and the visibility, crosswinds, turbulence, etc. associated with those weather norms. Any simulator can, however, be used to cover some aspects of the task. History has seen some very successful demonstrations of the procedural aspects being learned by ESL (English as a Second Language) students, following a chalked in circuit pattern on the floor and going through the procedural aspects in real time.

*Simulation as an Instructional Procedure*

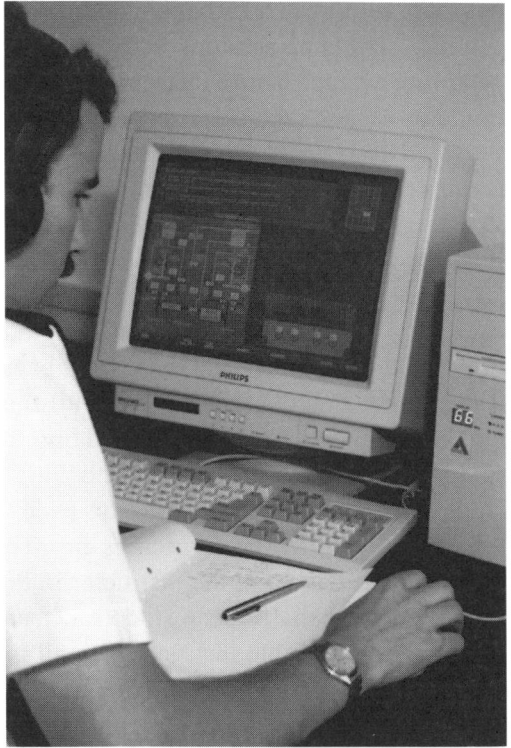

**Figure 5.15 Engineering CBT prior to type conversion**

The implementation and the instruction of simulator syllabuses require a number of improved methods of delivering instruction to be successful. The simple formula of:

- Agree on content;
- Design the lesson;
- Develop practical exercises; and
- Deliver the training product,

remains appropriate however, a number of qualifications need to be made as a result of this chapter. First, motivation is a key strategy and one of the general determinants of behaviour in the simulator. Pre-arranged and contingent methods of increasing student arousal levels need to be a part of each exercise. Second, chaining is an essential element for continuity. This may be achieved with the use of CBT, workbooks or just study guides and preferably a combination of all three such that a workbook leads the student through the theory, CBT, simulator sessions and thence the aircraft in a logical sequence of learning events. Third, the removal of distractions. The capacity of the brain to absorb and take cognizance of more than the task at hand is a well documented fact. This serves to highlight the likelihood of distraction if it is available. If a simulator can conduct aerobatics, you can bet your bottom dollar the students will make use of the fact well before it comes up in their syllabus. Equally, teaching basic IF skills with a myriad of gauges, buttons, dials and radios regardless of the aircraft type. Captain Dick Wilkinson successfully got a number of Qantas upgrade candidates in the B747 who were finding trouble with their base work, back on the rails by blanking out all but the essential flight instruments until they were back to just flying the big jet comfortably before gradually adding the 'distractions' to the primary task. Finally, the role of the instructor in this environment must be clearly defined. The instructor as a facilitator needs to be given the flexibility to progress the training as she or he sees fit. The variability of both instructors and students demand that the instructor in this role becomes a time and resource manager on behalf of the student whose requirement is the demonstration of competency to that instructor. In all things simulated, the relationship between syllabus, training and testing must be maintained as a living and evolutionary relationship.

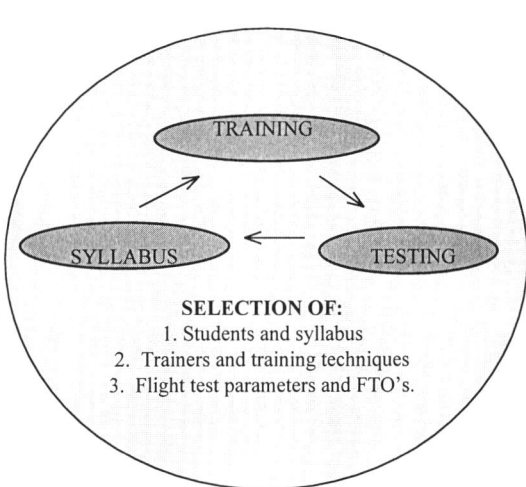

**Figure 5.16 The syllabus, training and testing inter-relationship**

## Testing and evaluation

*Evaluating the effectiveness of the outcomes*

These issues are necessarily related to two different, though equally important aspects in relation to the rest of this book. First, we must consider the evaluation of exercises within the simulator, and second, the evaluation of the simulator within the total training context.

The fairly prohibitive costs of aviation training have resulted in a norm at licensing level of just meeting the minimum requirements rather than a striving for excellence. Simulation, however is one area of flight training where the opportunity to excel often does exist. Simulators provide the capacity for formative evaluation of learning rather than the industry norm of summative evaluation. The New Zealand Qualifications Authority (NZQA) initiatives towards achievement levels in which candidates need to jump through a number of hoops prior to progression on to the next level of training is somewhat akin to the block system of training used in some educational institutions. This system generally devolves the assessment of student formative evaluation to the flight instructors with some form of criterion referenced word pictures which include the objective parameters where they exist. The capacity of simulators to undertake the measurement of those objective parameters and for the candidate to have an audit trail in the form of a video tape or computer printout provides a permanent record of achievement and of student learning rates. For the tasks that can be reasonably completed within the simulator environment this obviates the necessity for the snapshot, summative testing of those parameters in the flight test because the student already has a demonstrated and measured performance in that area. This same capability also provides instructors with the remote monitoring capability either in real time or as feedback sheets/videos on student progress.

*Simulated Total Electric Failure*

**Figure 5.17 Just testing!**

As discussed by Hunt, Macfarlane and Colbourne (1995), the purpose of human factors development in aviation is to affect positive differences in flight crew performance. While much effort has been expended in seeking to define what these construct differences might look like in the aircraft, less effort has been put into defining the baseline behaviour which defines acceptable behaviour in this context. The need here is for statements of attitudinal measures that support the usefulness of CRM training. Until valid and reliable norms of number and types of interactions become acceptable measures, the word picture is likely to be the most comfortable equation for instructors and testing officers alike. Arguably, a solution to the problem at this evolutionary stage would be to separate the human factors aspects from the technical aspects. While they are inseparable at operational level, it is feasible to devise separate syllabus parameters for technical and human factor requirements in the simulator, and indeed to conduct training targeting those specific requirements which may by either technical or human factor based. It is at this stage that the flight test parameters for each must be clearly established with word pictures to enable feedback into the syllabus development. Test item 1 of a human factors bank might look something like the following:

*Simulation as an Instructional Procedure*

Task: The aim of the exercise is to assess the candidate's personal preparation at the professional licensing level.
Objective: To determine that the candidate demonstrates professionalism by:

    a. Presenting him or herself for the test:

        1. Punctually
        2. Neatly dressed, in uniform and in accordance with the School's code of dress and personal appearance.
        3. Enthusiastic and fit for flying.

    b. Demonstrates preparedness by presenting:
       Up to date, neat and correctly summarized and certified Pilots Log Book, Student Training Records and flight documents including Aircraft Flight Manual, Load Sheets, current local weather data and Flight Guide.

    c. Demonstrates a thorough knowledge of the licensing and currency requirements for a commercial pilot engaged in Air Transport Operations.

Action:

The examiner will:

1. By examination of the candidate's Log book and training records, determine that all statutory flight time requirements have been met and that the flight training syllabus has been completed.
2. Determine that the candidate's appearance and dress is in accordance with the School's dress code unless dispensation has been obtained from the Director of Flight Systems.
3. Determine that the candidate has a sound knowledge of the privileges, currency and renewal requirements of the Commercial Pilot licence and is aware of the additional requirements for Air Transport Operations.
4. Determine as far as is available that the candidate's physical and mental state will permit the test to proceed successfully.

Rating:

| 1 | 2 | 3 | 4 | 5 | 6 | 7 | 8 | 9 | 10 |
|---|---|---|---|---|---|---|---|---|----|
| | | FAIL | | PASS | | | | | |

| | | | |
|---|---|---|---|
| 1. Does not show up | 1. Is unacceptably late. | 1. Punctual or late with acceptable excuse. | 1. Arrives punctually at the flight test venue and reports to examiner. |
| 2. Dress and appearance totally at variance with dress code. | 2. Dress and appearance unacceptable. | 2. Dress and appearance acceptable. | 2. Dress and appearance strictly in accordance with school dress code. |
| 3. Illegal health status. Is physically or mentally unfit for test. | 3. Not well enough to undertake sortie. | 3. Fit but clearly nervous. | 3. Fit and enthusiastic. |
| 4. Log book and training records missing or forges. | 4. Log book untidy or incomplete and training records incomplete. | 4. Log book and training records substantially complete. | 4. Log book and training records are neat and complete in all respects. |
| 5. Training syllabus at variance with requirements and unaware of licensing requirements. | 5. Training syllabus not completed. | 5. Demonstrates basic knowledge of licensing requirements. | 5. Demonstrates complete knowledge of licensing requirements. |
| 6. Shows no initiative to obtain weather and flight documentation requirements. | 6. Needs prompting to obtain weather and flight documentation. | 6. Obtains weather and flight documentation after reporting to examiner. | 6. Has obtained the latest weather information and has on hand all the documentation required for the flight. |

Assessment of the value of the simulator in the overall perspective is a far more difficult task. Issues such as transfer effectiveness, usage rates and cost benefit need to be addressed. These are dealt with effectively in other texts and so will not form part of this chapter. It is essential that these factors are considered, however. Feedback for an organization is as critical as it is for staff members as it is for students.

**Conclusion**

*Simulation is the training future of our industry*

The role of most pilots in industry is to transport people or goods from one place to another safely, effectively and efficiently in that order of priority and training to that aim is the goal of most institutions. The gradual automation of cockpits is leading a subtle change in the role of the pilot to achieve those objectives. Education in the broader sense is becoming an advantage for the job seeker and training in the technical sense a functional corequisite of that education. Philosophically, the advantages of simulation in both education and the more focused aspects of training and assessment are many fold but misuse of the systems and the reluctance of the aviation authorities to legislate to the capabilities has led to an industry prejudice against them. This misguidance has resulted in the training and evaluation system remaining static for many years while the most dynamic industry in the world forges ahead. Our present training inertia will lead to a gradual phasing out of pilots in the cockpit as a redundant luxury.

This chapter has endeavoured to explain some of the rational training advantages of simulators with some methodology explanation to guard against misuse. The primary lessons to observe are: that simulators are like aircraft in that you need to choose the correct machine for the job; there is a consumate distinction between skill acquisition and skill maintenance that needs to be addressed both at the procurement stage and in the instructional delivery; the aim of training in the educational context is to bring the classroom into the cockpit and the capacity of simulators to meet this need is profound if and only if it is well managed; and that the capacity of simulator feedback to measure objective performance parameters in a controlled environment provides the potential to be able to grade pilots according in both technical and human factor competencies within a single set of SOP's. Finally, 'the instructor is the single biggest variable affecting a student pilot's learning' (Telfer and Biggs, 1985) is no less true with the use of simulators than it is with aircraft. The methodology employed by instructors to facilitate student learning needs to be addressed as a structured framework of learning needs with some delivery flexibility built in to allow for individual instructor student variables.

## References

Caro, P.W. (1979) 'The Relationship between Flight Simulator Motion and Training Requirements'. *Human Factors.* 21 493 - 501.

Caro, P.W. (1988) 'Flight Training and Simulation'. In E.L. Wiener and D.C.Nagel (eds) *Human Factors in Aviation.* San Diego, CA : Academic Press.

Fleishman, E.A. and Quaintance, M.K.(1989) *Taxonomies of Human Performance.* Orlando, FL: Academic Press.

Flexman, R.E.; Roscoe, S.N.; Williams Jnr, A. C.; and Williges, B.H. (1972) 'Studies in pilot training: The anatomy of transfer'. *Aviation Research Monographs,* 2.

Gagne, R.M. (1987) *Instructional Technology: Foundations* Hillsdale, New Jersey: Lawrence Earlbaum Associates

Hays, R.T. and Singer, M.J., (1989) *Simulator Fidelity in Training Systems De-sign: Bridging the Gap Between Reality and Training.* New York: Springer-Verlag.

Hays, R.T.; Jacobs, J.W.; Prince, C. and Salas, E. (1992a) 'Flight simulator training effectiveness: A. meta-analysis'. *Military Psychology,* 4, 63 - 74.

Hays, R.T.; Jacobs, J.W.; Prince, C. and Salas, E. (1992b) 'Requirements for future research in flight simulation training: Guidance based on a meta-analytic review'. *The International Journal of Aviation Psychology* 2 (2), 143 - 158.

Jacobs R.S. (1976) *Simulator Cockpit Motion and the Transfer of Initial Flight Training.* Unpublished paper.

Jacobs, R.S. and Roscoe, S.N. (1980) 'Simulator cockpit motion and the transfer of flight training'. In S.N. Roscoe (ed) *Aviation Psychology.* Ames : Iowa State University Press.

Jacobs, J.W.; Prince, C.; Hays, R.T. and Salas, E. (1990) *A Meta-analysis of the flight simulator training research.* Orlando, RL; Naval Training Systems Centre.

Jensen, R.S. (1989) *Aviation Psychology.* Hants : Avebury Technical.

Kennedy, R.S. and Fowlkes, J.E. (1992) 'Simulator sickness is polygenic and polysymptomatic: Implications for research'. *The International Journal of Aviation Psychology,* 2(1), 23-38.

Kraemer, R.A. (1984) *An Overview of the Literature on Human Factors and Part-Task Training with Implications for Visual Simulation in Primary Flight Training.* Unpublished: Miami-Dade Community College.

Lintern, G. (1980) 'Transfer of landing skill after training with supplementary visual cues'. *Human Factors.* 22 (1), 81 - 88.

Lintern, G. (1987) *Flight Simulator Motion Systems Revisited.* PLET, 30 12.

Lintern, G. (1988) *Fidelity for Flight Simulation.: Meeting the Challenge* Unpublished paper.

Lintern, G. and Kennedy, R.S. (1984) 'Video games as a covariate for carrier landing research'. *Perceptual and Motor Skills*, 58, 167 - 172.

Lintern, G. and Koonce, J.M. (1992) 'Visual augmentation and scene detail effects in flight training'. *The International Journal of Aviation Psychology.* 2(4), 281 - 301.

Lintern, G. and Roscoe, S. N. (1980) *Visual Cue Augmentation in Contact Flight Simulators.* In S. N. Roscoe (ed) Aviation Psychology. Ames: Iowa State University Press.

Lintern, G.; Sheppard, D.J.; Parker, D.L.; Yates, K.E. and Nolan, M.D. (1989) 'Simulator design and instructional features for air-to ground attack: A transfer study'. *Human Factors.* 31, 87- 89.

Macfarlane, R. and Crosthwaite, R.G.B. (1993) *Workshop on Simulator Fidelity.* Seventh Aviation Psychology Symposium, Ohio State University.

Phelan, P. (1994) 'Cultivating safety'. *Flight International.* 24 - 30 August.

Povenmire, H.K. and Roscoe, S.N. (1973) 'The Incremental Transfer Effectiveness of a Ground Based General Aviation Trainer'. *Human Factors.* 15, 534 - 542.

Povenmire, H.K. and Roscoe, S.N. (1971) 'An evaluation of ground based flight trainers in routine primary flight training'. *Human Factors.* 13, 109 - 116.

Roscoe, S.N. (1980) *Aviation Psychology.* Ames: Iowa State University Press.

Roscoe, S.N. and Eisele, J.E. (1980) *Visual Cue Requirements in Contact Flight Simulators.* In S.N. Roscoe (ed) Aviation Psychology. Ames: Iowa State University Press.

Ross, M.J. (1989) *An Evaluation of the Training Effectiveness of a Low Cost Computer Based Flight Simulator.* Proceedings of the Workshop on Flight Instruction for the 1990's. Newcastle : Institute of Aviation.

Stark, E.A.(1989) 'Simulation'. In R.S. Jensen *Aviation Psychology.* Aldershot: Gower Technical.

Telfer, R.A. and Biggs, J.B. (1985) *The Psychology of Flight Training* Cessnock: Aircrew Training Centre.

Wightman, D.C. and Lintern, G. (1985) 'Part-task training for tracking and manual control'. *Human Factors.* 27(3) 267 - 283.

Westra, D.P.; Lintern, G.; Sheppard, D.J.; Thomley, K.E.; Mauk, R.; Wightman, D.C. and Chambers, W.S. (1986) *Simulator Design and Instructional Features for Carrier Landing: A Transfer Study.* Orlando, FL; Naval Training Systems Centre.

# 6 Object technology and simulation life-cycle costs

*Peter G. Fairweather*

**Introduction: The beguiling promise**

Ironically, the luster of the promise of object-oriented software technology to computer-based training simulations in the aviation industry remains as untarnished as it does unfulfilled. We crave software-engineering relief from the painful costs of developing training simulations. Given this pain, do we too quickly accept the object-oriented potion the same way that we grasped at structured programming, for example, or is there really something there that can dramatically increase the cost-effectiveness of aviation simulations?

*The first sign of trouble in paradise*

The necessity to explain why object-oriented software technology will revolutionize aviation training hints that its proponents' claims warrant scrutiny. However, the value of object-oriented software technology tends to be expressed in terms that differ markedly from those used to evaluate the cost-effectiveness of training simulations. Our first task, then, of assessing its value involves defining the language of one domain with terms of the other.

## What does it mean to be object-oriented?

Immediately we notice that the names of the attributes that enable us to decide whether an approach is 'object-oriented' do not number themselves in the lexicon of those charged with developing training or performance support systems in general or simulations in particular.

The names of these attributes themselves vary depending on whether the discussion centers on programming language features, software engineering approaches, or simulation development. Programming linguistics tends to emphasize attributes including 'inheritance;, 'classes', and 'polymorphism'. Software engineering practice, on the other hand, tends to value 'encapsulation', 'abstraction', 'information hiding', and 'composition'. These are not on the tongue nor in the mind of the training specialist developing simulations, so we should first try to establish their value outside of the domains of programming linguistics and software engineering and then determine whatever might be missing.

*Programming language features vs. software engineering approach*

The seeds of object-oriented development as a major software engineering strategy lay in early object-oriented languages, in particular, Simula (Dahl, Myrhaug, and Nygaard, 1970) and Smalltalk (Goldberg and Robson, 1983). These languages, and others such as CLOS (Steele, 1984) and C++ (Stroustrup, 1991) joining them, offered constructs particularly well-suited for handling complexity. This aramentarium propelled object-orientation from a language attribute to a software engineering strategy.

*Semantic distance*

Because aviation equipment is so expensive to produce, training developers tend to focus first on faithfully replicating its behavior in software, yielding a relatively low-cost device upon which to practice procedures, for example. Developers must abstract equipment behavior as software constructs, a process made more or less difficult by the *semantic distance* separating that behavior from the constructs that must represent them.

*Designing Instruction for Human Factors Training in Aviation*

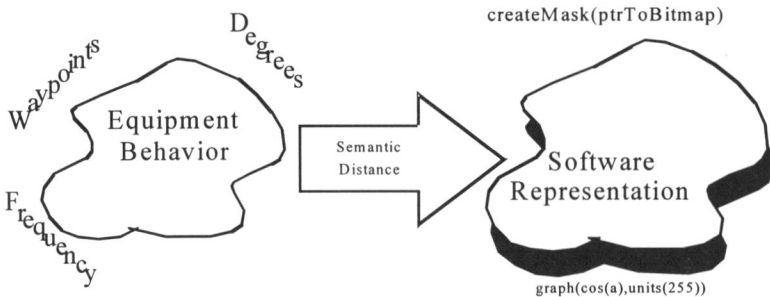

**Figure 6.1  The trip from real to simulated**

As figure 6.1 suggests, development implies moving from a design space defined by one set of dimensions to one defined by another. This trek has to be undertaken not only during the initial creation of the simulation, but repeated during its whole life-cycle. Understanding is crucial to maintaining simulations during its life and anything that reduces the semantic gap increases that understanding and reduces life-cycle costs.

*Encapsulation and the semantic gap*

Encapsulation pushes the problem and solution domains together by creating a interface between the inside of each object in the simulation and the rest of the application, as in figure 6.2.

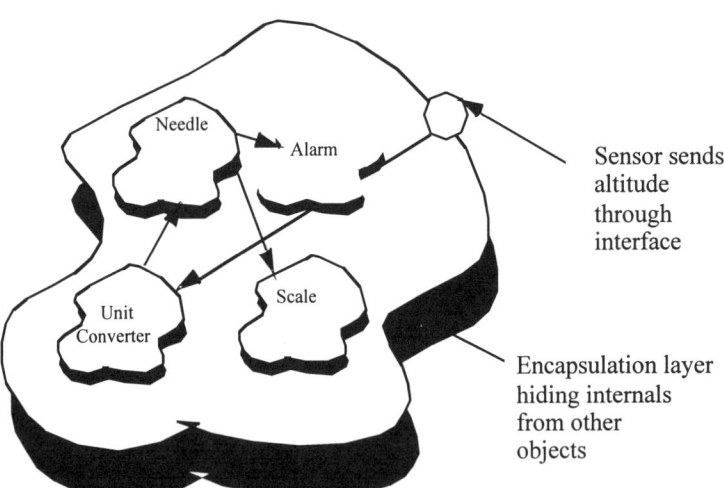

**Figure 6.2  Encapsulation produces boundaries**

The object, in this case an altimeter, appears as a dyad of hidden implementation and exposed interface. Development deals only with the interface which accepts input in the form of whatever the altitude sensor sends. Moreover, the hidden implementation can be changed without modifying any other part of the simulation.

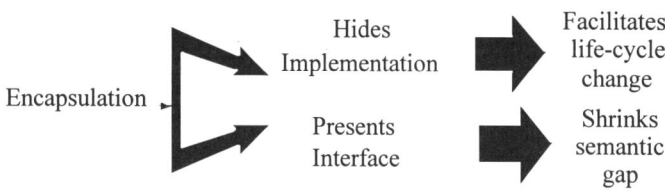

**Figure 6.3  How encapsulation yields value**

**Change**

Change buffets training and performance support courseware more than typical application programs. For example, experience with a large airframe manufacturer with frame-based authoring system showed that 25% of the frames across all courseware units changed each year after their release from development. By contrast, during the first five years of development and release of this courseware, the authoring tool used to develop the courseware changed less than 1% of its code and the run time interpreter less than 10%. In other words, proportion of change of the courseware to the authoring system that built it over the same period of time was about 12.5:1 (25%/yr * 5 yr: 10%/ 5yr).

The rate of courseware change is higher than other forms of application software, but even in that spectrum of flux, aviation courseware stands out, exhibiting high life-cycle costs. Consider a few of the range of demands for change on aviation training simulations:

- emerging equipment systems require that simulations be built before the systems they are to simulate have become stable,
- procedural changes promulgated by a regulatory authority (e.g., NTSB, FAA) must be incorporated into training simulations,
- carrier specific changes must be incorporated into airframe manufacturer supplied courseware,

- airframe configuration combinations require that simulations be adapted to the appearance and behavior of the different combinations,
- the requirement that tail-number specific training change as aircraft are modified,
- changes to the simulation interface to increase ease-of-use or fidelity, for example, mandated by data collected during initial phases of deployment,
- maintenance changes,
- changes required to re-host simulations on different hardware.

Because of the complex interrelations of simulation components, changes must be localized. Encapsulation is the most powerful localizer, ideally establishing an unbreachable boundary between an object's internal behavior (its implementation) and the way it appears to the rest of the application (its interface).

For example as abstracted in figure 6.2, if a simulation used a fuel gauge that indicated pounds of fuel available, other components of the simulation should not have to adjust their behavior if the fuel gauge were changed to report kilograms instead of pounds. Moreover, it should make no difference to the other simulation components if the gauge were changed from a dial display to one resembling a thermometer. The implementation of the gauge remains encapsulated within itself, hidden from the rest of the courseware.

*Encapsulation, abstraction, yes, but reuse?*

The virtues of encapsulation are often associated with the Holy Grail of software engineering: reusable components. Although object technology promises reuse, the emperor really has no clothes: *aviation training simulation does not benefit from significant software reuse.* This disappointment has little to do with software technology, however, but with how that technology is applied.

The first question for the development organization trying to take advantage of object-oriented technology is to identify the objects to be constructed. At this early point in development, virtually all organizations make a mistake that blocks significant component reuse. They adopt a development strategy shaped by the development tool they have selected and continue it in the wrong direction.

Most tools designed to support the creation of training simulations promise to reduce development costs by eliminating some of the development tasks.

Object-oriented tools do this by providing various object classes predicted to be most useful to developers To attract users, the vendor picks object types that virtually every simulation will use, such as windows, sliders, media players, or ordered collections. Although generally useful, such objects relate only distantly to the real purpose of the simulation: training.

The development organization picks up where the vendor leaves off and continues the definition and construction of object classes particular to the simulation needs, such as horizon indicators, altimeters, or flight management systems. As a result, simulation construction usually reduces to the enumeration of the classes of objects that make up the systems to be simulated. After all, if the goal is to produce a part-task trainer simulation of an inertial navigation system, then what else is there but creating the components and getting them to work together?

Taking a step aback and looking at two equipment simulations for maintenance training, one involving the flight management system and other involving the manual landing gear override system, we see that with the exception of vendor-supplied classes such as windows, buttons, bitmaps, or collections, none of the classes developed for one simulation would be used for the other. However, if both simulations were to be used for fault-classification training, we should expect to exploit common object classes, shouldn't we? Absolutely. That expectation hardly ever bears fruit, however, *because simulation builders rarely get around to building components that can be shared.*

Instead of building a set of object classes that model the acquisition of fault-classification knowledge and model how it is taught, developers stop at creating the object classes that simulate the behavior of the equipment involved. Failure to extend object-oriented technology to the support of the actual training purpose is the principal reason why reuse evades developers in the aviation simulation courseware business.

*Designing Instruction for Human Factors Training in Aviation*

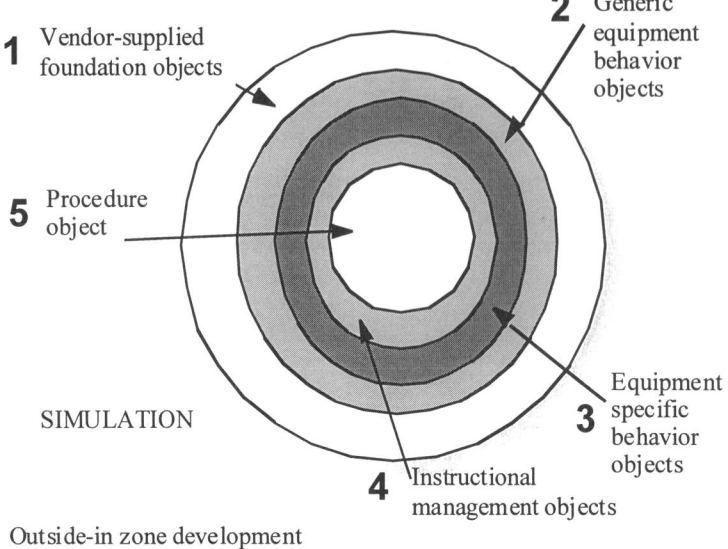

Figure 6.4  **Outside-in zone development**

Developers follow this 'outside-in' path of object-class designation, or *abstraction*, beginning with the typically vendor-supplied foundation classes and moving toward those that represent the core classes that capture the essential simulation components (see figure 6.4). If they manage to complete a runnable complex of objects that represents the device or system to be simulated, they consider the effort successful. In so doing, they omit the development of that set of classes most predictably useful for training simulations, namely those that model learning and teaching functions.

**Instructional objects**

Prior to object-oriented technology, instructional development used frame-based authoring systems. Indeed, at this point, far more aviation part-task training simulations have been implemented with such tools than with newer object-oriented technologies. As developers' usage patterns matured, new tools emerged to define how frames could be linked together to represent instructional patterns such as those needed to teach procedures, principle-using, or fact memorization, for example.

To create objects that do the same things that frames do means conceding the battle to close the semantic gap between the developers' representation system and those things to be represented. Indeed, if objects are built to do what frames did, they bring developers no closer to the problem domain space than the frames. Alternatively, however, developers could create objects that model such things as 'a procedure,' the most common instructional pattern in avionics simulation training.

Abstracting a procedure might mean decomposing it into a set of steps, each of which has a set of conditions that initiates it (possibly null), another set that blocks it (possibly null), and a mechanism for changing the state of the simulation as a consequence.

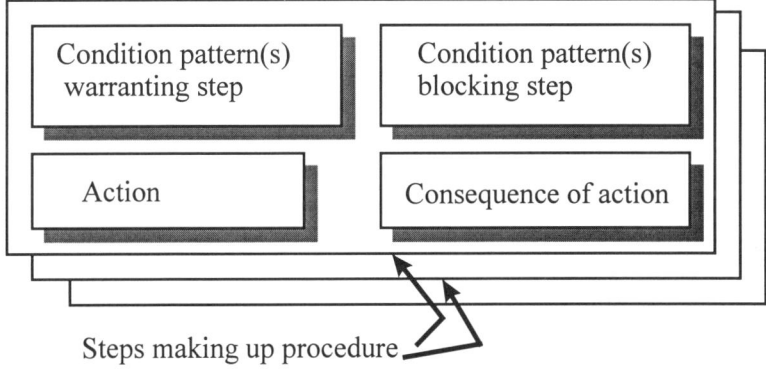

Possible composition of a procedure object

**Figure 6.5  Possible composition of a procedure object**

Difficulties abstracting object classes such as this one (figure 6.5), to say nothing of their implementation, prevent most developers from creating those objects which predictably make up aviation simulations used for instruction or assessment.

## The reuse of instructional objects

Although instructional domains vary (e.g., flight, maintenance, avionics, hydraulics), that which guides learning and assessment by modeling student cognitive skill acquisition or instructional strategy should remain constant across the content domains. However one abstracts a procedure, for example, will be the same no matter what the domain, a notion convincingly articulated by instructional systems theorists (e.g., Merrill and Tennyson, 1977; Gagné, 1966).

Although they outline instructional concepts such as procedures or principles and give examples of how tutorial instruction might be formed using them, they do not specify an implementation architecture. Others have worked through such details, however, although with other goals in mind. Anderson and his co-workers (Anderson, 1993), for example, have aimed at perfecting a cognitive architecture that explains skill acquisition, its generalization, and its automatization, for example, using the production rule as their building block. These not only conveniently represent the kinds of knowledge we expect within procedures we try to train, but they also can be operated upon by meta-procedures to simulate the effects of practice, transfer, or forgetting, for example.

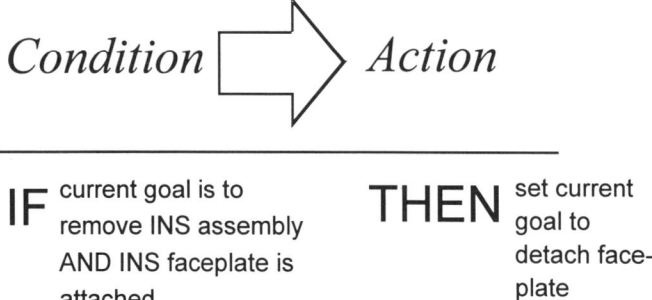

IF current goal is to remove INS assembly AND INS faceplate is attached   THEN set current goal to detach faceplate

**Figure 6.6   Abstract anatomy of a production rule and a simple example**

It would appear that production rules as in figure 6.6 offer the best bridge over the semantic gap (see figure 6.1), if for no other reason than the descriptions manifest in both their condition and action sides seem to derive from the problem domain and not the computer or authoring system. Because these rules are content domain specific, they are attractive candidates for embedding within objects that represent more general abstractions such as procedures. Such objects invite reuse and the development of authoring views that permit their rapid construction, testing, and modification.

## Conclusions

Object-oriented software development technology will not markedly reduce the costs of simulation construction until developers add abstract instructional objects to those that they have developed to represent the problem domain. These objects can be reused across domains within aviation and offer a weapon against the waves of change that buffet courseware during its life-cycle.

## References

Anderson, John R. (1993) *Rules of the Mind.* Hillsdale, New Jersey: Lawrence Erlbaum and Associates, Inc.

Dahl, O-J. Myrhaug, B. and K. Nygaard. (1970) *SIMULA Common Base Language.* Norwegian Computing Center S-22. Oslo, Norway.

Gagné, R.M. (1966) *The Conditions of Learning.* New York: Holt, Rinehart, and Winston.

Goldberg, Adele and Robson, David (1983) *Smalltalk-80: The Language and Its Implementation.* Reading, Massachusetts: Addison-Wesley Publishing Company.

Merrill, M. David and Robert D. Tennyson (1977) *Teaching Concepts: An Instructional Design Guide.* Englewood-Cliffs, New Jersey: Educational Technology Publications.

Steele, Guy L., Jr. (1984) *Common Lisp: The Language.* Bedford, Massachusetts: Digital Press.

Stroustrup, Bjarne (1991) *The C++ Programming Language.* Reading, Massachusetts: Addison-Wesley Publishing Company.

# 7 Evaluators and extended feedback models in aviation CBT

*Andrew S. Gibbons*

**Introduction**

Over the past two decades, a family of low-cost problem solving simulations called 'evaluators' has been created which demonstrate unusual surface characteristics, have important training benefits, and introduce new tools and design techniques into aviation Computer Based Training (CBT). This paper describes those simulations, their unique instructional features, the tools evolved to build them, and the new training concepts which they represent. These simulations are described in chronological order, giving a historical account of the issues each one raised and the problems which had to be solved. These simulations are described individually in Gibbons, Waki, & Fairweather (1990), Gibbons, Trollip, & Karim (1990), Gibbons, Rogers, & King (1991).

The simulations are called 'evaluators' because as well as creating a free-play simulation environment for problem solving, they provide an extended critique of the student's performance at the end of the problem, using the student's historical event trace as the basis for evaluating the student's choice of actions and their order. The theoretical background for the design of evaluators is provided in Gibbons, Fairweather, Anderson, & Merrill (in press). Early precedents for this type of simulation are found in training for guided missile maintenance (Gibbons, Cavagnol, & Lines, 1982) and medical diagnosis (O'Neal, 1981; see also Kuo, 1992 for a more recent example).

This chapter will concentrate on three successive aviation-related simulations of the evaluator type: the Flight Evaluator, the Maintenance Evaluator, and the Pilot Emergency Training Evaluator. These represent a single, intensive period in the development of the evaluator concept and were the most productive in terms of lessons learned and innovation of tools and design approaches, making evaluators affordable in quantity.

**The Flight Evaluator**

In the late 1980s Wicat Systems, then my employer, formed an agreement with the University of North Dakota and Northwest Airlines to create computer-based instructional materials for *ab initio* (from the beginning) pilot training. The organizations were represented by myself (Wicat), Stan Trollip (UND), and Mike Karim (Northwest). In brainstorming sessions, we decided it was possible to improve the standard of aviation instruction through the use of simulations. Hands-on experience provides instruction within a performance context and has always been respected as a vehicle for training. The problem was to make these simulations numerous yet affordable. Our team decided to produce a prototype of simulation-based aviation instruction. We designed two simulations and found it possible, before funds ran out, to produce one of them, called the Flight Evaluator.

The Flight Evaluator was to be a testing tool for students ready to perform their first cross-country solo flight. To ensure that these students were certified capable of making a safe and reasonable flight plan, the Flight Evaluator presented them with a cross-country planning problem, asking them to detail their plan on a series of worksheets which captured planning steps and intermediate computed values. At the end of the problem, this trace of planning events was inspected by an expert system capable of computing its own flight plan and then comparing the student's solution to the computed one. Probably the most interesting feature of the simulation was the environment created graphically of an airport, complete with Flight Service Station, aircraft, pilot's bag, and flight plan form. Within this environment, the student was able to move about from location to location, examining data and planning resources, performing actions, entering decisions, and ultimately completing the plan. The Flight Service Station (FSS) looked like an FSS interior, complete with radios, telephone, weather charts and maps, a computer, and full set of manuals. All of these sources of information were accessible by mouse-clicking on them. When the Airport facilities Directory was clicked, it opened to a table of contents, and from there further clicks allowed the student to 'turn' the page to a particular part of the manual. There, the student found accurate and realistic entries just as would be found in a real AFD. In this environment, telephones permitted calls to distant airfields to obtain visual weather, and radios allowed local weather forecasts and reports to be obtained. Computers produced standard weather summaries and reports which looked just as if they had been printed out by a real printer.

Students were free to move about within this simulated airport in a free, non-constrained fashion. Maps and regulations could be found in the pilot's flight bag, along with the pilot's flying certificate and log book. Aviation maps were displayed through the use of videodisc. The aircraft control panel displayed the hours of flight for the aircraft, and the aircraft's log, available in its usual place, showed the maintenance entries for the aircraft. With this arrangement of the data in various places, it was possible to tell from the student's motion around the environment what information had been checked and what had not. If the student forgot to ascertain the currency of his or her flight certification, then that could be noted and recorded for later comment. If the flight plan was made without checking specific weather reports or facilities dimensions, that became apparent, and other errors could be anticipated. This type of simulation is called a 'location' simulation, because it is not a functional model but an environmental model of a real place about which the student can move to gather data and perform realistic actions.

Except for one minor sequence (entering flight leg visual checkpoints on the flight map before entering leg data), no order was imposed on the student's planning activities. Moreover, as the student made decisions and expressed them, the data was recorded appropriately in the worksheets. For instance, a passenger list was given to the student, and one of the response options allowed the student to graphically 'load' passengers into the seats they would occupy during the flight. This in turn influenced weight and balance computations later and was automatically registered in the weight and balance section of the planning worksheet. But it did not constrain the student's planning activities nor force them into an order. It was left to the student to determine the order of actions and the magnitude of the values entered into the planning worksheets. No errors were identified during the planning problem.

Following the student's submission of the flight plan and accompanying worksheets, an expert system program was invoked. It opened the history trace file compiled during problem solution and (1) used the problem's 'given' values to compute a solution, and then (2) made comparisons between the computed values and the student's entered values. Since the planning computations take place in several waves, based on earlier decisions, this computation-comparison cycle had to be repeated several times until all of the entered planning data had been checked. At the beginning of each subsequent cycle, the expert took as input values the actual computed (and checked) values of the student so that the next round of comparison would produce reasonable values which the student might be expected to obtain through the same calculations. When an error was found, it was messaged to the student, and a diagnostic process was started to determine the source of the error. Since this was a prototype product, not every type of the error had a diagnostic, but if the error was in fuel computations, for instance, the student would be asked to solve the missed fuel computation again, this time under close scrutiny and with step-by-step results being recorded by the student on the computer. It was possible using this over-the-shoulder method to determine exactly where the student was making an error so that a remedial message could be produced that fit the error.

The tools used to create the Flight Evaluator consisted of the WISE authoring system for the simulation and OPS-5 (an expert system programming language) for the expert critic. The authoring system, though very powerful, was yet in its infancy with regard to simulations (one of the reasons we wanted to try it out), and it was a difficult programming task to make it do a simulation. Moreover, the programme became very large compared to the standards of the day (which thought a 20MB hard drive to be enormous). Yet the resulting simulation and critic were very satisfying. Not only was the high level of student involvement present, but the visual aspect of moving about a realistic environment somehow took the confining feeling away from working on a computer, and it was as if the computer had become a magic window that allowed us to move about freely an environment of any size. This was before the days of either Windows or virtual reality, but the simulation succeeded in creating the same kind of experience. Because the approach taken to producing the simulation required us to include all of the visuals and branching information for a vast reservoir of problem data into one program file, not only did the file become very large, but it was quite labour intensive to produce, and therefore although we liked the experience, we didn't like the cost, which was high.

The same was true of the expert system, which was hand-coded for each anticipated error. What we accomplished in this project was to prove to ourselves that this form of instruction was interaction-intensive and inherently interesting and that it could be used effectively as a training vehicle. It was a type of instruction to pursue, but the cost had to be cut dramatically for it to be practical. We set goals to do it again and waited for the opportunity.

## The Maintenance Evaluator

The next opportunity was not long in coming. Wicat was contracted by Dr Ken Govaertz of AMRTT (AMR Technical Training) to build a prototype evaluator for aviation maintenance training, and the budget was much smaller than for the Flight Evaluator. However, we had learned enough from the first experience that we were sure we could produce a similar product for much less, and we did succeed. The Maintenance Evaluator, like the Flight Evaluator was designed as an environment. In this case, it was the airport flight line maintenance shop for one airline. This shop consisted of a main area containing manuals, a maintenance data base computer, a maintenance manual microfilm reader, a printer, the door to a parts room, and view out the window of an aircraft just pulled in to the gate needing repairs (whose symptoms were described in the problem statement prior to the problem). A telephone on the shop wall permitted calls to cooperating organizations. At the aircraft, which was accessed by clicking on it, there was a second major environment: in the cockpit, the captain and flight attendant stood by, ready for questions and answers, a passenger cabin could be seen, cockpit panels could be observed closely with accurate readings visible, and on some panels controls could be operated, bringing about accurate responses. Below the cockpit, an equipment centre housing automated maintenance equipment could be entered, and some of the equipment panels operated and observed to give accurate responses. In the air conditioning compartment, the air conditioning unit (the target of this maintenance task) could be observed and repaired.

To provide a means for the student of acting within the environment, we invented a number of action icons which we arrayed along the bottom of the screen. Actions were universal to locations. If there was a person in the location you entered, you could use the 'speak to' icon to address this person. If there was an object in the location which could be lifted and carried, then you used the 'pick up' and 'put down' icons for that purpose. This expanded the range of possible responses by the student over those possible in the Flight Evaluator. The environment of the Maintenance Evaluator differed in another, very significant way from the Flight Evaluator's environment: a limited model of some parts of the air conditioning system was connected with controls and indicators in various locations of the aircraft. As the student moved to the location, the visible signs reflected the state of the model. In the cockpit, for instance, when zoomed into the maintenance computer display panel, the error messages originally viewed by the pilot were still visible. Just as in the Flight Evaluator, the student was free to move about, poke, and prod things at will.

Constructing this environment was an important learning experience in several ways. We discovered, for instance, that it was not necessary to simulate the entire aircraft in order to obtain significant training benefit from the simulation. It was pointed out to us by many observers that students would be sure to 'try everything' just to see what worked and what didn't and thereby be able to stumble onto the correct answer. The other half of this thinking was that we would have to simulate the entire aircraft and its systems in order to keep the student from bumping into walls and perceiving non-responsive aircraft systems (which would, of course, give clues to the right answer). Our response to this concern was that students free to do anything at any time might well experiment in a random fashion in order to obtain clues, but that would be evident in the historical trace of actions, and the expert would not be fooled by an answer reached by serendipity. It would not only detect the discrepancy between the answer and the path to it, but it would be able to identify in detail the erroneous steps and judgments that led to it. In short, the expert would reach the conclusion that the student had been fooling around. If the student knew that deviations from a reasonable path toward solution (of which there might be very many) were being noticed, then he or she would be more likely to confine activities to steps calculated to be effective.

The expert critic for the Maintenance Evaluator was improved greatly from the Flight Evaluator's because of greater experience with the expert system language and how to use it. We found it relatively easy to define not just one but several possible paths to a correct answer, and indeed to specify several possible correct answers and to judge between them. This showed us that the problems and solutions of an evaluator did not need to be deterministic. We evolved a way for expressing acceptable answers and solution paths toward an answer such that we would be able to evaluate judgment as easily as we could evaluate procedural behaviour. This was an important discovery for us, and it encouraged us to think that this type of simulation made possible a wide range of problem solving and judgment-related evaluations which before have been difficult for computer-based training to deliver.

Only one solvable problem was included in the Maintenance Evaluator - an air conditioning system fault. As in the Flight Evaluator, the problem was hard coded, but new features added to the authoring system made it possible to greatly reduce the size of the program file because graphic material could be stored in graphic libraries and called by reference rather than being stored within the programme itself. This was a major improvement and was the first necessary step towards rapid, high-volume production of simulations. As it was, with this new tool capability, we accomplished the goal of creating the simulation in one-third the time with one fifth the production team and for one-tenth the cost, despite the fact that we had interleaved a model simulation with the design of the environment simulation, making the suite more complex in some ways than the Flight Evaluator had been. We felt that we had taken a major step toward our ultimate goal of low-cost, high quantity production of high-quality simulations and evaluators.

**The Pilot Emergency Training Evaluator**

We realized this goal in the creation of the Pilot Emergency Training Evaluator (PETE), which was developed for Scandinavian Airlines with the cooperation of Otto Lagarhus. In this project we were able to create a family of seven simulation problems lasting from ten minutes to one and one-half hours and an expert critic matched to each problem, with the prospect of creating an unlimited number of additional problems for costs below that of a tutorial per problem. Moreover, we were able to do it for the same cost as the Maintenance Evaluator.

Though the environment of the PETE problems was much simpler than the environment for the previous evaluators in terms of number of locations, the problems themselves were in some cases much more complicated than any previous. For example, the most complicated problem created involved conditional events occurring to the student. A particular message from the tower to the pilot during the taxi-to-take off problem was not sent until the pilot had completed a particular procedure. The problem itself was given a kind of unfolding drama in this way. The problem involved heavy weather and the decision to take off on a snow-covered runway. It also involved the take-off distance required under adverse conditions, and many calculations and recalculations were required of the student in order to obtain a satisfactory decision. In the middle of this stressful setting, the conditions of the problem would change, as the airport first closed, then re-opened, but did so with limitations on its runway lengths.

The PETE evaluator made heavy use of interpersonal communications between the student-pilot and several other information or advice-giving resources. Radio calls to appropriate airports were provided, some relevant to the problem, and some decoys. The First Officer and Cabin Attendant could be addressed with questions and under some circumstances interrupted with information or questions for the pilot. In addition, many cockpit resources were made available to the pilot in their customary locations: emergency procedures checklists, approach plates, flight manuals, aircraft manuals, and other relevant (and some irrelevant) resources.

Without a doubt, the most important breakthrough in the development of this set of simulations was the ability to manufacture large numbers of problems at very low cost. This was accomplished by creating the simulation and expert critic as shell programs capable of executing the data placed in problem data files. By changing the contents of the data files, it was possible to change an entire problem and its expert evaluation of the solution. Moreover, except for new graphics which might be required, the creation of new problems consisted only of creating new problem and critic data files and giving their names to the driver programs.

The approach we have described does not create 'intelligent' instruction beyond the scope of the individual problem, but within the scope of the problem, the simulation and the expert critic do have a small amount of intelligent behaviour. More important to us that the appellation of 'intelligent' is the degree of flexibility that is afforded the designer by the low cost of each simulation problem relative to the cost of not only other simulators but of tutorial instruction as well. We found that the ability to make large numbers of simulation problems at low cost made the simulation of entire aircraft systems unnecessary except for those problems which involved the entire system. We found that a field of problems developed at low cost could supply the training effect of a full system simulation. Moreover, the large number of problems made it possible to provide the student with a wider variety of experiences with a higher degree of feedback tailored to the problem than would be possible in a larger system simulator.

## Implications

What is the importance of having reached the goal of low-cost, high quantity simulations with evaluative feedback? We feel that it opens a door to a whole new way of thinking about aviation training. Simulations have always been expensive, so their production and use has been rationed carefully. Low-cost simulations in quantity is an idea that most instructional designers are not ready for because the notion challenges the very foundations of traditional syllabus and curriculum thought. The preponderance of early-stage instruction both inside and outside of aviation training structures the curriculum into packages of instruction called 'lessons' which are most often verbal, lectures (or the equivalent) followed by verbal tests (often multiple choice). You are not likely to find a training designer able to give you a clear and specific definition of a 'lesson', despite the fact that ground school curricula are structured into packages called lessons.

The high-quantity simulation promises to revise this way of thinking. Students learn well through experience, and an appropriate field of simulation problems - properly structured, ordered, and stepped for the learner, and supplied with appropriate coaching and feedback functions - may become the preferred organization of even the ground school syllabus in the future. This is especially attractive in light of the principle called 'increasingly complex microworlds' which Burton, Brown, and Fischer (1984) point out has been applied for years to skiing instruction.

We think that the time is ripe for the exploration of simulations as the vehicle for aviation instruction. Not only is the evaluator concept appropriate as a testing vehicle, but our experience showed it to be viable as an instructional one also, developing in the student an extensive experience within a short period of time and providing feedback to maximize the impact of that experience.

**References**

Burton, R.R., Brown, J.S., Fischer, G. (1984) 'Skiing as a model of instruction'. In B. Rogoff and J. Lave (Eds.), *Everyday Cognition: Its Development in Social Context.* Cambridge, Harvard University Press.

Gibbons, A.S., Cavagnol, R.M., and Lines 'Distributed instructional system for Hawk training'. A paper presented at the Fourth Annual Conference on Interactive Videodisc in Education and Training, Society for Applied Learning Technology, Alexandria, VA.

Gibbons, A.S., Fairweather, P.G., Anderson, T.A., and Merrill, M.D. (in press) 'Simulation and computer-based instruction: A future view'. In C.R. Dills and A.J. Romizowski (Eds.), *Instructional Development: State of the Art.* Englewood Cliffs, Instructional Technology Publications.

Gibbons, A.S. and Rogers, D.H. (in preparation) *The Scandinavian Pilot Emergency Training System: Feedback Based on Assessment of Judgment.*

Gibbons, A.S., Rogers, D.H., and King R.V. (1991) 'The maintenance evaluator: Feedback for extended simulation problem's'. Paper presented at the Ninth Conference on Interactive Instruction Delivery, Society for Applied Learning Technology, Kissimmee, FL.

Gibbons, A.S., Trollip, S.R., and Karim, M. (1990). 'The expert flight plan critic: A merger of technologies'. Educational Technology, 30(4), 32 - 35.

Gibbons, A.S., Waki, R., and Fairweather, P.G. (1990) 'Adding an expert to the team: The expert flight plan critic'. *Interactive Learning International*, 6:63 - 72.

Kuo, G. (1992) *MacCAMPS author reference.* DACIS Software, Philadelphia, PA.

O'Neal, A.F. (1981) 'An analysis of eight interactive videodisc training programs'. A paper presented at the annual meeting of the Association for the Development of Computer-based Instructional Systems, Atlanta.

# Human factors instruction-airlines

# 8 Human factors training in airlines

*Ross Telfer, John Bent and Norm Dowd*

**Introduction**

There is a difference in the nature of learning and instruction about the effects of human factors (HF) in aviation safety. Much of technical training consists of skills and knowledge, suiting division into parts for understanding, demonstration, rehearsal and testing. Emergency drills are a simple example. In contrast, HF tend to pervade all operations and are difficult to isolate for separate assessment. Consider judgement and airmanship, for example. This distinctive characteristic of HF has inhibited industry's ability to integrate technical and non-technical training, and much of the effort of airlines to introduce HF training has been devoted to overcoming problems related to the nature of HF as an instructional focus.

It is only if training is interpreted in its widest form: as education (knowing why) as well as training (knowing how) that it can be linked with HF. Such a wide ambit is provided by a composite definition drawn from two sources: Lederer (1988) and Trollip and Jensen (1991). It describes human factors as 'the study of how airline pilots interact with their environments'. It thus includes such topics as adapting machines to human limitations; cockpit organization; crew interaction; fitness for duty; judgement; problem solving; sensory illusions; distraction, and complacency as result of equipment reliability.

For several reasons, the aviation industry is reshaping initial and recurrent training to incorporate HF. The authoritative support of ICAO and NASA, the demonstrable statistical link to major causes of incident and accident, and the recognition by insurers of the value of HF programmes such as LOFT and CRM, have combined to initiate and maintain the innovation. As is usually the case with change, the HF movement in aviation is not without opposition or constraint. These problems will be discussed in the next section.

**Problems in human factors training**

Predictably, there has been opposition at an individual level. This is entirely understandable in an industry in which individuals have acquired skills, knowledge and attitudes from thousands of hours of demanding experience. For highly experienced pilots to adopt a new basis for crew behaviour is asking a lot. Further, when such individuals occupy positions of power in airlines, it is also understandable that their corporate position would reflect personal values. For sceptics, hard facts to show the benefits of HF training are not easily found.

Unfortunately, this situation supports the stance of company accountants seeking to shave airline expenditures. A major constraint upon the effective implementation of HF training in aviation can be the lack of parity of esteem given non-technical training. Hardware (such as cockpit equipment, part-task trainers or full-fidelity simulators) appears to be much easier to justify and obtain than the software or human resources to support a HF course. The bean counters are especially aware of the costs to a company to withdraw a dozen pilots from the line for three days, or even to provide additional payment for facilitators for the time they give in developing and presenting HF courses. Many of the most successful airline HF programmes have depended heavily for their implementation on the commitment, professionalism and goodwill of the pilots who were the prime movers. Their enthusiasm swayed managements and overcame the logistical obstacles. Unfortunately, there remains the managerial view that facilitators, presenters and trainers in HF programmes provide a service as well as, rather than instead of, other airline duties.

There are indications, though, that this is changing. It is possible to see a place for career instructors in the field of HF provided the vital integration of technical and non-technical training continues. The trend towards utilization of non-jeopardy sessions for LOFT-type exercises has resulted in a seamless continuity of technical and non-technical simulator sessions. For example, Cathay Pacific has progressed on from the add-on CRM and Trainer Training. Conventional LOFT is being replaced by a form which is integrated into all training where possible. The airline now integrates CRM and LOFT into all training activities, and introduces training into line operations where possible. HF training consists of ten workshops, each with a specific training focus, but all contributing to HF training. The next stage is expected to be a rationalisation of the number of different workshops.

The merging of technical and non-technical at Cathay has reduced the potential for conflicting expectations. On the Airbus fleet the airline has achieved the blend by providing a dominant operational content. It is driven by operational procedures which provide understanding of systems through the ways in which they are used, rather than the traditional method of instruction in which topics were treated separately in a theory-to-simulator-to-flying sequence. All instructors, regardless of specialization, share objectives and are represented on a central steering team. The ground school, simulator and flying training specialists now belong to a single team. The aim is to validate this approach on Airbus training, then to extend it to other fleets.

The intent at Cathay is to eliminate differences in the process of instruction coming from separation and departmentalization. Under development in-house is a mechanism for this integration: a TRO computer based training programme which is procedure based. Using double-VGA monitors, it is highly interactive.

## What is taught?

Probably the most influential document on HF teaching in airlines have been the ICAO HF Digests, especially No 3 (1991), and the ICAO Journal devoted to HF in Aviation (48, 7. September, 1993). Together with the United Kingdom's 'Human Performance Limitations Requirements' (See Barnes, 1993), the contents have been reflected in both the Australian Civil Aviation Authority's HF Manual (Wilson, 1993) and the New Zealand Civil Aviation Authority's HF Syllabi (1993). Some regional variations are now becoming apparent, however.

The Joint European Pilot Licences (Johnston, 1993), and specific airlines' HF programs, such as that of JAL (Iwase, 1993) and those of Cathay Pacific (Telfer and Bent, 1992) and Air Canada, described below, have extended the range of content, the media of communication, and the variety of presentation. More recently, Transport Canada has undertaken a twelve-month development project to provide HF manuals for private pilots; advanced (Commercial, IF rated, and ATPL) pilots; and flight instructors. It is also establishing HF syllabi for these groups, and investigating ways in which HF can be tested.

Typically, HF coverage in airline training programmes includes:

1   *Basic physiology and the effects of flight* (such as sleep, fatigue, stress management, anatomy, health and fitness);

2   *Basic aviation psychology* (information processing, workload, bias, personality, perception);

3   *Judgement and decision making* (decision models, hazardous attitudes and the error chain);

4   *Social psychology, and group dynamics* (communication and crew resource management);

5   *Design of flight decks* (ergonomics, documentation and procedures);

6   *Learning and instruction* (with application to ground, simulator, LOFT, CRM and line instruction).

## How it is taught?

More complete accounts of means of improving the effectiveness of HF training are provided elsewhere (Telfer, 1993), but some general comments can indicate the range of HF methods. Since the mid-eighties, such programmes have developed basic characteristics which distinguish them from prior aviation training.

1   They are based on *adult education principles* of active learning. The chalk-and-talk, content-based briefings, or the standardised audio-tape and synchronised slide or video, have been replaced by discussion groups, simulations, critical incidents, interactive computer programmes and role play.

2   Although the constraints of bean-counting and off-line cost remain pre-eminent, pilots are being given HF training for *longer periods*, and immersed in the training programme which may be located in a non-aviation context overnight for the training period.

3   *Traditional training approaches are being supplemented or modified* by methods derived from other contexts, such as management and education. These include problem-based learning, focus on line examples, and personal development experiences.

4   *Airlines are moving away from generic programmes* developed by external agencies, towards in-house designs meeting the demands of company culture and parochial problems. Videotapes, usually short in duration, are also being scripted, acted and filmed in-house (usually in simulators now fitted with cameras). Less polished, perhaps, but with a credibility that comes from recognisable, expert participants. Both validity and humour are derived from familiar faces and relevant situations,

5   There is an *increasing evaluation* of the efficacy of training by means of special-purpose questionnaires at the formative and summative levels. This, in turn, contributes to ongoing refinement by application of the systems model of training.

## Developing HF training

The first stage of developing a human factor (HF) programme is to decide on what is needed. For example, in 1984 Air Canada commissioned a comprehensive needs analysis to examine the goals and priorities of over twelve hundred pilots. To assist in the design of HF training, the discrepancy between actual and desired HF behaviours was identified. Such a comprehensive analysis is rare in the industry because of its cost in both budget and time. For most airlines, these constraints will force a compromise. Instead of a structured survey to analyse needs, the judgement of a small group of experienced trainers, perhaps with the input of an external consultant, will be used as a basis for design.

Next comes the check on available resources. At Air Canada both company experts and outside consultants combined to identify resources and ways of presenting the program. Factors considered included effectiveness of training, time constraints, financial limitations, and the training needed for presenters. It was concluded that line pilots rather than management pilots would present the program, because of credibility with and acceptance by their peers. The resultant three-day crew resource management course included communication, team enhancement, problem-solving and decision making, judgement styles, crew co-ordination and resource management.

**Three phases in development**

Using the Air Canada and Cathay experiences as examples, three phases of HF training can be identified.

*Awareness*

In the first phase, the new focus requires a re-thinking of training needs, and a means of describing the new non-technical component. A language of communicating HF is initiated and disseminated in the company. For example, models of communication, leadership and decision making will usually be identified by acronyms or mnemonics. Styles of performance will be labelled by brief descriptors as a common language develops. Pilots will begin to perceive line activities in terms of the models, and will later begin to use the new descriptors.

Line incidents will appear in workshop discussions or as cases or critical incidents, making the course relevant. Simultaneously, workshop design and topics or modules are developed. Pre-workshop packages will be written and trialled, requiring participants to provide responses to questions which will later be raised in the workshop. Usually, this is done in a small group situation of around six pilots who develop a team response. Finally, the teams meet in a plenary session to compare approaches and conclusions. The practice of labelling 'right' or 'wrong' answers is avoided.

The modules are trialled on pilot volunteers or presenters-in-training, evaluating content, presentation, materials, aids, and timing. Finally, this phase concludes with the introduction and evaluation of the HF workshop. This leads to an awareness of the opportunity for participants to actually practise the HF skills they have acquired, and to receive feedback on their line applications of them.

This is where observations of other airlines helps. Other valuable techniques are attendance at international conferences (especially ICAO workshops), informal discussions, conducting a search of aviation literature for reports on the progress of other airlines, and writing for copies of manuals or course descriptions. This becomes a matching of airline needs with budget and available LOFT mechanisms. The criteria used by Air Canada were:

1   measurable effectiveness of the training;

2   limited simulator availability owing to present usage and costs;

3   the need to measure both technical and HF components;

4   Transport Canada had to approve the training for licence renewal in place of the traditional Pilot Proficiency Check (PPC) and Instrument Flight Training Rating Renewal (IFR).

*Practice and feedback*

In this second phase, crews gain experience in applying human factors training such as CRM techniques and interpersonal skills. Typically, this will occur by means of four opportunities:

1   Pre-LOFT packages;

2   Pre-Briefing;

3   LOFT session;

4   Debriefing.

The Air Canada Pre-LOFT package provides general guidance, clarifying the difference between 'evaluated training' and 'checking'. Performance objectives which must be achieved before the LOFT session are provided. There is an emphasis on crew rather than individual performance, and only a crew LOFT report is provided.

The Pre-Briefing is about an hour in length. Two of the eight HF components are reviewed and discussed in terms of line operations. The LOFTs flown that day are designed to include these two components.

The four hour LOFT session is divided into two line oriented legs taking about two and a half hours, and a procedures training session of one hour. This leaves half an hour to repeat any manoeuvres requiring practise.

The Debriefing is considered the key component of LOFT. This is when crews view their videotaped performance and undertake a personal assessment of their performance. An emphasis is given to self-critique. The basic objective is the integration of technical skills with Human Factors training. Evaluation is made on a five-point Likert scale on the following eight dimensions:

1   Communications;

2   Team enhancement;

3   Decision making and problem-solving;

4   Communication style;

5   Conflict resolution;

6   Judgement style;

7   Workload management;  and,

8   Resource management.

The facilitator is provided with a list of key behaviours as a guide to assessment. In the debrief the crew will attempt to identuify the chain of behaviours which contributed to any problem, and to the success of the flight.

*Reinforcement*

In the third phase at Air Canada, CRM was integrated with line flights, check flights, and simulator sessions. The next stage is team enhancement, enlarging the scope of HF training to include the entire corporation: management, maintenance, dispatchers and agents.

## Evaluating HF training

Probably one of the major obstacles which remains for airline HF training is the demonstration of efficacy. Individual programmes can be evaluated for the effectiveness and their efficiency, but HF training can only really be judged against its intention to improve safety. As organisers of HF programmes have discovered, it is no simple matter to demonstrate that an accident has NOT happened and that incidents have been avoided because of HF training.

On the other hand, the pressure of the need to develop a suitable mean of evaluating HF is itself an integrating factor. The fact that HF will need to be evaluated in actual flying operations will force its recognition as a component of flight, not simply a subject for study.

If the ultimate aim of HF training is to improve the safety of aviation operations, it follows that any evaluation must occur in line flight. Non-technical training needs to be assessed in the same ways as technical training. In LOFT or simulator sessions, there has been a gradual introduction of HF principles, especially in team work, decision making and problem solving aspects of exercises. With the use of video cameras and trained simulator instructors, HF aspects have been a natural component of the debrief.

A major problem has been *jeopardy*. What if the pilot is technically capable, but autocratically incapable of adjusting to participative decision procedures on the flight deck? Do inadequate listening skills cost a pilot's licence?

A possible solution lies in adopting a similar approach to that of making any pilot testing procedure as objective as possible. First, *reduce the focus of testing to its components*, and derive a performance criterion. We cannot test airmanship, judgement, vigilance or awareness satisfactorily because we cannot agree completely on what the terms mean. However, we recognise aspects of each when we see it.

Second, *make the evaluation criterion-referenced*. In HF this will rarely be an all-or-nothing, pass-fail approach. It is probable that the same flexibility which enables an examiner to discriminate shades of technical performance, will enable levels of HF attainment to be assessed. For example, a Likert-type scale (Never, Sometimes, Occasionally, Always) can provide a virtual assessment check-list.

Third, *introduce a transitional and compromise move to separate the licence jeopardy check* (currently in the simulator but perhaps a line check in the future) from the HF check. This is an artificial distinction and could be seen as a retrograde step in HF training. However, it would meet the needs of licensing authorities and ease the tension on the pilot. During this interim phase, further work on evaluation checklists could provide the refinement needed to satisfy regulatory authorities, airlines, and the pilots themselves. One aspect of such HF training is that it would reinforce the important notion that the application of HF is determined by the nature of the flying activity and its demands on pilots.

The application of the four part systems approach to developing evaluation, can help to refine HF evaluation in the same way as it improved programs of instruction. The systems approach starts with instructional objectives, then considers the controlled learning experiences, performance criteria and evaluation.

Change can be represented graphically by a sigmoidal curve. The 'S' profile is imposed on a graph in which the vertical axis represents the percentage of change, and the horizontal axis represents the time lapsed. On this basis, the airline industry has progressed along the horizontal tail of the 'S' and is now starting the climb as change occurs. To continue the climb, several factors will be influential. These include management support, financial backing, and the authoritative involvement of influential individuals. As with other organizational changes, ultimately it will probably take a generation of pilots to move through the system before full integration of technical and non-technical training to occur. These pilots will have experienced such training as *ab initio* trainees, and will expect it for the rest of their careers. This is when the top of the 'S' curve will be reached.

## References

Barnes, R.M. (1993) 'Human Performance Limitations Requirements - the United Kingdom experience'. *HF Digest No. 9.* Montreal:ICAO.

Civil Aviation Authority of New Zealand (1992) *Advisory Circular.* ISSN 1172-0778

ICAO (1991) HF Digest No. 3. *Training of Operational Personnel in HF.* Montreal. Circular 227-AN/136

Lederer, (1988) in *Human Factors in Aviation* edited by El.Weiner and D.C. Nagel, San Diego: Academic Press. p.xv.

Telfer, R. (1993) *Aviation Instruction and Training* Aldershot: Ashgate.

Telfer, R. and Bent, J. (1992) 'Producing a workshop for training airline instructors' *The Journal of Aviation/Aerospace Education and Research.* 2, 2. Spring. 31-38

Trollip, S.R. and Jensen, R.S. (1991) *Human Factors for General Aviation* Englewood: Jeppeson Sanderson.

Wilson, T. (1993) *Aircraft - Human Performance Limitations. Notes on the Performance and Limitations Syllabuses for the private and Commercial Pilot Licence.* Canberra: CAA.

# 9 Teaching human factors for airline operations

*Neil Johnston*

**Introduction**

This chapter considers theoretical, technical, policy and design issues relating to human factors training for airline cockpit crew. It starts by briefly reviewing the international legislative background and context. Given that the favoured approach to training is based on newly developing training principles, the relevant theoretical aspects are reviewed at some length. The implications for training design, training policy, training implementation and training practice are then considered, prior to outlining a number of criteria relevant to human factors training development. The overall aim of the chapter is to provide a strategic review of human factors training development methods and considerations, rather than airline human factors training specifics.

*The background*

In recent decades as the percentage of airline accidents caused by technical problems has steadily decreased, the percentage of accidents due to human error has correspondingly increased. Indeed it has now become an oft repeated aviation industry truism that most accidents are in some way caused by human error. It is widely recognized that this fact presents the aviation industry with a notable challenge, and that the consequences of human error must be reduced through multi-faceted human factors intervention programmes.

In respect of cockpit crew members, Crew Resource Management (CRM) training programmes were among the first and internationally best known responses to this human factors challenge (FAA, 1989; Wiener, Kanki & Helmreich, 1993). In addition, a considerable research effort is being directed to problems associated with the design and operation of aircraft automation, aircraft dispatch, maintenance, and so forth. As discussed below, ICAO (International Civil Aviation Organization) Annex modifications and other legislative provisions increasingly mandate systemic human factors interventions across the entire aviation system. These changes reflect the growing international and industry consensus on human factors and are collectively directed towards preventing, or ameliorating, the consequences of human error.

*The international context: legislative requirements and initiatives*

The first truly international initiatives in pilot human factors training followed the publication, in 1988, of the Eighth Edition of ICAO Annex 1 (Personnel Licensing). This mandated human factors *knowledge* training for each category of flight crew licence holder, specifying that this training be in:

> .... human performance and limitations relevant to...(the licence being issued).

This international requirement has the same status as the technical knowledge traditionally contained within the pilot training syllabus (Johnston and Maurino, 1990). In consequence, most contemporary commercial pilots are now equipped with basic human factors knowledge. The 1988 Annex 1 revision also included a slightly augmented requirement in respect of human factors skills. Hence, for example, the holder of an Airline Transport Pilot Licence must henceforth:

> demonstrate the ability ...to...
>
> (c) exercise good judgement and airmanship,...
> (f) understand and apply crew co-ordination and incapacitation procedures,
> (g) communicate effectively with the other flight crew members.

In an independent but supporting programme, the ICAO Flight Safety and Human Factors Study Group was formed to act as an international forum to discuss aviation human factors issues. ICAO also published an extensive series of Human Factors Digests, based upon the deliberations and efforts of this group (see, for example: International Civil Aviation Organization, 1989a, 1989b and 1991). A number of world symposia and regional seminars on human factors were also organized (Maurino, 1993). Moreover, ICAO recently (July 1995) published an amendment to Annex 6 (Operation of Aircraft), intended to strengthen training responses by Operators in respect of '...knowledge and skills related to human performance and limitations...'. With these changes to Annex 1 and Annex 6, ICAO has initiated far reaching human factors interventions in both the licensing and operational domains and their consequences will steadily permeate the aviation system over the coming years.

The U.S. AQP - Advanced Qualification Program (FAA, 1991) - is probably the best known and most sophisticated initiative by a single aviation administration to encourage the integration of human factors skills training within commercial aviation. European Aviation Authorities - the Joint Aviation Authorities (JAA) - have combined their efforts to produce new flight crew licensing (JAR-FCL) requirements. The JAR-FCL proposals include a comprehensive syllabus to cover human factors knowledge and an innovative proposal for applied human factors training to conclude the Commercial Pilot Licence (CPL) training phase (JAA, 1994; Johnston, 1993) this particular JAR-FCL initiative mandates Multi-Crew Cooperation (MCC) training which will incorporate both ground and simulator training phases. JAA requirements for operators (JAR-OPS) will mandate CRM training, including shared aspects for both cockpit and cabin crewmembers.

*Industry responses*

An increasing number of textbooks on human factors in aviation have been published in response to the growing interest in aviation human factors and the need to integrate the ICAO requirements into training syllabi. A developmental approach to the human factors knowledge requirement is being pursued in Canada (King, 1993). A number of university based pilot training courses, which include training for the CPL/IR, have been implemented in several countries; these aim to fully integrate human factors throughout the entire *ab initio* pilot training syllabus (Hunt, 1990, 1993; Telfer, 1993).

Crew Resource Management (Wiener, Kanki & Helmreich, 1994) is now the most widely established airline human factors training format. CRM training seeks to achieve optimal performance of aircraft crew members through the timely and proficient use of all available resources (Federal Aviation Administration, F.A.A., 1989). The primary goal is safe and efficient flight, achieved through effective cockpit team performance (Foushee, 1984). Appropriately trained crew members should promptly solicit or provide relevant operational information relevant to the efficiency and safety of flight. The intention is to achieve the best situational use of all available resources (Foushee & Helmreich, 1988). The strategic CRM objective is full incorporation of CRM attitudes and practices within all crew training activities. Successful achievement of this task represents a major challenge for the global aviation industry.

This brief summary illustrates how recent years have seen remarkable changes in the legislative and industry environment. Those involved in aviation human factors prior to the late 1980's would have been amazed to hear that these comprehensive legislative and training approaches to human factors training would be completed over such a short period. It would, however, be foolish to conclude that mere syllabus redesign and the provision of basic human factors knowledge can, of themselves, solve aviation human factors problems. Much more efficient and cost-effective pilot training in applied human factors is essential. This important avenue has yet to be fully exploited. While it is widely agreed that such training will necessarily concentrate on the successful integration of both technical and human factor skills, the effective design, implementation and quality control of such training manifestly presents a number of practical challenges.

The deficiencies of traditional approaches to training design are considered immediately below, since they are believed to present a significant constraint on the development of applied human factors training. Alternative approaches and perspectives will then be considered, and integrated technical and human factors training design criteria outlined.

## Learning theory and pilot training

*Introduction*

Contemporary approaches to learning theory increasingly reflect findings from research into human expertise (Chi, Glaser & Farr, 1989), including research into the nature of skill differences between novices and experts. These research findings suggest that learning context and domain-specific training methods merit particular attention (Glaser, 1992a; Chi & Bjork, 1991). There is an increasing consensus that an explicit understanding of learning theory is important when designing instructional courseware (Montague and Knirk, 1993a). Gelman and Greeno (1989) propose that any effective theory of instruction must consider; (a) a theory of the requisite knowledge required, (b) a theory of the learner, and, (c) a theory of the process of transition between the initial and desired states of knowledge.

A detailed analysis of the implications of these findings is beyond the scope of this chapter, though some theoretical considerations will be reviewed. Applied considerations and perspectives which derive from these alternative views of learning are subsequently addressed. The primary intention here is to demonstrate why traditional learning theories are inadequate to the task of developing applied human factors training.

*Traditional perspectives*

When we design or develop training we must have some underlying ideas - whether implicit or explicit - about human learning (Johnston, 1995). Traditional training approaches are based on variations of long established learning paradigms such as 'formal discipline', 'general transfer', 'stimulus-response similarity', or 'identical elements', all of which posit transfer of training from a learning context to an applied context (Hammerton, 1987; Rolfe, 1991). Learning is thus represented by the point to point 'mapping' between a training activity 'in' to the mind, storage as a mental representation, and back 'out' to the applied task (Cormier & Hagman, 1987, Ch. 1; Gick & Holyoak, 1987). Such ideas are reflected, for example, in Instructional Systems Design and certification criteria for flight training devices (O'Neil, 1979). In the latter case strong emphasis is placed upon physical fidelity to real aircraft - since training transfer is widely held to occur because of 'identical elements' or 'stimulus-response similarity' between the learning and applied contexts (Thorndike, 1903; Osgood, 1949; Baudhuin, 1987).

Operationally realistic tasks and situations are not normally taken to be an essential part of simulator-based learning, since contextual detail is believed to bring a complexity which interfers with clean training transfer. Within this paradigm factors which are typically believed to enhance training transfer include:

1   attaching meanings to goal oriented stimuli,

2   the development and contextual association of appropriate responses with stimuli by the trainee, and,

3   generalization of simulation-based learning to broader task demands (Baudhuin, 1987).

This leads to a segmented instructional design orientation which seeks the sequential mastery of constituent skills, often with behaviourally explicit testing at each learning stage. Knowledge is frequently treated as important for its own sake - as principles and theory - rather than being resource for direct application in practice. The learning and testing of formal declarative knowledge and computational skills is often a priority, with learning reinforcement paradigms dominating in actual training situations. There is also a tendency to treat learners as the passive recipients of those environmental reinforcement contingencies which are believed to effect actual learning.

Learning is thus treated as a kind of induction of sensed data from the external world. The task of the training and equipment designer is to facilitate the mental and learning processes - primarily by representing and exploiting identical elements between learning and applied tasks - while minimizing the presence of confounding variables. This frequently leads to decontextualization of training objectives and context. In consequence, the specification and testing of discrete units of declarative knowledge often has an elevated training priority. This entire approach to training is obviously predicated on the assumption that the requisite tasks and skills can first be successfully identified, compartmentalized and decontextualized - to subsequently be taught as discrete learning units (Montague & Knirk, 1993b).

*Applications of the traditional view*

In most applied training circumstances theory normally precedes the 'complexity' and fuzzy difficulties of practical training in most training contexts. For instance, we teach (and test) abstract mathematical skills to school-children to help them eventually deal with 'real life' calculation (Lave, 1988) and often proceed as though human expertise is somehow akin to 'theory in practice'. Aviation practice is no different to that in other domains. Thus in the case, for example, of aircraft type-transition training we take it for granted that we must train in linear sequential steps from theory to practice, with each step following 'naturally and necessarily' from the previous one.

It is normal to start with technical (systems) training, before moving on to drills and manipulative training exercises in procedural trainers and high fidelity simulators. Technical and manipulative procedures and drills are taught progressively as discrete and decontextualized exercises. As each discrete training exercise is mastered trainees progress to the next handling and procedural exercise. It is normal for traditional type transition training to be concerned with decontexualized *technical* realism rather than *operational* realism. The cost of simulator time invariably ensures that type transition training is focused on technical issues and aircraft handling skills. Technical drills typically finish when the pilot handles each operational/training problem as an independent technical or manipulative task.

Since pilots are checked and licensed as individuals, the syllabus often assumes that one crew member is learning PF (pilot-flying) skills, while the other is simultaneously learning PNF (pilot-not-flying) duties. In consequence little emphasis may be directed to crew co-ordination and CRM skills, other than those which arise as an artifact of the actual training exercise. 'Real world' operational considerations rarely figure, given that their incorporation is believed to unnecessarily increase training time and complexity. That complexity is generally is considered more appropriate to the final line operational training stage - when the trainee is expected to recall, combine and suitably orchestrate the requisite component skills, in order to achieve a suitable 'operational line standard'. Unstructured consolidation subsequently takes place during the passage of time following initial checkout.

*Limitations to traditional training approaches*

The implicit assumption underlying the type of training outlined above is that pilots will have little problem in applying various constituent technical, human factors and CRM training competencies when faced with real world operational problems. In other words it is assumed that pilots can easily link and integrate each of the discrete sub-skills necessary to successfully resolve technical and operational problems. This means that the declared objective of training - a fully and effectively qualified line pilot - is not normally considered to be an issue of significance until the very final stages of training, and then only for the purposes of a final 'check out'. Paradoxically, while the final operating standard and competencies of the trainee provide the ultimate focus and objective for the *entire* training effort, the reality almost seems to reduce or understate the significance of this fact. A further assumption, namely that co-pilots will 'pick-up' and develop more sophisticated insights and skills as they gain 'experience', then begins to play its ideological role.

It will be argued below that this approach to training is not compatible with the learning of *applied* human factors skills - especially since these skills are contingent and circumstances often require behaviour which in a slightly different context might be judged inadequate or inappropriate. There is a manifest difference between teaching CRM theory to pilots and ensuring that they have the requisite, generalized and applied CRM skills. Application is the key. Theoretical understanding is not of any applied benefit and may be far removed from the real needs of the operational world. It follows that we need to train exactly as we wish to see trainees operate.

It equally follows that the training and development of applied expertise in human factors skills must take place in operationally realistic contexts. Thus the only way to develop and refine the necessary skills is to practice in operationally realistic situations and circumstances. If we need to integrate different competencies in operational practice, the training and development of such skills must be within a comprehensive and integrated training format. In other words, a training orientation which can overcome the disadvantages of traditional 'building block' approaches. It will be argued below that such an inclusive and comprehensive training approach has even more radical implications than appear at first sight. For that reason we must first review research findings which will provide an alternative perspectives on training and learning.

*Learning theory and expertise*

A repeated criticism of traditional training approaches has been that the experiments upon which learning theory is built lack a bridge to the real world (Chapanis, 1988; Simon, 1987; Schneider, 1985). Glaser & Bassok (1989) observed that 'learning theorists have generally expected that principles so gleaned would be extrapolated eventually to explain complex forms of learning' (p. 632). However, these expectations have not been realized and the conditions and tasks used to investigate learning are frequently sterile and unrepresentative of the conditions in which most human learning actually takes place. This tends to lead to 'inert' or 'brittle' knowledge which cannot be accessed for use in practice.

Valuable insights into the nature of human expertise have been obtained from the analysis of human performance within a number of highly-specialized work domains (Chi, Glaser & Farr, 1988). This has contributed significantly to instructional psychology and added considerably to our understanding of superior work performances. Studies of the differences between experts and novices have provided numerous valuable findings and insights relevant to training development and design. The following paragraphs briefly summarize some of the relevant findings (for detailed information see: Bedard & Chi, 1992; Chaiklin & Lave, 1993; Chi & Bjork, 1991; Chi, Glaser & Farr, 1988; Chi & Greeno, 1988; Federico, 1995; Glaser, 1990, 1992a, 1992b; Montague & Knirk, 1993a; Ortega, 1989; Phillips, 1994; Resnick, 1989; Reimann & Chi, 1989; Seamster, Redding, Cannon, Ryder & Purcell, 1993).

Experts operate at a deeper and more principled level than novices when dealing with situational and problem assessment. It is often the case that the experience base of experts is built from long experience, rather than achieved through formal teaching. However, it is equally the case that that appropriately designed training appears likely to contribute to the early and more principled acquisition of expertise by novices. It is widely agreed that learning within complex domains merits greatly increased attention, specifically with respect to those conditions which enhance and delimit highly skilled performances. At a very basic level novice learning seems to be driven by failures of comprehension and the consequent reflective efforts to resolve problems and inconsistencies (Kolb, 1984). In consequence, learning challenges should be designed to be just beyond the trainee's current level of competence. Prototypical training situations can help to both provide, and develop, basic trainee mental models. This fosters the kind of applied reasoning frequently absent from formal problem representations.

In the absence of applied training, novices may know the relevant principles, rules, and operational vocabulary without being able to recognize the 'when and how' of their effective application, whereas experts possess an organized body of conceptual and procedural knowledge which can be readily accessed and applied to maximum effect. Experts use recognition processes which are based on a substantial repertoire of structured knowledge, and their skills mainly derive from the way in which their knowledge is organized. This knowledge structuring makes the knowledge more accessible, functional, and efficient. Experts tend to be highly effective at self-monitoring. To summarize; expertise is characterized by cognitive efficiency and principled understanding, in combination with domain specific pattern recognition and meta-cognitive monitoring.

Effective training within complex environments is invariably grounded in an explicit Cognitive Task Analysis which captures the salient characteristics of competent performances. Training programmes which incorporate learning in respect of specific and realistic problems are more successful than those which teach general propositions. Most investigators seem to agree that useful knowledge is acquired as a result of pursuing specific goals during active task involvement, especially when set within realistic contexts. The use of explicit and applied ('hands on') learning strategies is stressed, with the objective of helping trainees to reason, speak, and act like an experienced practitioner. Accordingly, a primary objective is to teach in a supportive task-oriented context, with a view to building a repertoire of realistic experiences for the trainee. This necessitates real or realistic problem spaces, contextually and socially nested within a real or simulated domain of practice.

*Situated learning*

Another valuable perspective on human learning is provided by anthropological accounts of everyday learning activities. These supplement the findings from research into the nature of human expertise. Lave (1988) considers why school mathematics fails to successfully transfer to the 'real world', drawing the conclusion that all learning is socially 'situated' and is therefore primarily and fundamentally a culturally structured activity. For this reason previous (existing) learning and culturally mediated understanding are held to be basic to all human learning. Skill and knowledge acquisition are thus considered to be critically dependent upon the varied social and applied contexts in which they are acquired and deployed.

The Situated Learning approach (Lave & Wenger, 1991) emphasizes the need for contextually rich, realistic and representative learning contexts. These are believed to shape the learning experiences of the trainee, whose unique self-organizing potential is also brought to bear upon these experiences. Learning thus has an emergent quality, which is partially shaped by tacit and dynamic cultural norms and values (Johnston, 1993a). The Situated Learning approach is also based on the idea that formal, or verbal, descriptions and reductions of behaviour are necessarily and irremediably incomplete (Winograd & Flores, 1986; Lintern, in press). From this perspective all learning is inherently social, rather than being a linear and cumulative process of personal knowledge construction. Successful acquisition of knowledge is actually demonstrated by effective and effortless engagement in practice - in other words by the smooth flow of activity we associate with skilled performances.

Cognitive and social processes are considered to be neither separate or separable - since the social activities within which knowledge is developed and deployed cannot be isolated from learning and cognition. Learning is thus an enculturation, or a kind of cognitive apprenticeship (Brown, Collins & Duguid, 1989). Aviation, especially in its *ab initio* training programmes, is continuously involved in turning non-pilots into pilots. From the Situated Learning viewpoint this learning transition transcends simple technical, academic or psychomotor learning activities. The process of becoming a pilot, or indeed becoming anything... is just that ... a becoming ... an apprenticeship of some form or other (Lave and Wenger, 1991).

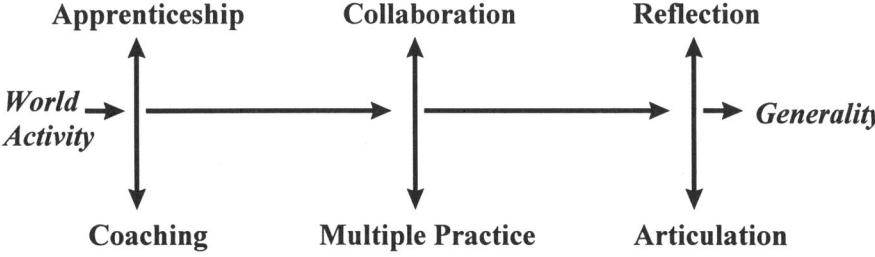

**Figure 9.1   From Brown, Collins and Duguid (1989)**

For this reason the learning of 'facts' and applied knowledge cannot be separated from the actual context of their acquisition and application. Hence all learning, including the transition from novice to expert, should ultimately be treated as a social activity, rather than the mere accumulation of more and more factual knowledge and raw skills. The key role of significant others in this learning transition is emphasized in Figure 1, which illustrates and summarizes the social processes of learning - and of 'becoming'.[1]

The insights of Situated Learning and research into expert performances suggest that improved training is both possible and necessary if we wish to optimize the teaching and development of high-level expertise and competence. Taken in combination with the failures of traditional learning theory, they collectively suggest a need for radical changes to our training design, development and implementation practices. Cognitive Task Analysis seems a likely candidate to help bridge the gap between both novices and expert knowledge structures, and between the expertise and situated learning research literatures.

*Cognitive Task Analysis*

Glaser & Bassok (1989) note that 'what is common to exemplary work in this area [analysis of training and expertise] is grounding in cognitive task analysis; that is the objectives of instruction are based on current knowledge of the characteristics of competence on a task'. Ryder and Redding (1993) discuss the integration of Cognitive Task Analysis (CTA) into the development of instructional systems. They suggest that CTA differs from traditional analytic approaches by concentrating on the domain-specific nature of expertise, and also in explicitly examining how expertise actually develops. Ryder and Redding (1993) contrast the concerns of the CTA with traditional methods, as outlined here:

**Table 9.1 Comparison of CTA and traditional methods**

| **Traditional** | **Cognitive** |
| --- | --- |
| Emphasizes behaviour | Emphasizes cognition |
| Analyzes target performance | Analyzes skill development |
| Evaluates knowledge for each task separately | Evaluates knowledge for whole job |
| Behaviourally-based task segmentation | Skill-based task segmentation |
| Mental models not addressed | Mental models addressed |

CTA considers knowledge organization for the entire job function, specifically seeking relationships between knowledge, concepts and actions (Schneider, 1985). Mental models, heuristics, mental simulations and meta-cognitive functioning are explicitly addressed (Redding, 1989b). These help to understand how expertise actually manifests itself within a particular domain and, crucially, the findings then become a key resource for structuring and guiding the training of novices (Seamster, Redding, Cannon, Ryder & Purcell, 1993). CTA thus helps us understand how a skill is actually learned in practice, and this provides important clues as to how this learning can be compressed, expedited and improved (Redding 1989a; 1989b). CTA also helps to identify stage-like knowledge and skill transformations during the learning process. This enables a qualitative differentiation to be made between experts and novices in a manner which facilitates progressive and efficient training to be designed around a cognitively relevant framework.

*Mental Models* Identifying relevant Mental Models is an important part of Cognitive Task Analysis. Ryder and Redding (1993) define these as; '...functional abstractions about a job or job task which provide a deductive framework for problem solving.' Mental models might best be considered as domain-specific problem representations which integrate key variables and salient perceptual clues. Mental models cognitively represent '... the structural, functional, and causal relations among ... components' (Chi & Bjork, 1991). It is the dynamic, computational and 'runnable' nature of mental models which helps to project and mentally simulate the implications of perceived situations and intended courses of action. Developing and learning to utilize basic mental models in a contextually appropriate manner is an important part of acquiring expertise.

*Learning theory and pilot training - summary review*

Resnick (1989) summarizes current cognitive theory as emphasizing three particular aspects of learning. He first notes that learning is 'a process of knowledge construction, not knowledge recording or absorption.' Second, that 'learning is knowledge-dependent' - we use existing knowledge to create new knowledge and, third, that 'learning is highly tuned to the situation in which it takes place'. In summarizing the burden of the foregoing discussion, each of these suggest that the development of effective human factors and technical training practices will generate:

- A need to identify the nature of domain-specific expertise and competencies,
- A need to identify and develop domain-specific training methods,
- A need for Cognitive Task Analyses to identify and develop domain-specific training materials and methods,
- A need to train in domain-specific and domain-relevant operational and social contexts,
- A need for a more global approach to training development and implementation.

These criteria have practical consequences and implications, which stand in some contrast to traditional training approaches and these will impact upon the design, economics, implementation, and quality control of pilot human factors training. A number of these are discussed below.

## Implications for human factors training

*Situated cognition and expertise*

The fundamental commitment in this chapter is to the view that the accumulation of aeronautical human factors skills can be accelerated through appropriately structured training. While effective new work habits are not easy to develop, established habits are even harder to replace - so the objective must be to train throughout as we intend our trainees to continue in practice. Moreover, it seems clear that if we want pilots to perform as a crew - as team members - we should train them as a crew from the beginning (Hackman, 1988; Swezey and Salas, 1992). In other words, we must provide initial and recurrent training which is consistent with the desired technical and human factors behaviours and competencies we wish to see manifested in operational practice.

Given such training imperatives it would appear necessary to combine and fuse a number of the different insights and research findings discussed above. There is, for instance, a need for integrated training methods which can avoid the inadequacies of overly decomposed and decontextualized training techniques. From the expertise literature there are important insights regarding the nature of expert performances and the qualitative differences found between experts and novices. From the situated learning literature we are reminded of the key social processes which contribute to the contextual settings within which expertise is learned and applied. Cognitive task analysis offers a valuable analytic technique by which to identify the salient aspects of expertise which practitioners need to acquire (Redding, 1990). These considerations, summarized in Figure 2, suggest that greater attention to task analysis, syllabus design and training delivery will be required in the future.

# Teaching Human Factors for Airline Operations

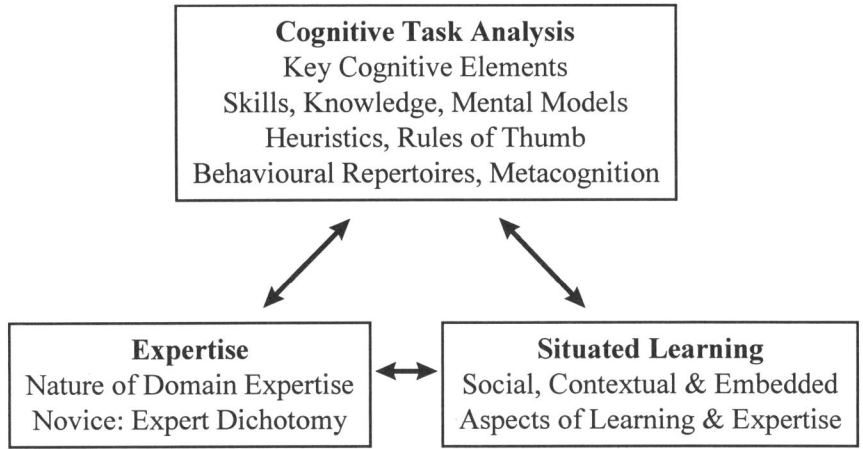

**Figure 9.2 Summary of CTA, expertise and situated learning**

*Training applied aviation human factors: Basic principles[2]*

A major challenge is to find cost-effective training and simulation methods which can help trainees organize their learning in an efficient manner. The objective must be to rapidly achieve more effective and efficient practice - in other words, to help trainees develop 'experience' by artificial and accelerated methods. Training should equip trainees to recognize particular situations as necessitating the utilization of the relevant skills. Effective training will also ensure that the requisite skills will be readily available as an applied resource for effortless deployment, as may be required. In order to achieve these objectives it is suggested that the optimal approach must be *Holistic, Applied, Realistic and Integrated* - or *'HARI'* - training principles:

- By *Holistic* it is meant that training will at all stages take the **totality** of domain expertise and task demands into account - as distinct from decontextualized and sequential knowledge, or skills. A strategic view of the entire job function must therefore be taken throughout training design and delivery, and all operationally significant connections between knowledge, concepts and actions must be explicitly addressed. No matter how rudimentary the training format may be, the contextual and cognitive integrity of the entire training event must always be maintained. This will be achieved by considering the constituent training elements; (a) within the context of the overall task, (b) at the functional level experienced by practitioners, and (c) with the final standard of operational competence as the strategic focus for all design and implementation activities. Perception, cognition and action should be treated as constituting a single system - as distinct from, for instance, mediated or unmediated stimulus: response couplings.

- By *Applied* it is meant that training will involve 'hands on' practice, or the active 'doing' of appropriately representative tasks. This will explicitly involve combined physical and cognitive activities and, where possible, suitable emotional involvement. Appropriate attentional demands will be combined with those task goals and sub-goals typically associated with 'real world' requirements and performances. This necessitates the availability and contextually appropriate use of paperwork, manuals and equipment - whither as exact replicas, or as generic facsimiles. Within the applied training context physical, cognitive, social and physical activities will be synthesized to reflect applied task demands, characteristics, 'action triggers' and 'action sequences'. Peer or instructor coaching, such as would typically be provided to support and assist trainees, will also be relevant when designing and implementating training. It is clearly desirable that training designers structure the types of peer support and guidance which occur both formally and informally in 'real world' situations.[3]

- By *Realistic* it is meant that training must achieve a suitable degree of realism, such as will create rich and operationally representative learning *content* and *contexts*. Each training unit or scenario must be perceived as credible by trainees for the designated training task. This will necessitate real-time training in socially, operationally and technically representative tasks and situations. The training tasks and situations should therefore be capable of training - and evoking - typical operational reactions and dispositions from trainees. 'Realism' here is not a reference to high simulation *device* fidelity, or even to 'real' tasks; it is rather to assert that the 'practice environment' should achieve sufficient cognitive and operational fidelity so as to adequately and purposively *engage* trainees at the relevant functional and cognitive levels. The degree of training device fidelity will vary from low to high, depending upon the learning development stage, operational content and precise training objectives.

- By *Integrated* it is meant that technical and procedural training (aircraft systems, operating procedures, etc.) will be *fully* integrated with non-technical (human factors and cockpit management) training (Johnston, 1994). This means that training design should never consider technical and procedural training as entities which exist independently of the supporting Crew Resource Management (Wiener, Kanki & Helmreich, 1993) and human factors skills. Integration requires that applied human factors be explicitly addressed and incorporated with technical training. Neither should be trained in the absence of the other, since in real operational contexts they never have an independent existence. Moreover, due attention must be paid to social and organizational factors which impact upon mission or job function. Training must also ensure that suitable aspects of teamwork are practised and that appropriate feedback is provided (Swezey & Salas 1992). Effective integration will therefore encompass the physical, cognitive, social, technical and operational aspects of work performance.

The central objective of integrated training is to effectively unite training in both technical and non-technical piloting skills. The primary human factors training objective is therefore to conduct training exercises within a realistic operational and social totality, through the medium of realistic operational problems and circumstances. This helps trainees develop techniques and repertoires of behaviour which can be 'hooked' or linked to the relevant operational activities. By using prototypical training tasks derived from Cognitive and Operational Task Analyses, general skills, heuristics and behavioural repertoires can be taught in a contextually representative fashion.

*Experiential learning: Line oriented flight training and line operational simulations*

These considerations beg the question as to how the required pilot learning can best be achieved and promoted. If we take the foregoing analysis as the point of departure, it seems clear that the participants in any training activity must be actively engaged in representative training events during which they can develop domain-specific expertise. In order to achieve this, various training techniques and technologies are available. Of these the most important are real time simulations of technical and operational events using Line Operational Simulation (LOS) and Line Oriented Flight Training (LOFT) training scenarios.

LOS - Line Operational Simulation - refers to the 'real time' simulation of operational activities in circumstances where full contextual realism is not at a premium and some instructional input may be considered appropriate or desirable (Johnston, 1992).

LOFT - Line Oriented Flight Training - refers to 'full mission' simulation used for pilot training purposes. Definitions and applications of LOS and LOFT vary considerably. Useful definitions and background information are contained in a FAA Advisory Circular on LOS/LOFT (FAA, 1990) and in LOFT guidance material developed by NASA (Lauber and Foushee, 1981). LOFT consists of entire flights, normally conducted in high fidelity simulators, during which various operational or technical problems are managed by the crew in 'real time'. Full operational documentation, pre-flight planning and normal aircraft operating practices are used throughout. There is no direct instructional input during the actual LOFT session. At the end of the LOFT exercise, the 'instructor' acts as facilitator of a debriefing discussion of how the exercise developed, and what could be learned from the experience. LOS/LOFT scenario design and training content may be varied, depending upon the level of trainee experience - ranging from basic skill training for *ab initio* trainees, through to skill development, enhancement and reinforcement for experienced pilots.

Fundamental to the successful use of LOS and LOFT are; (a) the quality of training scenario design, (b) the effective conduct of simulator training scenarios, and, (c) the quality of pilot briefing and debriefing. Pilot debriefing is of particular importance, since it is during debriefing that opportunities for open discussion arise, and this is when the development and modification of pre-existing understandings, beliefs and strategies - in other words, *learning* - actually takes place (Johnston, 1993b; Kolb, 1984). This learning is thus experiential - based upon direct experience - rather than being based upon formal or didactic learning methods. Pearson and Smith, (1985) note that 'reflection lies at the core of experience-based learning. Without it, experiences may remain as experiences and the full potential for learning by the participant may not be realized.' LOS and LOFT provide pilots with an opportunity for such reflection and experienced based - experiential - learning (Kolb, 1984; Schön, 1983). Effective debriefing builds upon the training opportunities presented by effective scenario design, mainly by structuring and exploiting the developmental and experiential learning cycle, as outlined in Figure 3.

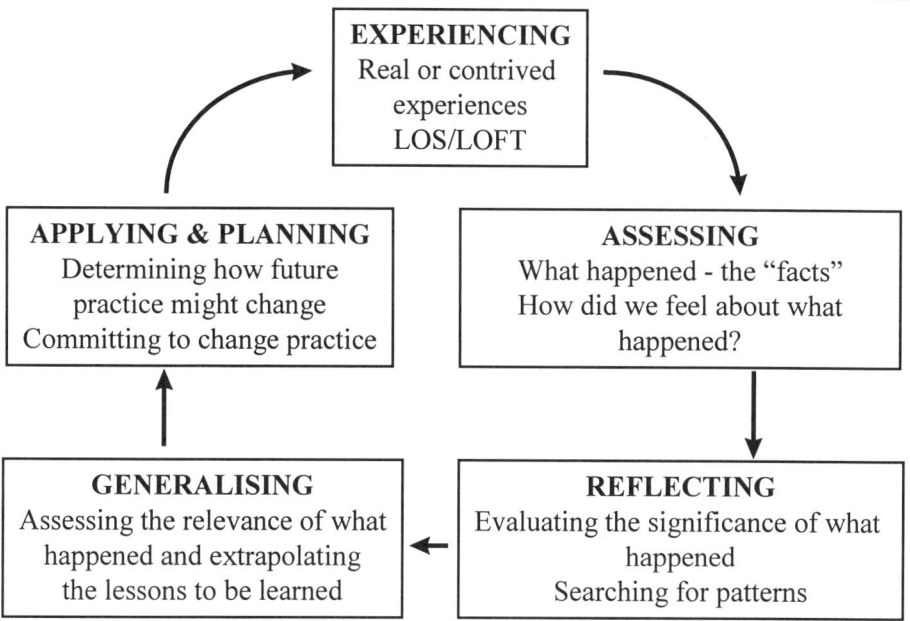

**Figure 9.3   The experiential learning cycle (from Johnston, 1993b)**

In respect of expertise development and consolidation, it is only through openness to the opportunities afforded by LOS/LOFT training, and the individual pilot's willingness to reflect critically on performance and behaviour, that its learning potential can be fully exploited (Miller, 1988). In any planned learning activity - such as LOS or LOFT - debriefing provides pilots with an opportunity to engage such in reflection. There are two essentials: (i) the exposure of trainees and practitioners to situations, circumstances, events and 'experiences' which they view as relevant, challenging and engaging, and, (ii) an openness to considering new ways of perceiving oneself, the situation, other crew-members, how such events might be managed differently in the future, and so forth.

The former is a matter of LOFT/LOS training scenario design, while the second depends heavily upon the facilitator and the participating pilots. The LOFT facilitator 'facilitates' - or enables and promotes - the overall learning process by chairing the debriefing session and creating an atmosphere within which reflective learning can occur. The attitudes of those involved ultimately contain the key to achieving its learning potential and this, in turn, depends upon the organizational training climate. An appropriate organizational training climate is essential for the success of such training techniques.

It should also be noted that these training considerations have traditionally been taken to imply a need for high fidelity simulation. An interesting implication of the analysis and *'HARI'* training principles introduced above is that high fidelity simulation is by no means essential for pilot training purposes, and that suitable low fidelity, generic and other simulation or training methods may be capable of providing sufficient operational, psychological and contextual realism to enable training to be successfully completed (Johnston, in review). Low fidelity methods are probably best suited to the training of inexperienced and *ab initio* pilots, while generic training has a much wider range of training applicability.

*Implications* There are a number of far reaching implications for training interventions based upon the combined criteria discussed above. These include the following:

- a need to break free from traditional technical and human factors training practice
- a move from individualistic pilot-based training to crew-based training
- a move from segmented to holistic training courseware and techniques
- the integration of Crew Resource Management (CRM) principles into all aspects of training practice
- an emphasis on the design of applied, rather than 'formalistic' training
- minimizing checking - 'dead' time - in order to maximize recurrent training opportunities
- significantly greater simulator training in real time, using operationally realistic training scenarios (e.g. LOS and LOFT)
- effective instructor training, with an emphasis on contemporary briefing and debriefing skills
- avoiding time consuming 'simulator training/checking rituals' which lack an explicit training role or value
- greater use of Cognitive Task Analyses for training development and to identify the salient characteristics of expertise in specific operational tasks and domains
- the development of a more incisive and 'rapid prototyping' Cognitive Task Analytic methodology
- a more pragmatic and developmental approach to evaluating the effectiveness of training devices

- emphasizing clarity of purpose in analyzing operational tasks and training needs
- the use of low-fidelity and/or generic training devices and techniques
- the use of technology for repetitive training, checking and quality assurance purposes
- the use of action research, survey and other feedback techniques to assess, modify and improve training courseware and delivery
- taking a broader and longer-term view of training cost-effectiveness

The preferred method or 'basic training technology' will be LOS/LOFT, conducted in either type-specific, generic or low fidelity simulators. In order to successfully introduce such training in practice, and to facilitate the ordered development of human factors training, some type of training policy framework is required. An example of such a framework is provided immediately below.

*Training implementation framework - the 4Ps: Philosophy, policies, procedures and practices*

In order to draw out the training management and administrative implications of the foregoing discussion, we can use the 4Ps framework - *Philosophy, Policies, Procedures* and *Practices* - to outline a number of provisional criteria which may be used to guide integrated human factors training design and implementation. The 4Ps provide a structure within which an organizational 'Training Mission Statement' can be formally instantiated. While the 4Ps were originally devised as a descriptive framework for Flight Operations (Degani & Wiener, 1994) it clearly has a wider analytic applicability. The particular contents suggested below serve only as an illustrative sample, since the actual content will necessarily vary with different legislative and organizational requirements and objectives:

## Training philosophy

- Pilot training will be crew-oriented, rather than pilot-oriented
- All pilot training will be designed to achieve operational relevance
- Training will replace checking to the greatest extent possible

- Wherever possible systemic Quality Assurance techniques will be adopted in preference to traditional checking and testing
- Training delivery will use flexible methods
- Pilot instructors and training equipment (including computers) are matched to those tasks to which they are best suited

**Training policy**

- Crew Resource Management principles will be integrated into all pilot training activities
- Training courseware and activities will aim to maximize operational realism and relevance
- To the maximum extent possible LOS/LOFT and variants thereof will be used for training purposes
- Technical, operational and CRM elements will be integrated into all classroom and simulator training
- Training and checking of basic manipulative skills will be highly formalized and designed for efficiency
- Theory will be taught only to the extent that it is required to support practical skills
- Repetitive recurrent training items will be achieved expeditiously, using standardized training courseware
- Supplementary human factors training will be specified for identified target groups (e.g. low-time pilots, those new to function, etc.)
- Training, including remedial activities, will be provided to meet the required standard
- Systems of training remediation will be developed and implemented, as required
- Appropriate instructor skills training will be provided
- Appropriate human factors training for instructors will be provided
- Guidance and/or 'calibration' training will be provided to all pilots regarding the characteristics of desired and acceptable cockpit performance

**Training procedures and methods**

- Applied - 'hands on' - training will be emphasized at all training stages

- A minimum of 50% of time on all type transition courses will involve line oriented training (LOS or LOFT)
- A minimum of 80% of time of all recurrent training will involve line oriented training (LOS or LOFT)
- All recurrent training will be highly structured according to a pre-published three year training cycle
- LOS/LOFT scenarios will be designed to explicitly incorporate technical, operational and CRM elements
- Single leg LOS/LOFT will be established as the recurrent training norm; 'branching' LOS/LOFT will be used as appropriate
- Applied training will be provided for pilots at airline entry and command transition stages

**Training practices - feedback and evaluation**

- Suitable feedback mechanisms will be established; these will provide appropriate feedback to line pilots, instructors and management
- All training implementation will be continuously evaluated for value and effectiveness
- Management and instructors will be provided with feedback on operational/training standards in accordance with an agreed plan/schedule
- Training courseware, materials and practices will be modified in accordance with information obtained from the Feedback and Evaluation systems.

*Human Factors training: Design and development*

Montague and Knirk (1993b) capture the essence of the actual training design and development task in their observation that; 'Anyone attempting to design and develop instruction has a substantial orchestration problem on their hands.' A comprehensive treatment of the many design and implementation implications of the foregoing discussion is beyond the scope of this chapter. (However, Cannon-Bowers, Tannebaum, Salas and Converse (1991) provide a useful overview of the relevant linkages between training theory and technique). On the other hand, the foregoing discussion provides sufficient material for some basic conclusions and guidelines to be outlined.

What Montague and Knirk refer to as the 'orchestration problem' should be considered in the overall context of the 'HARI' - *Holistic, Applied, Realistic & Integrated* - analytic framework introduced above. When addressing human factors training development the following general framework is relevant when considering most operational situations:

**Table 9.2 Training framework**

| OBJECTIVES | ORCHESTRATION | ACTION REPERTOIRES |
|---|---|---|
| **What are our global training objectives?** | **What activities needs to be orchestrated?** | **Linked repertoires of operational activities** |
| • line trained pilot<br>• crew (CRM) trained pilot<br>• procedurally equipped pilot<br>• SOP equipped pilot<br>• automation trained pilot<br>• technically trained pilot<br>• manipulatively trained pilot | • flying<br>• procedures<br>• callouts<br>• CRM skills<br>• automation skills<br>• using manuals/ documentation<br>• communications<br>  - cockpit, ATC & dispatch<br>  - cabin crew & passengers | • What is linked:<br>  - manipulative skills<br>  - instrument procedures<br>  - standard callouts<br>  - automation procedures<br>  - operating procedures<br>  - CRM skills<br>  - strategic operational tasks<br>  - tactical operational tasks |

These categorizations capture the essence of operational task demands in most airline operating environments. It will be noted that the general ordering of the 'global training objectives', starting - rather than concluding - with the 'line trained pilot', inverts the traditional 'cumulative building block' training approach. Using these general headings, the necessary generic or type-specific piloting skills can be readily identified for different operating circumstances. The basic competencies which need to be taken into account may, for convenience, be grouped under three basic headings; (a) Technical Skills, (b) Procedural Skills and (c) Human Factors Skills.

Obviously the required human factors and CRM skills are easier to learn if they are taught and practised in realistic training contexts. The key objective is therefore to develop training which will provide operationally relevant practice and demand the application of the relevant human factors skills within representative operational circumstances. The general categorizations introduced above therefore emphasize the importance of fully integrating all operational, technical, communications, documentation and flying tasks within real-time training scenarios. Optimal learning requires a high level of activity from the learner, supported by effective instruction; effective training design will ensure that these essential requirements are also taken into account.

*Courseware development and training implementation*

Training developers must also ensure that the overall training courseware is coherent, internally consistent and rigorous. To this end a number of analytic and feedback methods may be employed. One illustrative technique - involving rote learning - will be briefly discussed here. Rote learning and other 'traditional' training methods have a part to play in all training. It is clearly legitimate to expect trainees to memorize and 'know' certain essential information, especially where this is fundamental to their applied operational competencies. However, many training courses make unreasonable or unachievable demands of trainees, often because of a lack of rigour and clarity on the part of training designers. It is not surprising that implicit demands are frequently the source of training bottlenecks and problems. For example, it is obviously inappropriate for trainees to commence simulator training without knowing the key operational tasks they are expected to achieve and, especially, without grasping the techniques by which those tasks are to be achieved. Indeed, on many occasions such basic knowledge is fundamental to a successful operational performance.

If, prior to commencing a training event, or entering a simulator, trainees cannot articulate the necessary techniques and tactical objectives to be pursued, it should not then surprise us if the integration and application of the required human factors skills fails to meet expectations. However, on the other hand, trainees cannot be expected to rote learn everything in advance since this, of itself, is certainly no guarantee of a successful performance.

*Memorizing, understanding and doing.* Downs & Perry (1984) suggest that training materials and learning activities preparatory to applied training tasks should be prepared according to the following basic - MUD - framework:

**M** - memorizing facts
**U** - understanding and applying ideas and concepts
**D** - doing and practising tasks

This simple framework has considerable analytic and training benefits, particularly if used to support a Cognitive Task Analysis. The MUD framework encourages clarity in training design, and will ensure that fundamental questions regarding training courseware are addressed. The sequential listing of memory and comprehension items is not, however, a one-way street. While it is legitimate to expect trainees to memorize and 'know' essential information, the task for training designers must be to identify and *clearly* specify the required information. Moreover, the relevant materials must then be provided in an unambiguous and coherent format, and presented at a pace which trainees can successfully accomplish. The discipline of achieving this will help training designers to structure training courseware appropriately when translating different task analyses into applied training materials. In respect of the human factors elements of training, it is also important to carefully address the critical gulf between human factors *knowledge* and *skills* training.

In summary, while there is an obligation on the trainee to rote learn certain fundamental information, there is also an obligation on the training system to provide the necessary courseware and to sequence training delivery appropriately for achievable learning. Determining training sequencing, what courseware and materials should fall under each 'MUD' heading, the importance of strictly limiting the amount of rote learning and, in particular, addressing the key distinction between training human factors skills and knowledge - these are all useful disciplines for training designers when developing integrated human factors training courseware.

**Summary and conclusion**

This chapter has taken it to be axiomatic that technical, manipulative, human factors, procedural and CRM piloting skills never have an independent existence in actual operational practice. While they may be separated for analytic, design or research purposes, it is totally inappropriate to sustain such an artificial analytic division in operational and training practice, since this generates a fundamental breech between trainee knowledge and the applied competencies demanded in the real operational world.

A particular emphasis in this chapter has been upon *Holistic, Applied, Realistic* and *Integrated* - 'HARI' - training courseware and techniques. The fundamental importance of full training integration and the fusing of technical and human factors aspects of cockpit management at all training levels has also been emphasized. Our objective must *always* be to train pilots exactly as we intend them to function in operational practice. Moreover, it equally follows that if we need pilots to perform as a crew we should train them as a crew on all possible occasions, including airline entry and during type/command transition phases.

For each operating environment, and each aircraft type, Cognitive Task Analysis can be used to identify the relevant operational knowledge, skills, routines, heuristics and mental models (Redding, Seamster & Kaempf, in preparation). The 4Ps framework was suggested as one method by which an airline 'training mission statement' could be prepared, in the particular context of achieving combined technical and human factors training.

Figure 4 summarizes the potential role of Cognitive Task Analysis and the MUD framework when linking Expertise and Situated Learning research insights to training courseware development. Figure 4 also summarizes the application of the 'HARI' training principles when exploiting the CTA and MUD frameworks for training implementation and delivery. Taken together, these techniques will help to ensure the overall coherence and operational relevance of all training courseware.

A number of important human factors training issues remain to be fully resolved by the aviation industry. Among the important issues which arise in relation to the preceding discussion is how airlines can best achieve cost-effectiveness and efficiency in human factors training design. In addition, we need to find methods of identifying exactly what constitutes effective and efficient human factors training, and how to specify the various methods by which this can be reliably measured. Issues relating to the evaluation of crew human factors skills remain one of the most important tasks facing the aviation industry. This, and the allied issue of ensuring effective and definitive methods of training validation, feedback and remediation will continue to be major challenges for aviation human factors training specialists for some time to come.

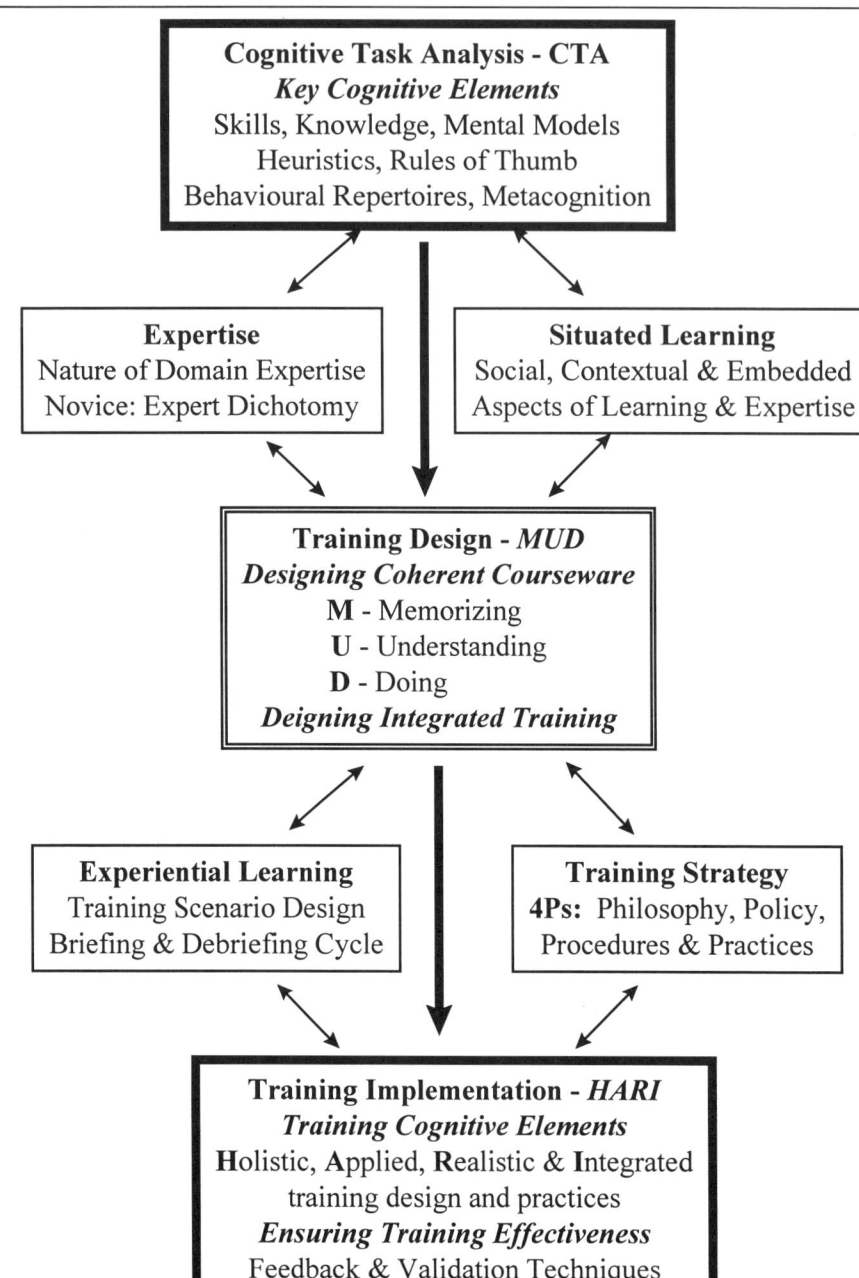

**Figure 9.4 Training analysis, development & implementation - summary framework**

**Notes**

1   This is all consistent with Vygotsky's concept of a 'Zone of Proximal Development' (Wertsch, 1979). Learning within the Zone of Proximal Development is enabled when learners work within their current level of knowledge and competence, while being aided by others towards yet higher levels of achievable competence - in other words, levels which are within their Zone of Proximal Development. Instructors and colleagues contribute the necessary learning resources, by providing, supporting and supplementing a 'knowledge scaffolding' through which understanding, meaning and signification are constructed by the learner (Kozulin & Presseisen, 1995).

2   The contents of this section are modified from similar material contained in Johnston (in review).

3   In some domains when trainees finish training and reach the operational stage they are often greeted by established colleagues with the statement 'forget everything you were taught in training, we'll now show you how things work in the real world'. The true test of effective task analysis and training success is to discover that such statements disappear, and that established practitioners readily acknowledge the quality and relevance of the skills possessed by new colleagues.

**References**

Baudhuin, E.S. (1987) 'The design of industrial and flight simulators'. In Cormier, S.M., & Hagman, J.D. (Eds), *Transfer of Learning*. (pp. 217-237). San Diego: Academic Press.

Bedard, J., & Chi, M.T.H. (1992) 'Expertise'. *Current Directions in Psychological Science*, 1(4), 135-139.

Brown, J.S., Collins, A., & Duguid, P. (1989) 'Situated cognition and the culture of learning'. *Educational Researcher*. 18(1), 32-42.

Cannon-Bowers, J.A., Tannenbaum, S.I., Salas E., & Converse, S.A. (1991) 'Toward an integration of training theory and technique'. *Human Factors*, 33(3), 281-292.

Chaiklin, S., & Lave, J. (1993) *Understanding Practice*. Cambridge: Cambridge University Press.

Chapanis, A. (1988) 'Some generalizations about generalization'. *Human Factors*, 30, 253-267.

Chi, M.T.H., Glaser, R., & Farr, M.J. (1988) *The Nature of Expertise.* Hillsdale, NJ: Erlbaum.

Chi, M.T.H., & Bjork, R.A. (1991) 'Modeling expertise'. In D. Druckman & R.A. Bjork (Eds.), *In the Mind's Eye: Enhancing Human Performance.* Washington DC: National Academy Press.

Chi, M.T.H., & Greeno, J.G. (1988) 'Cognitive research relevant to education'. *Psychology and Educational Policy*, 51,39-57.

Cormier, S.M., & Hagman, J.D. (Eds.). (1987) *Transfer of Learning.* San Diego: Academic Press

Degani, A. & Wiener, E.L. (1994) 'Philosophy, policies, procedures, and practices: The four 'P's of flight-deck operations'. In Johnston, A.N., McDonald, N.J. and Fuller, R.G., (Eds.). *Aviation Psychology in Practice.* London: Ashgate.

Downs, S., & Perry, P. (1984) 'Developing skilled learners'. *Research and Development Series: No.22.* Sheffield, England: Manpower Services Commission,

Federal Aviation Administration, (1989) 'Cockpit Resource Management Training'. Advisory Circular 120-51, Washington: FAA: Author.

Federal Aviation Administration, (1990) 'Line Operational Simulations'. Advisory Circular 120-35B, Washington: FAA: Author.

Federal Aviation Administration, (1991) 'Advanced Qualification Program'. Advisory Circular 120-54, Washington: FAA: Author.

Foushee, H.C. (1984) 'Dyads and triads at 35,000 feet: Factors affecting group process and aircrew performance'. *American Psychologist*, 39: 885-893.

Foushee, H.C., & Helmreich, R.L. (1988) 'Group interaction and flight crew performance'. In Wiener, E.L., & Nagel, D.C. (Eds) *Human Factors in Aviation* (pp. 189-227). San Diego: Academic Press.

Frederico, P. (1995). 'Expert and novice recognition of similar situations'. *Human Factors*, 37(1), 105-122.

Gick, M.L., & Holyoak, K.J. (1987) 'The cognitive basis of knowledge transfer'. In Cormier, S.M., & Hagman, J.D. (Eds.), *Transfer of Learning.* (pp. 9-46). San Diego: Academic Press.

Gelman, R., & Greeno, J.G. (1989) 'On the nature of competence: Principles for understanding in a domain'. In L.B. Resnick (Ed.). *Knowing, Learning and Instruction: Essays in Honor of Rober Glaser.* Hillsdale, NJ: Erlbaum.

Glaser, R. (1990) 'The reemergence of learning theory within instructional research'. *American Psychologist*, 45(1), 29-39.

Glaser, R. (1992a) 'Learning, cognition, and education: Then and now'. In Pick, P. van den Broek, & D. Knill (Eds), *Cognition: Conceptual and Methodological Issues*. Washington DC: American Psychological Association.

Glaser, R. (1992b) 'Expert knowledge and processes of thinking'. In D.F. Halpern (Ed.), *Enhancing Thinking Skills in the Sciences and Mathematics*. Hillsdale, NJ: Erlbaum.

Glaser, R., & Bassok, M. (1989) 'Learning theory and the study of instruction'. In M.R. Rosenzweig & L.W. Porter (Eds.), *Annual Review of Psychology*, 40, 631-666.

Hackman, J.R. (1988) 'Crew coordination issues'. *Proceedings of the 7th. General Flight Crew Meeting*, New Orleans. Montreal: International Air Transport Association.

Hammerton, M. (1987) 'Transfer of training'. In Gregory, R.L. (Ed.). *The Oxford Companion to the Mind*. (pp. 781-783). Oxford: Oxford University Press.

Hunt, G.J.F. (1990) 'An abilities-based approach to pilot competency and decision making'. In *Proceedings of the ICAO Human Factors Symposium, Leningrad: ICAO Circular 229-AN/137*. Montreal: International Civil Aviation Organization.

Hunt, G.J.F. (1993) 'New aviation professionalism: Knowledge systems that integrate human factor competencies in job performance'. In *Proceedings of the ICAO Human Factors Symposium, Washington, D.C.: ICAO Circular 243-AN/146*. Montreal: International Civil Aviation Organization.

International Civil Aviation Organization. (1989a) *Human Factors Digest No.1: Fundamental Human Factors Concepts*. Circular 216-AN/131. Montreal, Canada: Author.

International Civil Aviation Organization. (1989b) *Human Factors Digest No.2: Flight Crew Training: Cockpit Resource Management and Line-Oriented Flight Training*. 217-AN/132. Montreal, Canada: Author.

International Civil Aviation Organization. (1991) *Human Factors Digest No.3: Training of Operational Personnel in Human Factors*. Circular 227-AN/136. Montreal, Canada: Author.

Johnston, A.N. (1992) 'Airline "bridge" training'. *Proceedings of the Eighth Flight Crew Training Symposium*, Stockholm. (pp. 91-144). Montreal: International Air Transport Association.

Johnston, A.N. (1993) 'Human factors training for the new joint European pilot licences'. *In Proceedings of the Seventh International Symposium on Aviation Psychology.* Columbus, Ohio: Ohio State University, Department of Aviation.

Johnston, A.N. (1993a) 'CRM: Cross-cultural perspectives'. In Wiener E.L., Kanki, B.G. and Helmreich, R.L. (Eds.). *Cockpit Resource Management.* San Diego, CA: Academic Press.

Johnston, A.N. (1993b) 'LOS/LOFT debriefing skills and techniques'. *Proceedings of the Seventh International Symposium on Aviation Psychology.* (pp. 542a-f). Columbus, Ohio: Ohio State University, Department of Aviation.

Johnston, A.N. (1994) 'Integrating human factors into airline training curricula'. *Proceedings of the ICAO Flight Safety & Human Factors Regional Seminar*, Amsterdam. (pp. 183-198). Montreal: International Civil Aviation Organization.

Johnston, A.N. (1995) 'Continental philosophy and aviation psychology'. *Proceedings of the Eighth International Symposium on Aviation Psychology.* Columbus, Ohio: Ohio State University, Department of Aviation.

Johnston, A.N. (in review) *Simulation and Training: Perspectives on Theory and Practice.*

Johnston, A.N. & Mauriño, D. (1990, May) 'Human factors training for aviation personnel'. *ICAO Journal*, (pp. 16-19).

Joint Aviation Authorities. (1994) *Flight Crew Licensing Proposals for the Joint Aviation Authorities.* Fifth Draft, November. JAA: Hoofddorp, Holland: Author.

King, J.H. (1993) 'Implementation of human factors knowledge requirements in Canadian flight training system. *Proceedings of the ICAO Human Factors Symposium*, Washington, D.C., April 1993. Montreal: International Civil Aviation Organization.

Kolb, D.A. (1984) *Experiential Learning.* Englewood Cliffs, New Jersey: Prentice-Hall.

Kozulin, A., & Pressien, B.Z. (1995) 'Mediated learning experience and psychological tools: Vygotsky's and Feurstein's perspectives in a study of student learning'. *Educational Psychologist*, 30(2), 67-75.

Lauber, J.K. and Foushee, H.C. (1981) *Guidelines for Line-Oriented Flight Training.* NASA Ames: Conference Publication 2184.

Lave, J. (1988) *Cognition in Practice: Mind, Mathematics and Culture in Everyday Life.* Cambridge University Press.

Lave, J., & Wenger H. (1991) *Situated Learning*. Cambridge University Press.

Lintern, G. (in press) 'Flight instruction: The challenge from situated cognition'. *The International Journal of Aviation Psychology*.

Miller, A. (1988) 'Who would like to share their experiences?: Debriefing and experiential learning'. In D. Saunders, A. Coote, & D. Crookall, (Eds.) *Perspectives on Gaming and Simulation: Proceedings of the 1987 SAGSET Conference*. (pp. 23-34). Loughborough, U.K: SAGSET.

Montague, W.E. & Knirk, F.G. (1993a) 'What works in adult instruction: The management, design and delivery of instruction' [Special issue]. *International Journal of Educational Research*. 19(4).

Montague, W.E. & Knirk, F.G. (1993b) 'What works in adult instruction: Overview of the special issue'. *International Journal of Educational Research*. 19(4), 333-344.

O'Neil, H.F. (Ed.). (1979) *Procedures for Instructional Systems Development*. New York: Academic Press.

Ortega, K.A. (1989) 'Problem-solving: Expert/novice differences'. *Human Factors Society Bulletin*, 32(3), 1-5.

Osgood, C.E. (1949) 'The similarity paradox in human learning: A resolution'. *Psychological Review*, 56, 132-43.

Pearson, M. & Smith, D. (1985) 'Debriefing in experience-based learning'. In D. Boud, R. Keogh, & D. Walker, (Eds.) *Reflection: Turning Experience into Learning*, (pp. 18-40). London: Kogan Page.

Phillips, D.C. (1994) 'Epistemological perspectives on educational psychology'. [Special issue]. *Educational Psychologist*. 29(1).

Redding, R.E. (1989a) 'Perspectives on cognitive task analysis: the state of the state of the art'. *Proceedings of the 33rd. Annual Meeting of the Human Factors Society*, 2, 1348-1356. Santa Monica, CA: Human Factors Society.

Redding, R.E. (1989b) 'Trainers teaching thinking skills: applications of recent research in metacognition to training'. *Proceedings of the 33rd. Annual Meeting of the Human Factors Society*, 2, 1353-1357. Santa Monica, CA: Human Factors Society.

Redding, R.E. (1990) 'Taking cognitive task analysis into the field: bridging the gap from research to application'. *Proceedings of the 34th. Annual Meeting of the Human Factors Society*, 2, 1304-1308. Santa Monica CA: Human Factors Society.

Redding, R. E., Seamster, T. L., & Kaempf, G. A. (In preparation) *Applied Cognitive Task Analysis in Aviation*. Aldershot: Avebury Press.

Reimann, P., & Chi, M.T.H. (1989) 'Human expertise'. In K.J. Gilhooly (Ed.), *Human and machine problem solving*, (pp. 161-191). New Yourk: Plenum.

Resnick, L.B. (Ed.). (1989) *Knowing, Learning and Instruction*. Hillsdale, NJ: Erlbaum.

Rolfe, J. (1991) 'Transfer of training'. *Proceedings of a Conference on Training Transfer*, (pp 1.1-1.8). London: Royal Aeronautical Society.

Ryder, J.M., & Redding, R.E. (1993) 'Integrating cognitive task analysis into instructional systems development (ISD)' *Educational Technology Research & Development*, 1, 45-57.

Schneider, W. (1985) 'Training high performance skills: Fallacies and guidelines'. *Human Factors*, 27(3), 297-312.

Schön, D.A. (1983) *The Reflective Practitioner: How Professionals Think in Action*. London: Maurice Temple Smith.

Seamster, T.L., Redding, R.E., Cannon, J.R., Ryder, J.M. & Purcell, J.A. (1993) 'Cognitive task analysis of expertise in Air Traffic Control'. *International Journal of Aviation Psychology*. 3(4), 257-283.

Simon, C.W. (1987) 'Will egg-sucking ever become a science?'. *Human Factors Society Bulletin*, 30(6), 1-4.

Swezey, R.W., & Salas, E. (1992) *Teams: Their Training and Performance*. Norwood: Ablex.

Telfer R. (1993) 'Human factors in learning and instruction'. In, *Proceedings of the ICAO Human Factors Symposium*, Washington, D.C., April 1993. Montreal: International Civil Aviation Organization.

Thorndike, E.L. (1903) *Educational Psychology*. New York: Lemcke & Buechner.

Wertsch, J.V. (Ed.) (1979) *The Concept of Activity in Soviet Psychology*. Armonk, NY: Sharpe.

Wiener E.L., Kanki, B.G., & Helmreich, R.L. (Eds.). (1993) *Cockpit Resource Management*. San Diego: Academic Press.

Winograd, T., & Flores, C.F. (1986) *Understanding Computers and Cognition: A New Foundation for Design*. Norwood, NJ: Ablex.

# 10 The university airline internship programme: Educational entrance to professional airline employment

*Graham J.F. Hunt*

**Introduction**

The proficiency gap between flying a light single or twin-engined aircraft in general aviation, and operating as a co-pilot in an air transport twin jet airliner is substantial. Educationalists in university aviation education should be as interested in addressing this deficiency in student performance, as medical educators have been in integrating academic, technical and clinical knowledge to the real-world of health in hospitals and the community for student medical practitioners. When in 1989, New Zealand's multi-faculty state university Massey created its School of Aviation as a new applied profession's faculty, it did so seeking to replicate the traditions of schools of medicine and law. These faculties had long understood the need to teach academic and technical theory in a way which *integrated* within the practical and operational requirements of contemporary professional job performance. Massey sought to do the same in aviation. It purchased a fleet of single and twin engined aircraft and *integrated* the ICAO commercial and air transport licensing requirements into its Flight Crew Development major of its Bachelor of Aviation (B.Av) degree. The missing link was getting the university administrators to agree to purchase a fleet of twin-jet, glass cockpit, passenger aircraft to assist students in extending their knowledge and practice into airline type aircraft and route flying operations! In the absence of the university establishing such a resource, the solution was to develop *partnerships* with airlines so that this professional level of educational experience could be achieved within the requirements of the undergraduate aviation degree. This model posited that whereas the university provided aircraft and simulators as laboratory resources for the basic *ab initio* phase of pilot training, the airlines would provide the jet airliners for the advanced airline laboratory phase. This has become known as the 'University Airline Internship' option within the Bachelor of Aviation.

**Massey's University Airline Internship model**

Massey University's aviation model has been explicitly developed along the lines of university professional schools, such as medicine. These schools have integrated three dimensions of content within a professional degree qualification; scientific theory; technical knowledge; and practical skill development. These content areas are taught in lectures, laboratories and clinical practice sessions. While this teaching programme can provide the basic knowledge and skill components of professional development, the real-world context in which these competencies must be applied comes at the 'internship' stage, when the student, though technically qualified, is required to apply these knowledges within the context of a hospital or other medical facility. Here, under the joint supervision of the hospital's administration and the university's teaching faculty, the student learns to apply the knowledge and skills that he or she has been taught, to the real world of patients, supervisors, administrators, and the financial and regulatory structures of the work environment. This is the experiential setting in which the individual moves from student to professional. The same should be true in aviation.

Unlike most *ab initio* pilot training programmes, Massey's Flight Crew Development major assumes that students are being trained and educated for entrance directly into the air transport industry, rather than general aviation. As a result, the ICAO air crew licensing requirements are embedded into an academic aviation qualification which recognizes the professional and operational importance of aviation human factors (of which 'crew resource management' - CRM forms a critical component), science, technology and aviation management. Thus, by the end of two calendar years (*three* academic years, given that aviation students work to *trimesters* rather than semesters), students will have met all of the requirements for an ICAO defined Commercial Pilot Licence (CPL) with single and multi-engine instrument ratings, plus the examinations for the Air Transport Pilot Licence. These licensing qualifications are taught and examined within the context and practice of aviation science, technology, management and psychology.

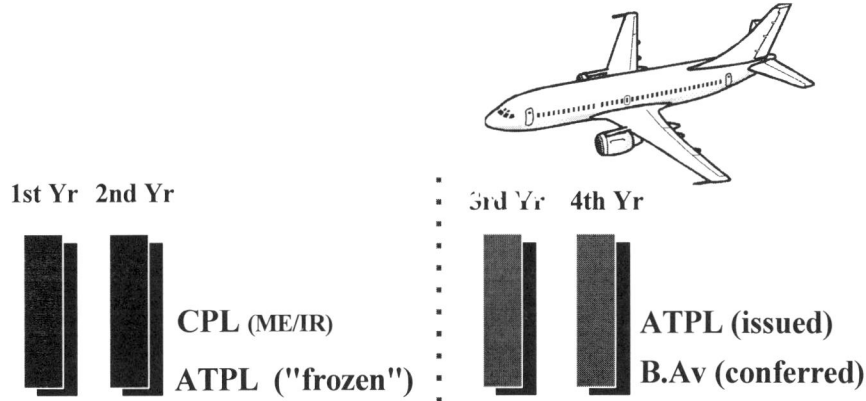

**Figure 10.1 Way points in Airline Internship Programme**

In the third and fourth years of the degree programme (*fifth* and *sixth* academic years) students join an airline as *Student* First Officers. The designator 'student' is a reflection of their educational status, rather than any degradation of their professional flight crew license status. Studies by Jean Pariès (Pariès, 1994) have indicated that pilots on initial transition to glass cockpit aircraft require up 1100 hours of experience with flight management computer systems and procedures before their use of these systems becomes 'automated' in their performance. Massey's experience with its students on Boeing 737-400 type operations indicate that this conclusion is probably true. The 1200 to 1500 hours of flight time allocated for the two year internship programme provides an ideal structured learning environment for these skills to become professionally 'automated'. On completion of their ground and simulator training they undertake extensive base and route training prior to going on the line as Student First Officers.

## Traditional entry into airline operations via general aviation

The award of a Commercial Pilot Licence should be simply one of the entry requirements into professional aircrew employment. Unfortunately, the traditional track to airline employment for pilots has required little more than this licence plus some ill-defined experience, usually expressed as a minimal number of pilot-in-command hours - 2000, 3000 or whatever the airline chooses. Candidates who enter the airline from general aviation usually reflect the following six typical characteristics of this approach to employment.

*Students trained not educated in aviation* Current licensing requirements emphasize an essentially 'training' rather an 'educational' approach to professional development. One of the expected characteristics of the 'educated' as opposed to 'trained' person is that individual's ability, through an expanded breadth of content, to be able to think at levels of complexity which result in applying rules and procedures, problem-solving and hypothesizing at high levels of abstraction. In a study designed to examine this training-education differentiation (Hunt and Hunt, 1993) a number of different civil aviation authority's Commercial Pilot Licence examinations were investigated. The results indicated that instead of requiring candidates to apply a lot of their knowledge in terms of rules and procedures, more than half of the items in their examinations simply required pilots to remember *facts, concepts* and *rules*. This is not what the authorities had expected, nor what they wanted.

*Assumption that hours equal experience* Most examples of *ab initio* pilot training and pre-requisite experience for airline employment follow the craft-based model of competency development. Experience is defined by regulatory authorities in terms of logged hours. Criteria for the award of private or professional licences and minimum hours prior to initial airline type training are based upon prescribed flight hours. Little attention is paid to *how* those hours might have been achieved, nor the types of environmental or human factor conditions which might be required to optimize acceptable performance. The broader disciplines for problem solving, decision making, and multi-crew performance are absent.

*Slow productivity* In most countries, the time between an individual's award of a Commercial Pilot Licence, and that person's initial type training for airline operations is measured in many years. It is not unusual for a pilot to spend between 4 and 8 years in general aviation before achieving the 2000 to 3000 hours required before being acceptable for an initial airline conversion course.

*Non standardized operations* Each operator in general aviation has their own method of getting the job done. Few conform to airline standard operating procedures. For example, it is common to find in general charter operations substantial deviations practised from set procedures for circuit entry, or in formal pre-flight and post-flight briefings. Further, the prime emphasis in these operations is on checking, rather than training. As a consequence, operational requirements such as emergency procedures are reduced to minimal mandatory checks.

*Single pilot performance* The least experienced pilots in a charter fleet operation are required to fly single pilot operations, only graduating in time to two pilot aircraft. This practice of requiring the least experienced pilots to operate commercially without the support and assistance of a more experienced pilot in the left hand seat is one of the many anomalies of general aviation. It is also one of the major contributors to 'bad practices'.

*Highly variable discipline* Given the unsupervised nature of general aviation, pilots are encouraged to focus on achieving the highest economic return for the owner. Often concepts and practices in relation to duty limits, crew rest, prescribed drug usage and fitness levels are ignored or deemed to be irrelevant.

## The alternative approach to airline entry - the university airline internship programme

The deficiencies of a craft-based approach to entering an airline are clear. An alternative is the development of a university airline internship programme which bridges the gap between the basic professional qualification - the Commercial Pilot Licence, and the minimal airline requirement - a qualified First Officer. In such a programme, internship students are paid a university student allowance and are required to meet both university and airline education, training and standards requirements.

## Characteristics of the University Airline Internship Programme

*Students are educated as well as appropriately trained* Throughout the implementation of the internship programme, the dual emphasis is on both *education* and *training*. At each phase, students are required to meet university *and* airline standards. Similarly, the development of academic, technical and practicum requirements are jointly defined by the two organizations. Education and training is required to extend the professional competence of each student first officer, while remaining relevant to the operational requirements of the airline.

*Airline standardized experience.* Students are required to complete between 1200 and 1500 hours of operational experience within the two-year period. All of this experience is defined by the airline's operating practices and procedures. The airlines training and operational philosophies and policies are embedded in the students behaviour. There is no learning 'bad practices' which will need to be unlearned at a later date.

*Multi-crew operations.* Student first officers are assigned to a training captain for flight operations and apply their previously learned multi-crew experience to their new aircraft type. Understanding crew dynamics within the pressures of a jet operation and often with the positive advantages of age and culture differences provide valuable learning experiences for future career development.

*Airline operating philosophy.* Airline operating philosophies are very different from that experienced in *ab initio* training, or in general aviation employment. In an increasingly internationally de-regulated environment, in which airlines, as part of multi-national conglomerates are required to adapt to changing regional alliances, an understanding of the airline's economic and philosophical imperatives is likely to lead to far more harmonious employee-employer relationships. Industrial relation experts have long argued that a major cause of labour unrest in enterprises is the lack of understanding by management and line operators about the organization's mission and the obstacles it faces in achieving it.

*Financially advantageous to the airline.* Many airlines have invested substantial sums of money in achieving their own *ab initio* airline programme. Arguably, in market driven economies, the cost of education should rest with the individual candidate, rather than the airlines. This may be seen as an extreme position. The Massey programme operates on both airline funded and individual student funded models. However, which ever model is employed, the key financial point is that the candidate is a student until fully graduated - that is, until he or she has met the requirements of the Bachelor of Aviation degree, with a First Officer type rating and ATPL licence (if the regulatory 1500 hours and flight test requirements for the licence have been met), they will continue to be educationally and financially treated as students.

*Fast Productivity.* The award of the internationally recognized degree is a four-year education and training process. However, by the end of approximately 30 months, the airline is already achieving an operational benefit - students have completed route training and are able to operate as line student first officers. By the end of 48 months, the candidate has fully graduated, both academically and technically, and is able to undertake increasing operational and management responsibilities within the airline.

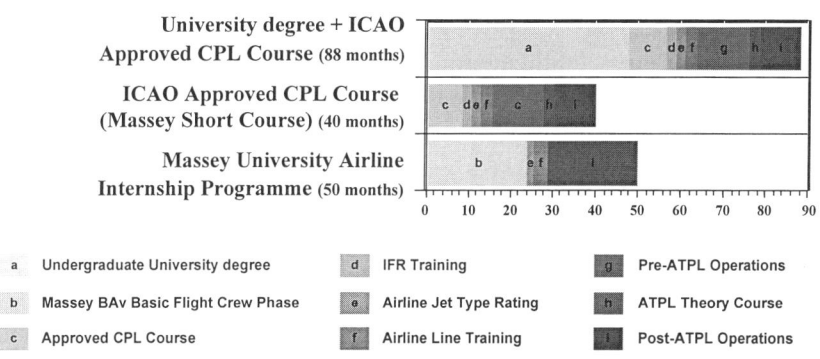

**Figure 10.2 Comparison of direct entry ab initio to airline pilots at 1500 hours criterion with a jet first officer rating**

As figure 11.2 illustrates, Massey's programme achieves a professional aviation degree qualification with approximately 1500 hours of jet airline experience in not much more time than it takes for a traditional ICAO approved course. But in this time, the pilot has not just learned how to meet technical requirements, but has qualified as a true aviation professional.

**Results of programme to date**

Over the past three years the Massey University Airline Internship Programme has involved the advanced education and training of 53 students with Garuda Indonesia. These students have been type rated as First Officers on that airlines Boeing 737-400 series twin jet aircraft. Flight operations include both domestic and international routes and range from short field and relatively primitive airfields such as Balikpapan to busy international airports such as Singapore's Changi International. Student nationalities on the programme have included New Zealand, Australian, Indonesian and Dutch. While rigorous empirical data is still being analyzed from the project, some preliminary observations are pertinent.

*Ground training* Students undertook both computer-based and instructor delivered instruction for the ground training aspects of their Boeing 737-400 type rating course. Over 90 percent of the students completed this aspect of their conversion to the jet with little or no difficulty in learning. This result is not surprising, since recent previous technical and academic study would be expected to have had a positive transfer effect on technical type training.

*Simulator training* Unlike ground training, with its high dependency on carefully structured learning resources (eg., computer-based training), the simulator training phase was much more reflective of differential instructor quality. Where the simulator instructor provided a well structured programme and the student was encouraged to ask questions and clarify specific concepts and procedures, progress through the simulator details was much faster and the overall effect, much better. Approximately 5 percent of the students found that they had to 'learn through their mistakes'. These students found this phase much more difficult to get through.

*Route training* The single most important variable in route training was the degree of standardization adopted by training captains. Some of them applied different procedures to situations leaving the student with the problem of having to learn each captain's 'preferred style'.

*Overall quality of flight performance* This study indicated no significant differences between the level of flight hours experience and overall flight performance on B737-400 type aircraft (Chi-square 6.38, p›.05). However, the single most important characteristic in coping with intense training, especially in new environments (full-flight simulation; EFIS flight deck; new social and cultural environments, etc.) was *attitude*. Students who were able to manage their mood and motivation, accommodate change and difficult learning conditions, were much more likely to be successful in both specific training situations, and in their overall flight performance than their colleagues with more restrictive attitudes. Student with high levels of cultural sensitivity and achievement motivation also tended to be more comfortable in exercising assertive behaviour in routing operating situations.

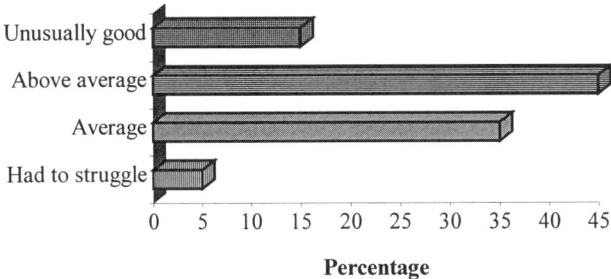

**Figure 10.3 Assessment of overall quality of B737-400 flight performance**

## Conclusions

University-airline internship programmes such as Massey's are increasingly likely to become the recognized induction model for pilots entering airline operations. As this institution-based method for entry into professional air transportation develops, so too will the need to review and change the regulatory requirements for *ab initio* pilot training. Arguably, current Part 61 civil aviation regulations with their emphasis on single pilot general aviation handling requirements, will need to be examined in the light of advanced technology multi-crew operations with their requirements for standardized aircraft and airline operating procedures. Now is the time for airlines, regulatory authorities and university aviation faculties to combine to develop new professional flight crew prescriptions and standards for the 21$^{st}$ century.

The advantages of the university airline internship programme over traditional air crew entry approaches are clear; the enhanced professionalization of pilots; greater technical competency - particularly in the area of airline operations; increased operational safety; improved productivity and lowered airline training costs. Through the development and application of this model aviation may achieve the same kinds of professional benefit that has long been characteristic of the induction programmes of medicine, law and other established professions. More importantly, airlines and their paying public will have greater assurance that pilots entering the profession and occupying the right-hand seat of the aircraft are better prepared and more capable of contributing to *safe and efficient airline flight operations*.

**References**

Hunt, G.J.F., and Hunt, L.M. (1993) 'Computer-based testing in flight crew licensing.' In R.A. Telfer (Ed.), *Aviation Instruction and Training*. Ashgate, Aldershot, Hants.

Pariès, J. (1994) 'The pilot, actor of a complex system'. In R. Amalberti (Ed.), *Briefings*. IFSA-Dédale, Paris, France.

# Human factors instruction-
# air traffic control

# 11 Teaching human factors for air traffic control

*V. David Hopkin*

**Introduction**

The ultimate objectives in applying human factors to air traffic control are similar to those of air traffic control itself. They are to achieve the safe, orderly and expeditious flow of air traffic, to meet further more tacit requirements including impartiality, cost-effectiveness, noise abatement and fuel conservation, to ensure that air traffic control does not harm those who are employed in it, and to attract and keep a fulfilled, dedicated and satisfied professional workforce. Human factors as a discipline seeks to achieve these objectives by several means. These are intended to ensure that the consequent human roles and functions are compatible with human capabilities and limitations, that the human-machine interfaces effectively harmonize human knowledge, abilities, and skills with air traffic control requirements, that trained controllers can implement safely and efficiently all the devised procedures and instructions which enable them to discharge their responsibilities, and that the system and conditions of employment are never harmful but contribute positively towards air traffic control as a job that satisfies human needs and aspirations at work.

The scope and content of human factors as a discipline are becoming more structured, clear and crystallized than they formerly were. Its range of applications has expanded comparatively recently, in belated response to criticisms of the narrowness of its approach, voiced many years ago but seldom heeded then (Fitts et al, 1951; Taylor & Garvey, 1959; Jordan,

1968). Many topics once treated separately are now recognized as interacting with human factors or encompassed within it, including team roles and structures, organizational influences, management practices, conditions of employment, and the development of norms and standards (Hopkin, 1994). The acknowledged relevance of human factors extends to a further range of activities which are not part of air traffic control but relate to it, including maintenance, validation, and certification (Shepherd & Johnson, 1991; Wise et al, 1993, Wise et al, 1994,) where some of the work conducted has relied mainly on air traffic control examples. Reviews and texts on human factors in air traffic control address specific air traffic control issues in detail but their lists of contents share many headings with other human factors texts on different applications (Hopkin, 1982; Hopkin, 1988; ICAO, 1993). The reason is that human factors focuses on the abiding characteristics of human beings, which remain broadly similar wherever human factors as a discipline is applied. However, many of the detailed ways in which human factors are applied and many of the preferred solutions of human factors problems become specific to air traffic control where air traffic control requirements differ significantly in human factors terms from requirements elsewhere.

Human factors is an applied discipline. It is judged by its results. Its products are reflected in the efficiency and safety of real air traffic control systems. Therefore human factors teaching is not primarily theoretical. Human factors as a discipline draws on and combines evidence and techniques from several other disciplines. It is applied in an inter-disciplinary context since the planning, design, procurement and operation of air traffic control systems are all multi-disciplinary enterprises. The successful collaborative application of human factors to air traffic control requires knowledge not only of human factors and of air traffic control but also of the strength of the evidence underpinning human factors recommendations and of the conditions for their validity. In practice the human factors specialist in air traffic control must know how far optimum human factors recommendations may be compromised in the interests of inter-disciplinary harmony and agreement, and when they must be compromised no further.

Human factors evidence of many different kinds can be applied to air traffic control. Compendia of human factors data have become very voluminous (Boff & Lincoln, 1988). Many relevant themes are each the subject not merely of journal articles but of whole textbooks devoted to them. The sheer amount of relevant information probably now exceeds the capacity of any single specialist to know it all. There is far too much to teach all of it in detail, except perhaps in full length degree courses devoted exclusively to it.

An essential starting point for all human factors teaching is to emphasize the interactive nature of human factors in air traffic control. Any change of any kind that could affect the controller will always have multiple human factors consequences and these consequences will interact. A main reason for particular emphasis on this point is that all human factors texts applicable to air traffic control are potentially misleading in this respect. They partition the subject matter under headings as a matter of expediency in order to deal with it, but real human factors issues in air traffic control are never so neat or wholly within a single heading. It is vital that they are not taught as if they were.

The first stage in teaching human factors for air traffic control must be to define the purposes of the teaching. When the objectives - why to teach - have been agreed, the traditional questions - whom to teach, what to teach and how to teach - should become answerable in terms of the defined objectives.

## Why to teach?

The human factors content of what is taught for application to air traffic control depends greatly on the purposes of teaching it. The following purposes of teaching human factors differ in their content requirements:

1. To instil a knowledge of human factors in air traffic control at some pre-defined level of detail.

2. To enable others to recognize human factors problems well enough to know when they need professional human factors assistance to deal with them.

3. To learn where professional human factors expertise and assistance may be obtained.

4. To inform those in air traffic control about human factors evidence and its applicability.

5  To obtain benefits from the application of human factors evidence and guidelines.

6  To prevent deficiencies with human factors origins or human factors consequences, and to minimize human error.

7  To promote the safety and efficiency of air traffic control.

8  To gain formal qualifications related to the application of human factors in air traffic control.

9  To provide a common level of human factors knowledge among human factors specialists in air traffic control.

10  To increase the acceptability and acknowledgement of human factors contributions to air traffic control.

11  To provide those concerned with the planning, operation, and evaluation of air traffic control systems with sufficient human factors knowledge for their own jobs.

12  To explain the full range of human factors influences on air traffic control, and the interactions between them.

13  To explain the role and methods of the human factors specialist.

14  To ensure that all decisions about the human factors aspects of air traffic control are as well informed as possible, particularly in terms of the full range of their human factors consequences.

15  To carry out human factors audits and checks of actual or planned air traffic control systems.

16  To standardize human factors applications to air traffic control and their associated methodologies.

17  To apply human factors evidence and standards to verification, validation and certification procedures.

18  To identify gaps in human factors knowledge and commission work to fill those gaps before the new knowledge is needed.

19  To expand the available human factors specialist resources until supply and demand are reasonably matched.

In teaching human factors for air traffic control it is essential to define how specific to air traffic control the teaching should be. In this context human factors topics can be classified into four levels of specificity. From the most specific to air traffic control to the least specific they are:

1  Topics that are wholly specific to air traffic control, so that solutions to problems must either be found within air traffic control or must be validated for air traffic control if they originate elsewhere.

2  Topics that are confined to aviation environments but not to air traffic control, so that guidance on appropriate solutions may be obtained from other aviation contexts but acceptable solutions of problems must be compatible with the solutions of corresponding human factors problems elsewhere in aviation, such as in cockpits or air to ground communications systems.

3  Topics that are endemic in all complex human-machine systems, so that evidence of successes and failures in other systems may be helpful, subject to confirmation for air traffic control.

4  Topics related to fundamental human capabilities and limitations, so that practical aims should be to utilize human strengths and circumvent human weaknesses rather than to alter human characteristics that cannot really be changed much.

A common purpose of teaching human factors for air traffic control is so that everyone can learn to recognize the presence of a human factors problem. For policy makers and managers, this may be the main objective and nearly all that is needed. At the other extreme, for practising human factors specialists this marks the starting point, for the recognition of a problem is the first step in the application of human factors evidence to resolve it.

In future, human factors may be taught in air traffic control not primarily to apply what has been learned but to obtain a broader professional qualification. It may be deemed that a controller must pass a human factors course in order to be licensed as a controller. The purpose of this kind of teaching, as far as the student is concerned, is to pass the course. Such a situation implies acknowledgement of the relevance of human factors for the job, but the teaching acquires the dual functions of conveying the human factors content, and convincing students that the study of human factors deserves to become compulsory.

This raises the issue of whether the teachers of human factors for air traffic control should be professional instructors or human factors specialists. If professional instructors, they themselves must have been instructed by human factors specialists on the application of human factors to air traffic control. However the human factors specialists may not have the qualifications, the ability or the willingness to teach well. This raises some ethical human factors issues. Most disciplines insist that the teaching of their discipline is under their own control, in terms of the content of what is taught and the expertise of the teachers. It would generally be advocated that human factors should be taught by human factors specialists.

This problem is not unique to human factors but affects other disciplines and this suggests a practical criterion to resolve the dilemma. Often the same course also has some medical content. If the medical profession is willing to train the professional instructors to teach the medical aspects of the course, then the human factors profession should be willing to train the same instructors to teach the human factors aspects of the course. If the medical profession insists that its own specialists teach the medical aspects of the course, the human factors profession should likewise insist that its own specialists teach the human factors aspects of the course. It is fairest to adopt a standard practice across disciplines. This issue tends to arise mostly with shorter courses. For more intensive instruction, there is little choice but to employ human factors specialists for teaching and to train them as instructors.

**Whom to teach?**

The purposes of teaching and the intended practical results of teaching are likely to differ greatly depending on who the students are, and this should lead to major differences in the content, methods and timing of what is taught. The main identifiable categories of people who should be taught human factors in air traffic control at some level are listed below. The actual human factors teaching content would normally differ between the categories in the list, and some content differences may also be needed within each category. The categories are listed in the approximate order of the level of detail of human factors knowledge appropriate for their responsibilities, progressing from least detail to most detail.

1   Those in national and international regulatory authorities dealing with air traffic control.

2   Those concerned with air traffic control policy, financing, resources, and higher management.

3   Those in public relations and the media concerned with the interface between air traffic control and the travelling public.

4   Those who work in supporting services for air traffic control, such as system maintenance.

5   Those who work with human factors specialists during air traffic control system building, procurement or operation, such as engineers, computer scientists and medical specialists.

6   Those in disciplines such as operational research and analysis, quality control and certification which seek to explicate air traffic control.

7   Those who officially represent air traffic controllers as a profession through international or national unions or guilds.

8   Human factors professionals who work primarily in other applications where they may encounter human factors problems that parallel those in air traffic control.

9   Air traffic controllers themselves.

10  Those concerned professionally with the recruitment, selection, training, licensing, career development and job allocation of air traffic controllers.

11  Those who have line management responsibility for controllers, and their conditions of work and employment.

12  Those who model, evaluate or conduct research on current or future air traffic control systems.

13  Those who plan or design future air traffic control systems.

14  Those who have charge of air traffic control safety, investigate air traffic control incidents, or recommend changes in air traffic control based on operational experience.

15  Those under training to be human factors specialists and to apply their human factors knowledge to air traffic control systems.

The teaching of human factors for air traffic control must acknowledge that in the past air traffic control has not been very orientated towards human factors, although some of the earliest and most influential human factors publications dealt with it. Far fewer human factors resources have been applied to air traffic control than to cockpits. The regular inclusion of papers on air traffic control in aviation human factors textbooks is quite a recent development, and the inclusion of more than one paper on air traffic control in a textbook of this kind is even more recent.

Many of the categories of people listed above as appropriate recipients of teaching of human factors in air traffic control have little or no initial knowledge of human factors, and some may not have much knowledge of air traffic control either. Much of the teaching therefore has to start from scratch. Air traffic control shares with many other applications a chronic under-utilization of existing human factors evidence (Heller, 1991), particularly during the planning, design and procurement of air traffic control systems. Human factors specialists in air traffic control must take the lead to make their discipline and what it offers more widely known. Teachers may also have to be proselytes for human factors.

**What to teach?**

In teaching human factors for air traffic control, all human factors topics that are relevant to air traffic control should be mentioned. Although there can be quibbles about details, there is now broad agreement on what human factors in air traffic control encompasses and this can be translated into a broad list of course contents, not every item of which will be relevant to every course. There follows an outline description of appropriate course contents. On the basis of this outline, the topics to be included in each course on human factors in air traffic control can be selected, and the relative emphasis on topics planned.

A brief historical introduction can outline the evolutionary development of human factors as a separate discipline, and its application to air traffic control. It can trace the progressive expansion of the range of human factors topics acknowledged to be relevant and draw lessons from the previous exclusion of factors now known to be important. From current trends, the direction of the further evolution of human factors applied to air traffic control may be discernible, such as concern with cultural ergonomics. Whether a course on human factors in air traffic control should include some coverage of air traffic control principles and practices will depend on the purposes of the teaching and on the obligatory prior knowledge of the students.

Many questions about controllers are posed in terms which treat the human as a system component. It is therefore necessary to define clearly the ways in which the human controller can be treated as a system component and those in which it is invalid to do so. Consideration of the controller as a system component raises issues such as the allocation of functions to human or machine (which tends to have been treated over-simplistically in the past); the importance of the specification of the human-machine interface as the main means for transmitting information between human and machine; the impact of automation and computer assistance on human roles, jobs, tasks, and functions; the reliability of the human as a system component; and the sources of human error and fallibility. Principles for the successful matching of human and machine can then be adduced, the correction of common mismatches can be discussed, and crucial human characteristics can be emphasized which have often been ignored in the allocation of functions to human or machine because they have no machine counterpart. Adaptability has to be treated dually, in terms of the ways in which the system can adapt to humans and the ways in which humans can adapt to the system.

Some principles of psychology are taught within the framework of the human as a system component. Basic capabilities and limitations of humans which affect their behaviour as system components can be classified under three headings, as inputs to, processing by, and outputs from the human. The input of data to the human is studied mainly through principles of perception since displays are the main means of input, and the output of information by the human to the system is studied mainly through the performance of tasks using input devices. Aspects of human information processing concern such cognitive attributes as learning, memory, attention, and understanding which deal with the capabilities and limitations of the human as an information processor and also with the extent to which these can be modified by knowledge, experience and skill. Information processing encompasses higher mental functions such as those involved in planning, problem solving, decision making, prediction, the allocation of resources and the formulation of strategies. Human capacity as reflected in workload is explained. Effects of individual differences, for example in motivation, are described. In some teaching contexts, it may be advisable to relate cognitive evidence to relevant psychological theories and constructs, and to other means to ascertain the validity, applicability and generalisability of psychological evidence. Simple laboratory experiments and simple visual materials can often make students realize some of their own fundamental limitations for the first time.

A useful topic to teach is the different kinds of human factors contributions that should be made at various appropriate stages in the evolution of an air traffic control system. This starts from the deduction of the broad human factors consequences of initial planning concepts, through more specific human factors problems and influences that become apparent progressively during the system planning and specification stages, culminating in system design where specific human factors evidence and recommendations can be applied directly. It can be salutary to demonstrate that many of the most significant and recalcitrant human factors problems originate from the system design stage and are identifiable at that stage. If they are not prevented then, attempts to resolve them by retrospective changes later in the system evolution are unlikely to be as effective, and they may fail altogether if the options required to resolve the problems have been precluded by other changes and constraints in the meantime. Human factors expertise is commonly applied when the system design is converted into prototypes for testing and evaluation, but at that stage the main human factors contributions are often on how to measure the human being, what to measure, appropriate measurement techniques, and the design and conduct of studies to yield unambiguous findings. Further human factors contributions are to operational systems, to resolve any residual human factors problems in them, either directly or by ensuring that they do not recur in revised or subsequent systems. Evidence from operational systems comes from direct observation by human factors specialists and from records of incidents or errors that have occurred.

During system evolution the functions that controllers must fulfil are deduced, and converted into tasks, procedures, instructions, and specifications of requisite information and equipment. Tasks are grouped into jobs, and jobs matched with system demands. Requirements for individual knowledge, experience, skills, and the satisfaction of human needs and aspirations at work are identified. Task analysis is one of several techniques that can be used. It is important to check that different tasks in the same job require compatible human skills and are mutually compatible in other ways. Air traffic control in many countries is subject to very gross fluctuations in traffic demands which entail the splitting or amalgamation of jobs in order to match capacities, traffic demands and staffing levels. Jobs, tasks, human machine interfaces and workspaces all have to be devised to facilitate splitting and amalgamation of the work. Air traffic control jobs and the tasks of each controller cannot be studied in isolation, for controllers function as teams. The team functions and the jobs of supervisors and assistants have to be considered concurrently with the controllers' jobs so that they complement and match each other.

Air traffic control requires a workforce of skilled, able and dedicated air traffic controllers. Human factors therefore advises on recruitment and on the motivations and expectations of applicants for air traffic control jobs. The extensive human factors contributions to the selection procedures for air traffic controllers include the identification of relevant human attributes, the devising of appropriate measures and tests of these attributes, and the formulation and proving of other measures such as formal tests, interviews, and biodata. Advice is given on how candidates can be screened, on the relevance of factors such as personality and aviation knowledge, and on how to validate the selection procedures themselves. A current preoccupation concerns the effects of automation on selection: this covers both the automation of the selection procedures themselves, and devising measures of each candidate's ability to work effectively in a more automated system. Human factors is also concerned with the evolution of the selection procedures in response to air traffic control changes.

Following selection is controller training. Human factors is concerned with defining training objectives and the content of training courses, and with defining future training problems (Hopkin, 1989). Human factors evidence is applied on the efficacy for learning of alternative kinds of instruction, and on the respective roles of self instruction, of formal teaching, of demonstration, of simulation, and of on-the-job training. Human factors advice is also applied to retraining: this covers how to learn new tasks most effectively and how to forget previous knowledge and skills that have become irrelevant or misleading. Human factors contributions include the objective assessment of progress during training, the devising of impartial criteria to judge success, and the establishment of the reliability and validity of the training content. At the end of training, human factors measures of individuals and of their achievements can guide the allocation of individual controllers towards jobs which match the particular capabilities that they have demonstrated.

Perhaps the most familiar applications of human factors to air traffic control concern aspects of the workspace and the work environment, commonly equated with ergonomics. Air traffic control centres and towers pose somewhat different human factors problems: for example the visual environment in centres can usually be controlled, specified and optimized in relation to the tasks, the visual displays, the decor and eyesight standards, whereas in towers it is very variable since the tower must function in conditions of exterior darkness or bright direct sunlight and flexibility rather than optimization becomes the objective. A good practical exercise for students can be to trace the sources of glare in a tower, and recommend how to prevent them. Generally the basic principles of workspace design contained in human factors handbooks about the construction of suites and consoles, the characteristics of seating, anthropometric evidence, the principles of accessibility, and staffing levels can all be applied in air traffic control. Much of the evidence about the desirable physical environments, concerning lighting, acoustics, heating, ventilation, air flow, radiation and decor for example, can also be applied, although often modifications have to be made. For example in most air traffic control towers, it is not possible to meet the normal recommendations for background noise levels because of the proximity of aircraft.

Within the workspace are visual displays which are the main means of conveying information from the system to the human controller. On the basis of human factors evidence, recommendations are made on the location of suites within the workspace and of displays within suites, on the physical dimensions of displays and their relative positioning, and on suitable information content and formats for the full range of tasks required for the planned and intended air traffic control functions at that workspace. Principles of visual information coding are applied, including recommendations on the shape and size of characters, on alphanumerics, on the use of colour and monochrome, on contrast and brightness, on textures and inversion, and on other visual codings such as flashing and underlining. Different codings suit different functions and appropriate guiding principles should be followed, although the fine detail of the recommendations may have to be modified to match particular air traffic control requirements or conditions, such as aspects of the physical environment, the ambient lighting, minimum eyesight requirements, and the visual scanning patterns implied by tasks. The information must be stable and clear, legible and readable. It may also often be desirable to include qualitative information to indicate how far the information should be trusted and to indicate any failures. New display developments and technical innovations always introduce new human factors implications; a current example concerns the usage of electronic windows within the radar displays, and a future example will concern possible applications of virtual reality. The human factors consequences of introducing innovations into air traffic control are examined in terms of their implications for tasks, the kinds of assistance that they afford the controllers, and the kinds of errors that could be made with them. Teaching can be based on a human factors audit of a real tower or centre, which can bring out the main interactions and any potentially conflicting requirements.

The main means by which the controller transmits information to the system are through the use of input devices. The human-machine interface design concerns these, as well as displays and the relationship between displays and input devices. Types of input device include keys, touch sensitive inputs, off-screen movable devices, voice activation, and a multiplicity of traditional controls such as knobs, dials, buttons, and switches. Human factors is concerned not only with the class of input device, but also with its gain and sensitivity, and the functions for which it is appropriate. Different input devices or controls have to be compatible with each other in their usage. The location of controls within the workspace in relation to each other is related to anthropometric evidence, to the forces required for activation, and to comfort.

Air traffic control deals with communications. Information transmitted within the system is of direct human factors concern only to the extent that the human controller can or should know of it or can be influenced by it. Information transmitted between air and ground is of human factors concern in terms of its intelligibility and the appropriateness of its content for the human tasks; when there are proposals to change the air to ground information by the introduction of satellites or data links, then the human factors consequences of this need to be addressed. Information is also communicated between human and machine through displays and controls. Some information is communicated directly between humans, so that the machine knows nothing of it unless there is also provision to enter it into the machine. There are also particular communications problems arising from specific air traffic control functions, such as those during the handover of responsibility from one controller to another at the end of a shift or watch. A teaching example is to predict what the human factors consequences of data links will be for air traffic control.

Air traffic control has relied very extensively on speech in the past and will continue to do so, although to a smaller extent. Speech will probably remain crucial for safety. Air traffic control has evolved its own language, terminology, and message formats, which were originally the outcome of extensive human factors research to make them as good as they could be. There is now the problem of adapting or changing the traditional language and terminology, optimized for human speech and listening, to meet the possible needs of automated speech recognition and speech synthesis, for which it may not be optimum. Other auditory information is communicated as auditory warnings, which must not be too frequent or numerous lest they become counterproductive. Generally air traffic control communications quite deliberately employ considerable redundancy of information so that even minor misinterpretations that are not crucial for safety are nevertheless likely to become apparent. A potentially contentious human factors issue is the desirable level of redundancy of communicated information. Identifying instances of redundancy of information can be a good exercise for students. On the whole safety is fostered by redundancy, but redundancy occupies time which cannot always be spared.

A great deal of current human factors work addresses the existing or proposed introduction of various forms of computer assistance into air traffic control. Many of the earliest forms of computer assistance are now common in operational air traffic control systems, being concerned primarily with the manipulation of data gathering, storage, compilation, synthesis, retrieval, distribution and presentation. Generally this assistance was very helpful to the controller and alleviated routine work. The next stage is to assist human tasks in order to increase system capacity, by enabling each controller to spend less time in dealing with each aircraft, without in any way jeopardizing the efficiency and safety of the air traffic control service provided.

There have been proposed aids for problem solving, decision making, prediction, planning and scheduling. Automated assistance may take the form of appropriately designed menus and dialogues, or of automated prompts and reminders to support human memory. Some forms of assistance can be provided as directives, instructions or commands, or as aids to organize work more effectively through better management of available resources. These and similar forms of automated assistance raise issues about whether they should be optional or mandatory, what their legal status is, and how they impinge on the controller's responsibility for the safe conduct of air traffic. Some human factors problems are specific to particular forms of computer assistance such as conflict detection, conflict resolution, direct or random routing, the automated updating of information, or the detection of an aircraft straying from its planned route. Not the least of the human factors problems is the discovery that the removal of routine tasks often impairs the controller's understanding because the information does not need to be processed by the human so deeply, and subjectively it can seem to involve a loss of the controller's 'picture' of the air traffic.

Some human factors implications of the forms of computer assistance provided are unintended, are different in kind to the implications normally considered, or pose problems which may be serious and difficult to resolve. Discovering instances of these can be an effective teaching example. Many changes cast the controller in the role of monitor, yet humans are poor monitors generally and cannot normally be trained to become good monitors, so this is not a function that is usually performed very well by the human. Another trend is for computer assistance to result in more passive human roles, which may involve some perceived loss of responsibilities and therefore meet resistance. Many forms of computer assistance have the potential to disguise human incompetence and to hide and compensate for human inadequacy.

Computer assistance may often curtail many traditional team roles and render traditional means of supervision impractical because most of these forms of computer assistance do not assist teams but only assist individuals, yet they are introduced into an air traffic control context where much of the work has hitherto been done by teams. The team functioning, though vital, is often tacit rather than overt, and therefore not always apparent to the system planner. The identification of tacit team functions can be an interesting exercise for students. Because computer assistance often makes the performance of individual air traffic control tasks less observable by others, it can affect the development of norms and standards which depend on observability. One issue concerns the level of human understanding about how the system functions that the controller needs to have. There is debate on how human intentionality may be conveyed to the machine so that the automated assistance can be employed to achieve human objectives and not to thwart human intentions.

One aspect of human factors is to look at the effects of the system on the individual controller. A list of factors under this heading may illustrate their importance. They include experience, workload, stress, boredom, health, attitudes, trust and job satisfaction. Practical examples of these in air traffic control can be used to look at their causes and consequences. Much traditional evaluation and study has concentrated on the effects of the human on the system, in terms of achievable human performance, the ability of humans to follow procedures and instructions, and the like, but there is growing recognition that the effects of the system on the individual controller can be just as crucial and must be taken seriously.

There is also more widespread human factors recognition of the importance of conditions of employment. Perhaps the most publicized of these are management-controller relations. Controllers, as others, wish to have means of consultation and access to management, to have good career prospects, and to have work environments which can satisfy human needs and aspirations. They need to feel that their jobs are worthwhile, to believe that others respect their professionalism, to see how their job fits within the system, to obtain feedback in the form of knowledge of results and praise for work done well, and to have opportunities to gain the esteem and respect of colleagues and others. The factors which influence morale are therefore highly pertinent to human factors. So are the more mundane but very important aspects of conditions of employment such as rostering, hours of work, work-rest cycles and flexibility in staffing. One effect of the system on the human concerns occupational health. Human factors experts work with medical specialists in this context since many of the health implications derive from the designs of workspaces and tasks, and collaboration is needed to ensure that both medical and human factors requirements are met in these designs. A final aspect of conditions of employment concerns retirement and the preparations for it.

The human factors specialist in air traffic control requires expertise on how to measure controllers in their work environment. There are numerous reasons for doing so. At the broadest level are measures of the performance of the air traffic control system as a whole, in such terms as traffic handling capacities, channel occupancy times, delays, and the like. Another measure is of human activity through some form of activity analysis. This should be distinguished from task performance measures which are not simply measures of activity but include some scoring or evaluation so that performance is judged as well as measured. One aspect of task measurement concerns consistency of performance for example, and individual differences between controllers in what they do. Most of the sources of human error are built in at the design stage, but measurements of human errors that occur aim to trace their causes and consequences, to prevent those that are preventable and to ensure that others cannot remain undetected. Human factors covers not only what occurs but also what does not occur but should have occurred. Some human factors measures are concerned with omissions.

Physiological and biochemical indices have been employed in the past to measure controllers for various purposes. Subjective measures are widely used, including discussions, questionnaires, ratings and a multiplicity of other techniques. It is quite common to include in air traffic control some social measures of how teams are operating, supervision is conducted, assistance is given, and co-ordination and liaison are achieved. Another kind of measurement is human health and well-being and the implications of air traffic control on health in terms of postural or visual problems, stress, sleep patterns, and morbidity and mortality rates. Since air traffic controllers normally work shifts, the effects of shift work on safety, efficiency, fatigue, health, sleep, and family life are studied, and recommendations made accordingly. Standardized psychological tests are employed for a variety of purposes, but especially in selection. Biographical data give evidence about individuals and their history that is relevant to their performance of air traffic control. Various modelling and other techniques allow system performance to be measured in more formalized or mathematical terms and these can be used in conjunction with human factors measures, for example by linking real-time and fast-time simulations. One kind of measurement gaining in importance is of air traffic control as an organization, including the ways in which decisions are reached, the kinds of evidence needed to influence decisions, and its responsiveness to the needs and wishes of its employees.

The human factors approach puts much emphasis on interactions between measures since the interpretation of any one of the above measurement categories is influenced by several of the others. To take only one kind of measure will be at best an oversimplification and at worst totally misleading. There has not been sufficient work to verify and validate measures, particularly those of the whole functioning system. Teaching can be based on a clash of evidence and how to interpret it, for example when subjective measures say that colour coding has improved performance, but direct measures of performance show that it has not.

Human factors as a discipline is heavily involved in much of the research and development for evolving future air traffic control systems, in the deduction and eduction of the human factors consequences during the planning, specification, design, and system procurement stages, and in the various kinds of evaluation conducted during iterative procurement processes. Human factors identifies relevant variables and specifies how to control them and is concerned with the interpretation of the findings in human factors terms. In this context there is also extensive international collaboration. The research and development resources for air traffic control are not plentiful anywhere and therefore it is in the interests of everyone to deploy these resources effectively for the common good, so that studies avoid duplication and complement each other whenever possible. This entails international collaboration which is also fostered because many of the technological advances in the offing in air traffic control could be used world wide and therefore give rise to similar human factors problems in relation to them in many nations at about the same time. An international example, such as the evolution of the ICAO alphabet, can be studied. Human factors as a discipline must be interfaced with the numerous other disciplines also applied to air traffic control. These include management, public relations, operational research and analysis, quality assurance, maintenance, certification, and engineering developments concerned with the sensing and processing of data. Human factors solutions to air traffic control problems must always be practical in technical and engineering terms, and must conform with various national and international standards, directly or indirectly related to human factors.

The above is intended to constitute a broad outline of most of the topic headings within the province of human factors as a discipline that are relevant to the application of human factors to air traffic control. It therefore follows that they should all be considered for inclusion in any course teaching human factors for air traffic control purposes. If they are excluded then some vital human factors, and even perhaps the most crucial ones, may be omitted from consideration altogether when decisions about air traffic control are taken. This is highly undesirable. Human factors as a discipline is always most effective when applied during the planning and procurement stages of systems, and least effective when attempts are made to apply human factors retrospectively to cure faults in systems that are already operational.

## What is taught and what is learned?

Human factors is an applied discipline in respect to air traffic control. When air traffic control is taught, the teaching inculcates the procedures, practices, methods, responsibilities, and objectives of air traffic control and converts the air traffic control workspace from an initially meaningless environment to one where every item of portrayed information is understood, the function of every data entry device is known thoroughly, and the usage of everything provided is familiar. The student is taught what all the tasks are, when and how it is appropriate to fulfil them, and how to choose what to do when. The student is also taught how to work as a member of a team and under supervision and what other controllers and pilots with whom he or she communicates are doing, in order to liaise and co-ordinate with them and support their work most effectively.

All this is taught. When the fledgling controller becomes an operational controller there is much still to learn that has not been taught and seldom is formally taught but is gleaned from the job itself. Examples of what is learned in this way include the attitudes of controllers as a group to each other, to management, to their conditions of employment, and to others with whom they come in contact. Further examples are the ethos and expectations of the air traffic control profession, and the norms and standards which constitute acceptable professional air traffic control and which the controller must conform with in order to gain and keep the respect and esteem of colleagues. Other forms of learning include the ways in which controllers are expected to help each other and when they are expected to refrain from interrupting a colleague. They include acceptance of and conformity with any local non-standard practices and shortcuts which are accepted and agreed by all those in a particular workplace and are a hallmark of it. Air traffic control itself provides an example of the importance of tacit knowledge. Individual controllers while they are working know a great deal about what their colleagues know and what they are doing, and this knowledge has a major influence on their own activities. Often controllers must also learn that it is their good fortune to have been posted to the place where the very best air traffic control service available anywhere is provided. The teaching can encourage students to identify as many of the above factors as possible themselves, and to judge which apply to their own jobs.

This point raises a parallel question about human factors. Just as all air traffic control expertise is not acquired from teaching, so all human factors expertise is not acquired from teaching either. Some of it is learned on the job by watching and understanding other specialists. Human factors specialists also make tacit assumptions about what their professional colleagues know, agree with, and can be relied upon to do. This aspect of professionalism is among the most difficult to teach.

Much of human factors is interdisciplinary. The successful practitioner must not be abrasive but can be firm, must be sure of the facts and know where further relevant data can be obtained, must not waffle, and must not be obstructive or intransigent to others in the interdisciplinary environment. Human factors recommendations and findings must not be wrapped in incomprehensible jargon. Nor must the teaching. Occasionally if a solution seems obvious in human factors terms but has not been educed by others, it may be necessary to make it seem less obvious so that others are not made to look naive or foolish, which is a sure way to lose their collaboration. One of the most difficult aspects of human factors to teach is that it does not follow because a human factors problem can be identified and methods to tackle it can be devised, that it must have a satisfactory solution, for there may be none.

**How to teach**

Human factors knowledge should be applied to the teaching of human factors. Different teaching methods yield different results and are appropriate for different kinds of knowledge. The range of teaching methods available includes the following: traditional classroom instruction; the use of air traffic control simulation which may be quite rudimentary particularly in the initial stages of learning; self-teaching by self-contained and self-administering computer packages; training by demonstrations; training by worked examples; on-the-job training; training through traditional forms of study including reading; training by traditional forms of output including essays; human-machine dialogues through an interface; and tests and assessments. The basic principles of instructional design and strategies described in this volume should be applied in the teaching of human factors in air traffic control. Several psychological principles, especially those concerned with learning, should be followed. A particular need is to ensure appropriate feedback at every stage of the teaching so that learning can take place and the student can entrench and expand knowledge already gained.

Almost inevitably, training has to progress from the teaching of very simple, obvious standard aspects towards greater complexity, exceptions and non-standard situations. The teaching has to build on what has already been learned at every stage. While the earliest aspects that are taught are frequently encountered in the subsequent teaching of more complex situations and thus become entrenched, the most complicated and difficult aspects have to be taught last, which often implies that the student has least experience, familiarity and practice with these exceptional and difficult items. This is not a sensible teaching principle. It is therefore prudent in the final stages of a teaching programme of human factors to devote extra time at the end to entrench and reinforce the final stages of teaching with extra examples so that students' familiarity and experience of the very difficult is commensurate with the students' familiarity and experience with the very easy. This is administratively difficult to arrange because it implies some overlearning of the final stages of the teaching programme, but such overlearning is also a sound human factors principle to follow and should not be neglected.

Some of the relevant points about the application of human factors to air traffic control can be made from the teaching environment. Two kinds of technique can be applied that are effective in involving the students. One is to perform a kind of human factors audit of the environment in which the teaching is conducted. This covers the room, the layouts, the furniture, the equipment, the decor, the lighting, heating, other environmental features, the relationship of instructor to students, the visual aids, the kinds of material used, the seating, the work-rest cycles, the forms of feedback, and the techniques employed. Often differences in interpretation of what is taught can be traced to differences in initial knowledge or attitudes so that what is taught is more easily integrated into existing knowledge by some students than by others. This approach of a human factors audit of the teaching environment as a workspace can be efficacious, and should also lead to an efficient human factors environment in which the teaching is conducted.

The second kind of technique is to take the teaching situation and note the human factors problems in it. It can be emphasized that the human factors problems of the teacher and of the listeners, although they are in the same room, are not the same. The listeners for example, may have problems of distraction, boredom, inattention, nodding off to sleep and impressions of the slow passage of time which are quite different from the problems of the instructor who may have stress or fatigue and may find the tasks demanding but has no difficulty in maintaining attention, no boredom, and will not go to sleep during the lecture. It is instructive to seek explanations for the differences between the instructor and students in their human factors problems within the same work environment. The role of the students is to be passive but the instructor is actively involved in a task which maintains attention, provides an opportunity to use and demonstrate professional knowledge and skills, and can be satisfying and exhilarating. This raises the question of why most forms of computer assistance being introduced into air traffic control will make future tasks in it more passive and monitoring like those of the students, and less active and involved like those of the instructor. In terms of the human factors implications and in terms of the lecturing situation itself, this does not seem the most sensible thing to do. This approach can provide a peg on which to hang a productive discussion about what the objectives of the computer assistance ought to be in relation to air traffic control. How can human factors as a discipline mediate between the satisfaction of human requirements in a work environment and the tendency in the interest of greater system capacity to reduce human involvement and responsibilities?

One aspect of teaching on which it is difficult to form judgements concerns the use of examples. In principle an example can be provided of almost any human factors point taught in relation to air traffic control. Unfortunately it is very seldom possible to provide an exact example, an exclusive example, a complete example, or an example which does not underplay the range of other factors which are relevant. Some examples at least must emphasize such deficiencies. A major application of human factors to air traffic and a major influence on success concerns the rigour with which every facet and implication of each problem is defined and traced, so that decisions about how to resolve it are taken with a full knowledge of all the implications, and not, as they often have been in the past, with a partial knowledge of only the most obvious implications.

One usage of examples can be particularly telling. This presents two sets of air traffic control situations which superficially look similar and are not, in the sense that the optimum solutions to the problems which they pose are not the same. In one traffic configuration, the best solution can be to do nothing, whereas in another traffic configuration which begins similarly, positive intervention is essential. Such pairs of examples can be very effective in drawing attention to the factors which are crucial and to critical conditions of those factors which require a change in tactics or strategy which alters the preferred solution. A further efficacious application of worked examples is for an instructor to demonstrate to pupils the correct resolution of a particularly complex air traffic control problem and then present the same problem to each pupil and invite each one to resolve it for themselves knowing, as has been demonstrated, that it does have a satisfactory solution. If examples are chosen where timing is all so that any precipitate or delayed interventions lead to difficulties, this is a good technique for revealing that factors which may not seem to be important such as the timing, scheduling and ordering of events, can be critical. While it is essential to know what to do, it is also essential to know when to do it and in what order. It can be salutary for pupils to practice such a difficult situation until they can resolve it consistently, for they can learn a lot in doing so about what is really important and what is not, and what is most difficult for them as individuals to get right.

A further kind of example is illustrated by studying paper flight progress strips. The work to convert them into an electronic form originally concentrated on their physical appearance and information content and on the ways in which the main tasks were performed using the information on them. It gradually became apparent that flight progress strips were more complex and subtle in their functionality than had been realized, and that an electronic replacement of them would have to be more elaborate than at first envisaged. Even then, it would not be able to capture their full functionality. The application of human factors therefore identified all the functions of paper flight strips with a view to deciding which could be discarded, which must be retained on electronic flight strips and which should be retained but could take alternative forms other than electronic flight strips. The human factors processes involved in identifying the functionality also are a good example to demonstrate the range of human factors and the interactive aspects of it. A flight strip is not just a tool but an emblem, a record, a history, and a legal document. Flight strips collectively convey other kinds of information: they can indicate that in a few minutes a particular controller will be very busy because there are numerous flight strips in the pending bay.

One role of human factors is to identify the full functionality within manual systems before computer assistance or automation is introduced. The purpose is not to demand that this full functionality must be retained, for often some of it may be superseded or become redundant. Rather the purpose is to ensure that when automation is introduced there are no unwelcome surprises because controllers unexpectedly find they cannot do what they thought they could or cannot fulfil functions deemed essential which normally they could fulfil. The purpose is therefore to enable fully informed and deliberate decisions to be taken about which functions should be retained and which should not, and to avoid any unsuspected loss of functionality.

Because human factors is an applied discipline the teaching of it must emphasize its applications. Because human factors utilizes knowledge of fundamental human attributes, the teaching must make some reference to them. Because these attributes always interact in air traffic control environments the teaching must illustrate some of these interactions. Examples provide the best means of tying these processes together, to show how human factors work.

Consider phonetic confusions as a simple example that can be treated in some depth for teaching purposes. It is best to start with some real ones from recorded accounts of incidents or accidents. The phonetic confusions will either be between categories, for example where a height has been interpreted as a heading, or between syllables which have led to human error because they sound too similar when spoken. These are identified causes of human errors that can be dangerous. The instructor should force the student to identify as many as possible of the factors that affect phonetic confusion. Some factors may be readily identified: the read-back of acknowledgements, clearer pronunciation, improved auditory characteristics of the communications channel, better headsets, lower ambient noise in the room, more rigorous standardization of the formats and sequences of message contents, discrepancies between what was actually said and what the listener expected to hear, instances where the speaker did not actually say what the speaker intended to say, etc. Other factors may be equally effective as means in alleviating phonetic confusions but be less obvious; examples include the reallocation callsigns to flights so that aircraft with phonetically similar callsigns are not in the same airspace at the same time, the conversion of an auditory message to a visually presented one, the duplicate transmission of messages in visual and auditory form, and the recognition that some words become ambiguous in some contexts but remain unambiguous in other contexts, etc. Examples of the last are 'climb 220' where the first '2' can be 'to' or 'two' and 'take off power', which can mean 'reduce engine power' in some circumstances and 'increase engine power ready for take off' in other circumstances. The point of the teaching at this stage is to impress on the students that there are many potential sources of confusion and that they must all be identified first. Only then does it become possible to decide what the best remedy for phonetic confusions will be in the particular circumstances because some of the sources of confusion will be changeable and some of them will not. The sources of the confusion have to be removed not according to some theoretical ideal, but employing whatever practical means are in fact available. The only way to identify the best combination of practical means is to list them all beforehand. The practical application of human factors to air traffic control eventually develops such listings into a mental check list or a written checklist for the human factors specialist which is then applied systematically.

The possible sources of confusion that have been identified in this way can be related to the large human factors literature about fundamental human abilities to discriminate auditory sounds and speech. These literature findings can then be applied not only to explain the errors which have been made but to understand why they have been made, and extended to formulate alternatives which should be free of identifiable phonetic confusions. This should be verified by preliminary checks that these formulated alternative are not themselves potentially sources of other confusions. For example if the alternative is adopted of replacing a phonetic auditory message with a visual one to be read on a display this is counterproductive if the visual characters are themselves ones which look too visually similar and are known to be a source of visual confusions. This is simply replacing one kind of human error with another. The application of principles, and the derivation of examples from principles, can assist the processes of checking that the new proposals do not violate these principles or add new examples of confusions. By application of these principles therefore, alternatives which are practical and should be as error free as spoken alphanumeric messages can be, are formulated and checked. They then have to be verified in the air traffic control setting because, although they may not violate any human factors principles, there may be other information in the same environment with which they could be confused.

A basic underlying principle is that most of the sources of human error can be derived from general human factors principles and therefore the sources of confusion can be largely eliminated. All human errors can never be completely prevented but those with identified common sources can and must be. In terms of teaching it is better and more memorable to force students to think out and volunteer as many as possible of these factors rather than list them or simply provide examples of each, although the latter is helpful. There will always be some factors which the instructor has to add because none of the students has identified them, and this can be a salutary demonstration that they must broaden their thinking and not be rigid in their approach. A practical point about the application of human factors is that the relevant influences range more broadly than may initially be recognized, and the options for solving problems are often correspondingly broader than those originally recognized. It is vital in finding the best solutions that all the factors are identified, and this is an essential practical point of the teaching.

Among the most difficult aspects of human factors to teach are the very extensive range of influences that may be relevant to any problem, decision, prediction, or incident, and the inevitability that any changes made will introduce a new crop of human factors problems which must be identified beforehand. The most crucial aspect of instruction is to force students to think through and identify what the new problems will be, starting with very simple examples and evolving towards more complex ones. The point is that even the simplest problems like callsign confusion have far more relevant factors than at first appears, but the positive side of this is that correspondingly numerous kinds of changes may be beneficial. If this process is done during system planning, the objective is to prevent human factors problems from arising. If it is done as a result of incidents that have occurred, the objectives are to prevent the recurrence of such incidents and of other similar incidents, and to forestall the occurrence of comparable incidents in future systems.

It is not of course enough to do all this. It is essential to check that it has been successful. Some kinds of evidence for success such as a diminution or cessation of incidents of a particular type will provide such evidence ultimately but they take far too long to accrue. Here the human factors principles and literature can be applied again. Do the solutions conform with the evidence they provide? In relation to the above example, do they avoid all known sources of phonetic confusion? Do they produce a combination of short term recommendations - what to do now to stop a recurrence of this incident in the current system - plus longer terms solutions of how to re-design future systems so that this kind of error cannot recur? These are the two ways in which we can learn from our mistakes.

Instructional methods can be taken further by formulating alternatives which should be free of phonetic confusions and by checking them against the principles. Whether this is done by the instructor, or by the students, or by both in collaboration, will vary with circumstances and objectives, but the objective is to demonstrate the practical application of human factors in a preventative role. This can be done in several stages. The simplest stage is to compare proposed phonetic message formats and contents with the basic human factors evidence to check that it conforms with the principles. If it does not, there is no point in progressing to other stages until it has been revised so that it does. When it does conform with the general principles so that there are no known phonetic confusions in it, it has to be evaluated in the context of its actual usage because there may be sources of confusion derived from the context itself. A solution for example that might be acceptable under all normal circumstances might not work if there are very noisy cooling fans in a room, a lot of overheard speech by other controllers, deficiencies in the communications channels, poor headsets or microphones, or particular similarities which are an artefact of air traffic control message formats and contents, either in general or in a specific air traffic control locality. Evaluations in air traffic control environments may be necessary to prove that these factors will not induce errors.

The outline of the subject matter of human factors can provide the framework for a comprehensive human factors check list. It can also serve to indicate what is important and what is not, since all the topics in the checklist or in the subject matter are not of equivalent significance for safety, for efficiency or wellbeing. A useful starting point is to note that most controllers very much enjoy doing air traffic control and to ask why. Again, with an informed instructor the burden can be put on students to list what they believe the satisfying attributes of work are, to compare their own work with that of controllers, to propose how their own job satisfaction could be measured and hence how that of controllers might be measured, and to suggest what sort of changes would make their own work more or less satisfying, and discover whether all are agreed about these. This process can promote discussion on how important it is that work should be satisfying, and what is affected if the work is not satisfying. Does it matter for safety, or for efficiency, or for attrition rates, or for health? Again the emphasis is on the sheer range of factors that may be affected. Will any forms of computer assistance being proposed take the challenge, the interest, the effort and the satisfaction out of the work? How could this be predicted in advance? What would the whole range of consequences be if it did? If the course is concerned with the costing of human factors contributions, this kind of example and the ones about phonetic confusions may also provide exercises in attempting to express the benefits of human factors in terms which are ultimately financial.

The teaching can and should raise questions and force students to think. Another effective topic for achieving this concerns the relationship between selection and training. Are controllers a very special type of person who justify an elaborate selection procedure and the rejection of most applicants because a rare combination of qualities is being sought? Or is successful air traffic control primarily a matter of training so that it is necessary to select people who are young, well educated, physically fit and emotionally stable, but superfluous to employ a more elaborate selection battery? If the selection procedure is inadequate, can good training compensate for it or can it never succeed unless the right people have been selected for training from the outset? What human factors evidence would be applicable? Even if the selection and training are satisfactory, could the best efforts of both be nullified because the recruitment procedures are so flawed that the most appropriate people never apply to become controllers, or because the job allocation procedures are faulty and controllers are posted to jobs on completion of training for which they are not suited? There are two purposes here. One is to think of such issues as practical human factors questions which can make a big difference to air traffic control if they are satisfactorily resolved. The other is to force students to ponder the range of evidence that is applicable to resolve these questions, and the kinds of data that could produce valid evidence.

It is important in allocating limited human factors specialist resources most productively to apply them where the benefits will be greatest. This means separating the important from the trivial, and to think through and obtain evidence on what is most important. Will a well motivated workforce provide a better air traffic control service with obsolete though reliable equipment than is provided by a poorly motivated workforce with modern equipment and up-to-date computer assistance? In general many of the ergonomic aspects do not make as big a difference to performance as is often implied, although they can induce characteristic human errors and must be checked to prevent them. Because controllers can normally learn skill and proficiency on non-optimal data input devices, optimization of the ergonomics, though it should always be done, may not result in gross improvements in performance. On the other hand a factor like working alongside a colleague who is not fully trusted can add greatly to workload and to the perceived duties and responsibilities of a controller, and hence can have a major effect on that controller's performance. The essential point is that the significance of various factors is not equivalent, and human factors resources, which are scarce, should be concentrated where they will have most effect.

People rationalize their actions. This can be demonstrated effectively by a staged incident. Present a film or video that is ostensibly on a completely different topic but in fact shows an accident or incident, unbeknown to the students but known to the instructor. The class is stopped. The students are told they have just witnessed an accident, and they are asked to prepare a written account at once of what they have just seen. The accounts can be compared, areas of disagreement and agreement identified, aspect of the incident that were reported but did not actually take place are also identified, and the original tape or film is replayed as necessary. This is a practical way to show that people whose testimony conflicts may not necessarily be speaking in bad faith or being devious or mischievous. Well-known distortions, biases and misperceptions can be demonstrated actively by such an unexpected example, whose unexpectedness is a vital aspect of it, as it is with real accidents and incidents. Such practical demonstrations aid the students' memory and understanding.

Another practical approach to teaching human factors is to issue accounts of incidents or accidents to students and ask them to comment on factors which are in fact not mentioned but would be expected to be mentioned. What is tacitly assumed because its significance was not recognized? What kinds of relevant information do not emerge from various procedures that are followed, for example in the investigation of incidents? Some of the commonest omissions are local disagreements, problems over lost face and seniority, misunderstandings of what colleagues are doing, failures to observe standardized procedures, tacit understandings that were wrong, confused team or supervisory responsibilities, loss of alertness accompanied by relief at solving a difficult problem, hearing what one expects to hear and seeing what one expects to see.

The framework of the subject matter taught within a course is defined at the outset. In it, the contents are classified in the approximate order of their presentation and some attempt is made to show the common logics among them and the interactions between the topics. If students have a framework of this kind at the beginning of the course, they can see where each topic fits within it as it is taught, and what it relates to. It is useful if the main points of each lecture can be provided in the form of handouts. If these can be illustrated, this can also be advantageous. If the handouts are fairly detailed and issued in advance, then the teaching can be considerably assisted if students have been encouraged to read the handout beforehand. If they are initially reluctant to do this, questions about the handout content near the beginning of each lecture can help students to realize that they are expected to have some advance familiarity with the handout. The series of handouts should themselves collectively represent a comprehensive and balance coverage of human factors in air traffic control and should follow a uniform design which facilitates this, for example by being tagged appropriately.

Since human factors as a discipline is essentially about people, each student brings knowledge of himself or herself to the course. This can be utilized in relation to some aspects of it. The course should seek not only to inform but to educate in the broadest sense by encouraging students to re-examine their assumptions and identify and question their prejudices, to defend their own views, and to identify the kinds of evidence that are valid for confirming or refuting various facts or opinions. One of the most vital aspects of human factors is to establish the criteria for determining which kinds of evidence are valid and which are not. Related to this is information about where relevant evidence can be obtained and how to evaluate it for purposes of applying it to air traffic control. It is a useful approach to force students to think this through for themselves, to take almost any issue and make students suggest what kinds of evidence would be valid in studying it, to appraise their suggestions as they are made, to show how suggestions are appraised in terms of their reliability, their validity and other criteria, and to make students realize that, in terms of the efficiency and safety of aviation and of air traffic control, mere opinions are not good enough. Reliable, valid proven facts are what constitute evidence.

It can be salutary to look at the difference between causes and correlations in this regard. A statistically significant relationship may be misleading without evidence to show what its correct interpretation is, and unless it derives from experimental designs or other procedures which do not allow other interpretations. Many views can be expressed and it is helpful to press for relevant evidence.

For example, stress is normally considered to have no benefits or advantages. If this is the case, why do people seek to avoid stress at work yet spend so much of their leisure time in pursuit of it? What is wrong with stress? What kinds of stress and causes of stress are harmful or unsafe and does stress bring any benefits, for example in terms of challenge or interest, job satisfaction, opportunities to use skills, pride in the work, opportunities to gain esteem and respect of colleagues, and so on. Similar points can be made about workload. The reduction of controller workload is often treated as a self-evidently sensible objective. Yet most people with control over their own workload choose to be busy and often overload themselves. What are the benefits of reducing workload and what disadvantages may its reduction have, such as reduced amounts and levels of information processing, reduced understanding of traffic scenarios, reduced capabilities of intervention, more boredom, and an increased potential to tinker with equipment when there is nothing to do? Are forms of computer assistance which reduce workload unselectively thereby disadvantaged in that they may reduce extreme workload to workload that can be coped with, at the cost of reducing workload that is already too low even further? The topic of boredom can also be critically examined. Is boredom unsafe? If it is claimed to be, where is the evidence for this? What kinds of evidence would be valid? Are people involved in incidents or accidents often bored at the time of their occurrence for example? Could it be that boredom is associated with good task performance rather than with poor task performance? Is it possible to study boredom experimentally? During teaching, are the instructors never bored when the students are, and why is boredom selective so that it does not affect everyone in the same work environment? What is it about the instructor's tasks which prevents boredom and about the students' tasks which encourages it?

## Postscript

The author has lectured widely on human factors for air traffic control to courses. A satisfactory outcome is more likely to result if the instructor follows some simple guidelines. The instructor must be fully briefed on the purposes of the course, on its other contents, on the backgrounds and previous knowledge of the students, on the forms of testing and assessment during and at the end of the course, and on the approaches and methods being adopted for other parts of the course and by other instructors, so that the human factors parts of it conform with the rest of it.

Course contents usually include extensive written material. All this material should exemplify established human factors principles for designing instruction. The same point applies to other aspects of the human factors course taught through human-machine dialogues: the dialogues should themselves exemplify good human factors practice.

## References

Boff, K.R. & Lincoln, J.E. (Eds) (1988) *Engineering Data Compendium: Human Perception and Performance.* (3 Vols). Ohio: Harry G. Armstrong Aerospace Medical Research Laboratory.

Fitts, P.M. (Ed.) (1951) *Human Engineering for an Effective Air-Navigation and Traffic Control System.* Washington DC: NRC Committee on Aviation Psychology.

Heller, F. (1991) 'The underutilization of applied psychology'. *European Work and Organizational Psychology*, 1, 1, 9-25.

Hopkin, V.D. (1982) 'Human factors in air traffic control'. Paris: NATO AGARDograph No 275. AGARD-AG-275.

Hopkin, V.D. (1988) 'Air traffic control'. In: Wiener, E.L. & Nagel, D.C. (Eds). *Human Factors in Aviation*. San Diego: Academic Press. 639-663.

Hopkin, V.D. (1989) 'Training implications of technological advances in air traffic control'. Keynote Address. Symposium on air traffic control training for tomorrow's technology. Oklahoma City: Federal Aviation Administration.

Hopkin, V.D. (1994) 'Organizational and team aspects of air traffic control training'. In G.E. Bradley & H.W. Hendrick (Eds.). *Human Factors in Organizational Design and Management* - IV. North Holland: Amsterdam. pp. 309314.

ICAO (1993) 'Human Factors Digest No 8'. Human Factors in Air Traffic Control. Montreal, Canada: International Civil Aviation Organization. Circular 241AN/145.

Jordan, N. (1968) *Themes in Speculative Psychology*. London: Tavistock Publications.

Shepherd, W.T. & Johnson, W.B. (1991) 'Aircraft maintenance challenges and human factors solutions'. Bangkok, Thailand: *Proceedings of the ICAO Flight Safety and Human Factors Seminar*. 204-220.

Taylor, F.V. & Garvey, W.D. (1959) 'The limitations of a 'Procrustean' approach to the optimization of man-machine systems'. *Ergonomics*, 2, 2, 187194.

Wise, J.A., Hopkin, V.D. & Stager, P. (Eds) (1993) *Verification and Validation of Complex Systems: Human Factors Issues*. Berlin: Springer-Verlag, NATO ASI Series F. Volume 110.

Wise, J.A., Hopkin, V.D. & Garland, D.J. (Eds). (1994) *Human Factors Certification of Advanced Aviation Technologies*. Daytona Beach, Florida: Embry-Riddle Aeronautical University Press.

# 12 Evaluating standards in air traffic operations and training

*Rod Baldwin*

**Introduction**

An Air Traffic Control system is a complex mix of technological systems, personnel for operational, technical and support functions, rules, regulations and procedures. Each aspect must be controlled to ensure suitable standards, but each will also require a methodology which is appropriate to its special nature. Safety critical aspects must, of course be treated rigorously to the highest standards but other aspects should be dealt with within the context of the activity.

Since the end users of the air traffic control system are the pilots of the aircraft which are being controlled, the results of their responses to the directions and advice given will be the ultimate test of the standards which are being applied. Thus the ultimate judgement must rest on the sapiential authority of expert controllers, providing that they are adequately trained and have a competent ATC system for their work.

To some extent, checking operational standards is fairly direct as the requirements are clear, according to ICAO requirements, and the end user will comment very quickly when standards fall below those required and expected. For support activities it is often not so easy to be so definite - or at least there are more opportunities to drift away from meeting direct objectives. Hence it is necessary to have a comprehensive checking procedure to ensure that the support functions are making the best efforts to meet the standards requirements for the end users of the system.

However, establishing criteria for the selection and training functions to meet the required standards in producing qualified controllers is a difficult process, as assessment of what the controller does is often dependent on how the individual operators apply the appropriate rules and regulations (Baldwin, 1993). The activity requires a controller to combine knowledge, skills and attitudes in a complex mix in order to achieve traffic safety and expedition within a time dependent framework.

The whole process of evaluating standards should be systematically applied in order to ensure fairness and all persons in the loop must be aware of what is expected of them; they must also have received proper training to be able to achieve the performance requirements. Unfortunately this degree of analysis is not always applied in ATC, with consequent difficulties in establishing sound common criteria for evaluating and enforcing standards.

In addition, the impact of other sectors of the ATC system must also be considered by taking account of the various stages leading up to producing a qualified controller. These include selection and recruitment, formal training and on-the-job training through to final operations and other tasks which a trained controller can perform.

Figure 1 shows the sequence of these major stages as well as demonstrating a systematic process for checking whether standards are being achieved in each stage (verification), and whether the objectives are actually, or not, those required for the total programme (validation).

*Verification of objectives*

The objectives of each stage should be set according to the entry requirements of the succeeding stage. Establishing the extent to which the objectives are successfully met is the process of verification for that stage. Appropriate action must be taken to adjust the programme when the objectives are not being met. As well as adapting for under achieving objectives, change should also be applied for over achieving objectives as this could be wasting the organisation's time, money and other resources.

*Validation of objectives*

As the stages are interlinked and impact upon each other, there must be a progressive procedure for checking back that the objectives of each stage are actually valid for the next stage of the programme.

The validation procedure must also consider whether a training programme is too long or too comprehensive and thus producing some controllers who are over achieving. Whilst this is obviously wasteful in time and money for the organisation, it must also be remembered that for the trainee it could represent delays in progressing to the actual job to be performed with, consequent build up of frustration and hindrance in career progression.

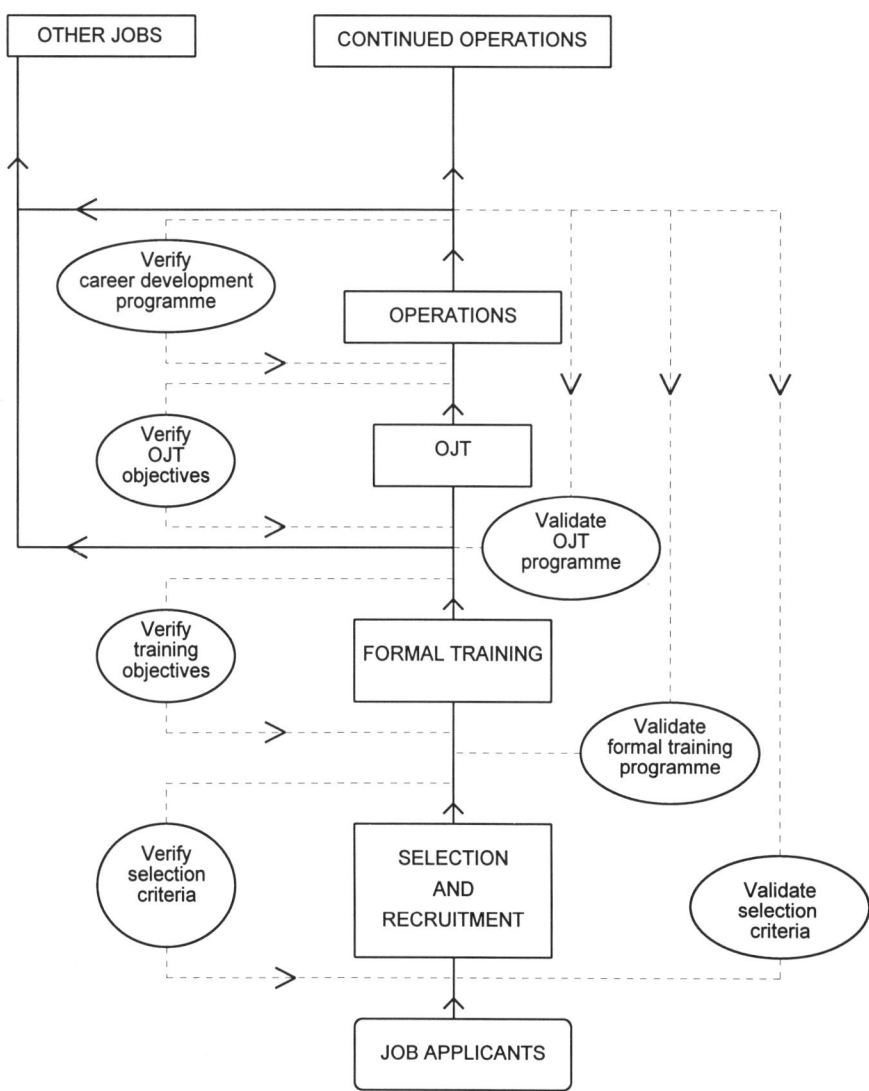

**Figure 12.1 Stages involved in evaluating standards**

However, the training process does include an educational element with the result that there might be a long term organisational requirements which are best met by including some extra training elements in the early stages of career development.

*Checking performance*

The process by which the objectives of each stage are achieved must also be checked in terms of the expected performance requirements. It is possible for stage objectives to be achieved through good staff performance even though the supporting conditions are poor. Whilst this might be adequate in ensuring standards are met, there is always the possibility that they might not continue to do so if any of the factors change. For instance, there might be a loss of key staff or supporting conditions might deteriorate. And the converse applies in that poorly performing staff might be sustained by a good system, or even helpful colleagues.

In order to check staff performance fairly and effectively, in any stage there must be:

1   A clear understanding of what tasks have to be achieved (job descriptions);

2   A clear understanding of how the tasks are to be achieved (job specifications);

3   An agreement about the level of performance to be achieved.

The level of performance needs to be carefully specified in terms of performance indicators so that staff clearly know what is expected of them and also so that they know the benchmarks against which they will be assessed. In addition, the criteria for establishing the standards should have been included in the basic, or updating, training programmes so that all staff have the requisite knowledge and skills to meet these standards.

Figure 2 illustrates the elements in an ATC organisation which can contribute to a performance checking procedure. The type and nature of the various elements will depend on each job under consideration, but for each job the performance indicators should be derived from the job description, a specification of how the tasks should be performed together with expected performance targets, and take account of the end user requirements.

Who performs the checks can be a sensitive issue as the actual staff are the only persons who have a complete current knowledge and experience of the specific details of the job which they are performing. However, there has to be an external check if failure of performance is to be arrested and adapted to the required standard. Even so, care must be taken to ensure that the assessed performance is oriented towards the objectives of the stage and not just to maximise the performance indicators. Studies in other areas (Davies, 1993) indicate that such exercises can result in suspicion and mistrust by staff and excessive top-down bureaucracy if the whole effort is not well managed.

Checking by external experts has the advantage of independent assessment. This can be particularly beneficial for smaller countries where it is not reasonable to have expert staff in a special standards unit which is only required a few times per year. However, the external expert must work in conjunction with internal staff in order to ensure that local conditions are fully understood. This situation is particularly pertinent in operation roles which are safety critical.

*Quality management*

In striving for high standards it is important to identify and establish priority items, such as safety critical ones, which must be met and supporting items which can contribute positively to maintaining, or improving, standards. In addition, attention should also be given to 'hygiene' items whose removal, or reduction, might reduce a negative impact on standards but will not necessarily add to improvements.

In practice, maintaining and checking standards can be more easily sustained if an organisation has a quality policy in accordance with the International Organisation for Standardisation's ISO 9000 series of requirements. Implementing and registering for ISO 9000 approval is a long and time consuming process but can be extremely beneficial in creating a systematic approach to providing a quality service. Amongst the many requirements to be met for the approval an organisation must have:

*Designing Instruction for Human Factors Training in Aviation*

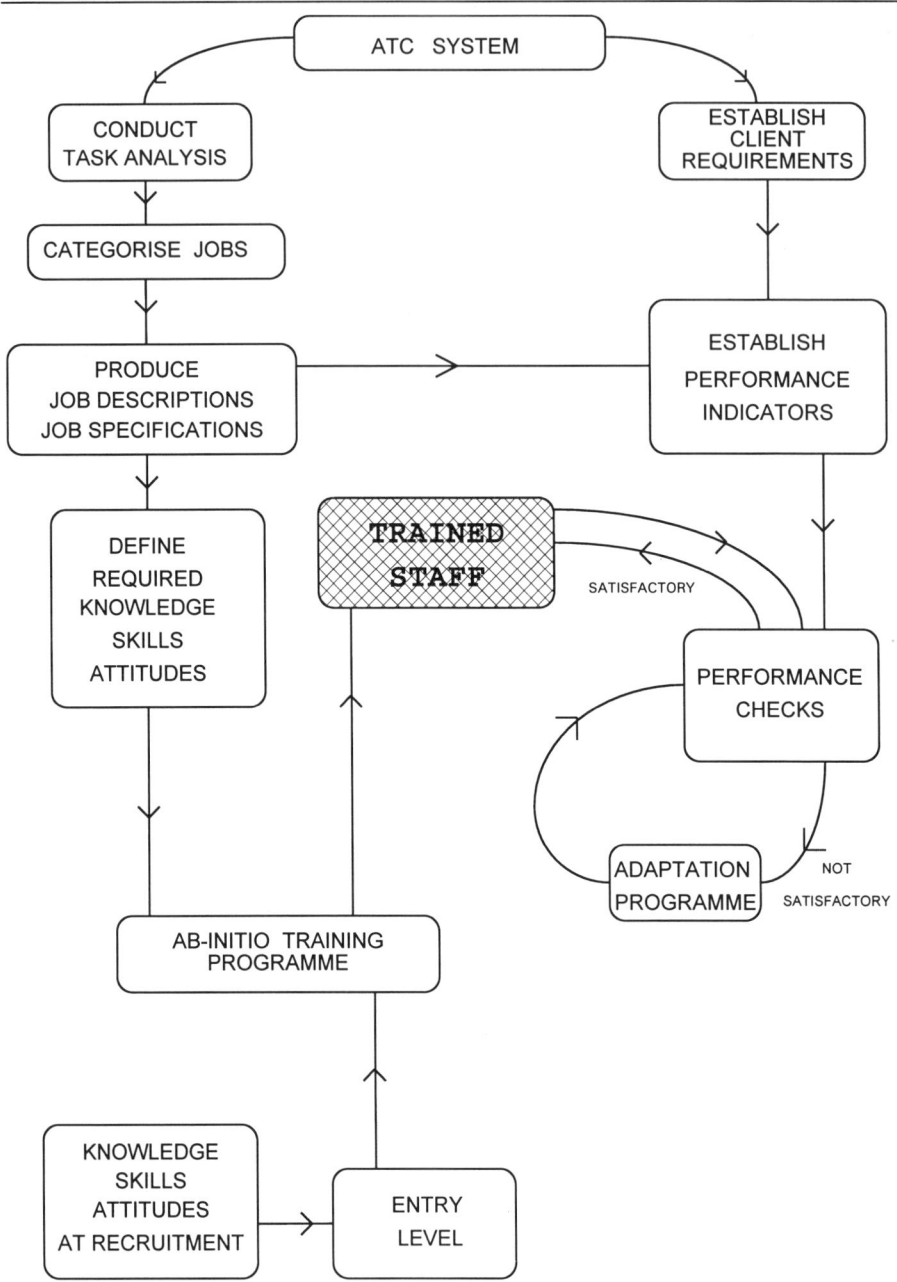

**Figure 12.2 Performance checking**

1    A quality policy manual;

2   Clearly written quality procedures;

3   Good written records, well controlled documents and good communication procedures;

4   Quality assurance procedures;

5   Appropriate workplace references.

**Operations**

Verification and validation of the operational activities must be made against the ATC organisation's defined objectives which in turn will be subject to the requirements of safety, other government regulations, ICAO requirements and pilot needs.

For the safety and regulation aspects, some governments do have separate safety and standards organisations which carefully check operational activities, whilst others delegate responsibility to the operating organisation.

With respect to the service provision, this feature has greatly improved in recent years and some ATC organisations do meet regularly with pilots and airline organisations in order to check the extent to which the service is meeting the standards offered.

Internal checking is nearly always performed in one way or another. Most units have a manual of operations which details procedures to be followed and it is against this that assessment of performance should be made. Some countries have also explicitly stated all the activities which a controller should perform. Thus they are able to establish the performance indicators shown in Figure 2 and carry out effective performance checks.

*The need for performance checking*

As the controller is regularly practicing the job it could be argued that there is no need for formal checking - and indeed many professions do not require such. However, there is agreement that whilst this performance checking does work, there is a problem in identifying and standing down anyone who is below a requisite competence level. In some areas a group can shield a weaker colleague but the advent of more automation into ATC and just sufficient staffing levels is making any such shielding extremely difficult.

When a check reveals an unsatisfactory performance, the adaptation programme can be of various forms depending on the degree by which the controller falls short of the required performance. This could take place in the operational centre, either on or off the job, or it could be a formal programme at a training centre. The availability of modern low cost skills trainers and simulators means that tailor made exercises can easily be developed and used at a convenient location.

Thus, regular formal checks, or currency checking, is the best way to maintain standards. Who should carry out the assessment raises a number of difficulties.

*The process of checking*

The immediate supervisor is able to continuously monitor the controllers performance in the environment which both know and understand. This certainly makes the controller appreciate that he is being judged by someone who understands all the problems. However, the downside is that the supervisor might make too many allowances, through knowing the practical difficulties of the job, either advantageously to the controller being assessed ('lets be realistic'!) or dis-advantageously ('the difficulties are not too hard, after all I did the job and managed'!) and consequently may be too harsh on the controller. In addition, the advent of automated systems makes it much more difficult for a supervisor to make such assessments (ICAO Circular).

It was mentioned earlier that checking by external experts has the advantage of independent assessment but this method must be carefully applied for operational roles which require a special understanding of the local situation and conditions.

Probably the best solution is a small check team consisting of the supervisor and an outside expert. Since the ATC world tends to be a close community the same system could also possibly be beneficial to even larger countries. Figure 3 lists some of the points requiring checks together with comments about how they need to be checked.

| Item | Comment |
|---|---|
| Evaluation policy | Determine how often checks are made. Does the policy include only operational activities or coaching for OJT as well? |
| Possession of a licence | Need to actually see the licence and check that it is up to date. |
| Possession of appropriate rating | Need to actually see the rating. |
| Demonstration of knowledge | Is this still current? Make an oral check. Make a written check. |
| Demonstration of experience | Are the checks appropriate to the amount of experience (ie. not antagonistic) |
| Demonstration of job performance | Who will do this? How long will it take? Is the check representative of all activities likely to be encountered before the next check? |
| Report | Are these discussed with the controller before being written? Who else is consulted? If there are unfavourable comments how are they communicated, and to whom? How long does this take? |
| Follow up | If a report is unfavourable: What corrective action is taken? Who ensures that the action is carried out? What is the procedure when the necessary action has been satisfactorily achieved? |

**Figure 12.3 Checking the standards of operational controllers**

*Scope of standards*

Thus standards in operational units can be verified against agreed criteria and these again can be referred back to the OJT, training and selection stages in order to validate the full programme against the operational requirements.

For the short term needs of the ATC organisation this process works well, but if long term needs are included then the validation process must include other job departments which will be part of the career chain.

For instance, there is much debate at the moment as to whether flow control positions should be occupied by only fully qualified air traffic controllers. If the answer is no then it is possible that in view of the need for a certain amount of ATC knowledge the positions could be taken by failed controller trainees (depending on level of failing) who have succeeded in other subjects. In this case should they be considered as successful trainees - and how would this affect the validation process?

## On the job training (OJT)

Strictly speaking this is the phase when a trainee actually works a position as an air traffic controller but under the supervision, and on the licence, of a controller who is qualified for that position. The situation of working on another persons licence means that the trainee must respect the controllers position. In return the controller should receive instruction in on-the-job training so that the two (or three) can work as a team with an understanding of each others needs and problems.

Therefore, the performance check in Figure 2. would be checking the skills of the on the job trainer as a coach.

*Pre - OJT*

For complex operational units there can be a pre-OJT phase which forms a bridge between the formal phase and the OJT. This is conducted by the operational controllers and ensures that the trainee is fully acquainted with the necessary local knowledge and procedures of the operating position before proceeding to operational duties. However, some of the benefits of this phase can be diminished if the controllers are no longer actually operational and the same status problems arise as occurs in formal training centres where some of the instructors might not have controlled for some time.

*Transfer of skills*

As in the formal training phase, the advent of computer based training aids, skills trainers and simulators has given a great impetus to OJT training and allows trainees to practice realistically complicated situations and procedures in safety and at times which are convenient to operational staff. The result is that in a busy operational environment the actual OJT time is used by the trainee mainly to gain the final experience of operating live. However there is still the question of the extent to which the acquired simulator skills transfer to the operational requirements and this will need to be carefully addressed as it was for line oriented flight training (Nash, 1992).

Whilst the operational controllers have all been through training courses similar to the new OJTs it is unfortunate that this may have been many years ago and the format might have changed - but no one has briefed the operational staff on their role in the training programme. Such information should be included in coaching courses; how many operational staff have attended an on-the-job training course? Without continuity of approach between the formal training and the OJT how can the former phase be validated?

Continuity is usually stronger in the smaller countries where trainee controllers may be recruited for particular stations, undergo their OJT there and eventually validate to become a qualified operator. Whilst this obviously saves time and money there can be problems in receiving on-the-job training and then being checked out by staff from the same operational centre. In addition the question could be raised as to whether the formal training was sufficiently generalised as to allow eventual transfer to another station. This is particularly pertinent for countries where the controllers wish to move around to different locations.

*Administration of OJT*

Whilst the above comments concern the practicalities of on-the-job training there are also many administrative features which can contribute to improving the standards through better involvement of the coach and better trainee motivation. These aspects should deal with such matters as:

1   How the trainees are assigned to an operational unit;
      Who makes the assignments;

2   Whether coaches receive details of the trainees formal training results;

3   Whether there is a pre-OJT induction briefing or course;
      If so, how long it should be and what it should contain;

4   Whether OJT is combined with simulated exercises;

5   Whether there continuity between the formal and the OJT training;
      If so - how this is achieved;

6   The nature and extent of feedback procedures/processes between coach and trainee;

7   How the OJT programme is assessed;

8   Who does the assessment.

**Formal training**

This is the phase of training which is concerned with the trainee acquiring the knowledge, basic skills and developing attitudes which are considered to be appropriate for the intended job. Since this is the bridge between the entry education level and actual OJT there must be a certain amount of education involved as well - especially in view of the increasing level of automation that is involved in modern ATC (Baldwin, 1991).

When using the results of a formal training programme to validate the selection and recruitment phase a much discussed aspect is the question of how much of the successful candidates personal data should be handed on to the training staff (Hopkin, 1991). It is often stated that none should be put forward so that all the trainees have an equal opportunity in the training phase; but this ignores the fact that the initial courses are short and the trainees differ in speed of learning skills.

Thus it seems sensible to give extra attention to trainees who need extra help in the early stages. After all, the early stages are the critical time and weakness or failure then can have repercussions well on into the training programme.

The opening chapter of this book pointed out Bruner's belief that an instructional system should specify ways of:

1   encouraging student learning;

2   structuring knowledge to enhance student learning;

3   sequencing instructional material in order to reduce learning difficulties;

4   providing reinforcement or punishment in the instructional process.

Of course a training programme which was individually adaptable, so as to ensure a trainees success, would be interpreted as a 100% validation of a successful selection and recruitment programme! To some extent this would be true as the results show that all the trainees possessed the necessary capabilities for the job.  In practice, the nature of the individualisation must be continuously analysed and fed back to the selectors with the aim of reducing factors which contribute to the expense and duration of the selection process and the training programme.

Fortunately the use of relatively cheap computer based learning aids in general and ATC simulators in particular enables the formal phase of training to become more realistic than ever and instructional staff have the opportunity for more scope in attending to the individual learning needs of trainees.

Consequently, in support Bruner's requirements, the evaluation of training standards should take into account aspects such as:

1   The location of the training centre;

2   The general quality of the facilities;

3   The extent and type of training equipment;

4   The quality and experience of instructional staff;

5   The support services given to trainees;

6   The course contents, structure, testing and exam arrangements.

*Location of the training centre*

There is often debate about whether the formal training should take place in a dedicated training institute, centre or school which can identify with educational and training centres of other disciplines, or whether it is best to conduct the formal training in an operational centre with an interchange of instructional and operational staff. This latter process may also be applicable in a separate institution which is close to an operational centre, but not if it is some way away.

Although the relative merits of each type of centre is dependent upon many factors, not least of which is the annual number of trainees, in practice the choice is often decided on logistical or historical grounds rather than as a matter of policy.

*Quality of facilities*

There are many features whose quality will support the standard of training, and other features which will have a negative impact on standards. These include:

1   Use of training aids;

2   Quantity and quality of teaching support services;

3   Catering facilities;

4   Study facilities;

5   Quality of accommodation;

6   Availability, and type of, of recreation facilities.

An ATC organisation must decide what value it places on these features, but as a minimum they should never be less that similar conditions which apply in other parts of the organisation.

*Quality of instruction*

This is an area where standards definitely affect the effectiveness of producing qualified operational staff and every effort must be made to meet the expected national and international standards. Features include:

1   Appropriateness of course content;

2   Quality and experience of staff;

3   Quality and quality of simulators and other training equipment;

4   Staff/Student ratios;

5   Quality and appropriateness of documentation;

6   Testing and examination methods and procedures;

7   Appeal procedures;

8   Degree of individualising training;

9   Evaluation methods and procedures;

10  Use of tests and examinations in later stages.

Each training manager must decide what degree of importance to attach to each issue and to what extent compliance with the required standard affects the quality of the training standards.

*Quality of instructional staff*

This is another area where standards definitely affect the training effectiveness. Often the best way of ensuring the highest standards is to give instructors a high status within the ATC organisation. Although this does not always ensure the best standards, the converse of low status resulting in low standards is all too often true.

However, in order to achieve a high status environment, instructors must keep their competence high and be regularly subjected to instructional performance checks, as in figure 2.

Maintaining practical operational skills is more difficult, but familiarity with current control activities is best when there is easy, and regular, access to an operation unit. Some organisations are able to utilise operational controllers in instructional capacities whilst others insist on rotation back to operations after a number of years. The latter method has a number of difficulties and complications, and so some organisations have allowed instructional staff to maintain their licence through performance checks on a simulator.

In general high quality instructional staff should:

1   have sufficient operational experience;

2   have recent operational experience;

3   be high performers;

4   be trained in educational and training knowledge and techniques;

5   be good instructors.

It is not easy in a modern, high technology environment to find a person who is currently a high performing operator and a high performing instructor. Consequently, this might necessitate a close co-operation of all ATC staff if standards are to be consistent and maintained.

A popular approach is to employ a very small core of permanent instructional staff and call on operational staff in numbers and type required for each particular course. This certainly satisfies the need for current operational experience and freshness of approach. Unfortunately, this method can in turn create a fragmented system with poor coherence of effort and it certainly weakens the continuity from selection, to formal training, to on-the-job training.

There is also a need for management to support the instructional staff by ensuring that they are sufficiently supported by adequate facilities, as shown above.

*Trainee needs*

Trainees learn in different ways and at different speeds so that each individual requires some flexibility in the training programme to cater for his or her own needs. They must, of course, learn to adapt their needs to a general approach used by the training centre, and for each particular course within the quality of instruction as detailed above. However, particular attention must be given to each trainee's needs and responses with respect to items such as testing, examinations, appeal procedures, degree of individualising training.

*Course content and examinations*

The content of ATC courses generally follow the recommendations of ICAO together with other subjects which an organisation wishes to include for internal reasons.

Sometimes, trainees question the need for subjects which do not meet the immediate needs of controlling aircraft, as these extra requirements make demands on available time and effort - especially if they are examined in the subjects. Unfortunately for the trainee, there can be additional subjects which need to be covered early in a trainees career and which should be examined. However, it would be more of a motivator if the results of the subjects were used only as indicators for use later, such as when considering career development. or even for guidance on alternative jobs if this is needed.

As many of the organisations have a long track record, there is usually a well established process of verifying whether course objectives have been met. However, validation programmes are much more difficult and are rarely implemented in a systematic manner.

Few ATC organisations have a standards department which is independent of the operations department, and indeed, operational staff are usually the final arbiters of the success or failure of a training programme. Whilst this is works well if the whole system is working well, and standards are high, there is the danger of meeting self-fulfilling objectives and great difficulty in adapting if standards are falling.

Since there is often an intrinsic danger of the training centre drifting away from the requirements of the operational units, there is a stronger case to be made for the use of external auditors to evaluate the standards of ATC training. Although, as in the case of the operational units, the outside experts might not have the specific knowledge and experience of the particular ATC system, their interest is more in the quality of instruction and whether the objectives are those required by the operational units. In this sense the external expert is able to address interface matters in an unbiased way.

The above condition is particularly apposite in the case of formal examinations. Although examination pass levels can vary from 50% to 75% and trainee rates can be as low as 25% or as high as 98%, each country has its own benchmark of what constitutes the pass level. This impacts on the degree of confidence that can be placed in the selection and training process, and in this situation the external expert can offer comparisons with other organisations and help to establish reasonable and realistic standards.

## Selection and recruitment

The length and nature of a training programme will depend on the objectives to be achieved and the entry level of knowledge, skills and attitudes. The objectives will differ for different organisations as each will have different long and short term requirements for their trained controllers. Although cross and continuation training will meet many of the future needs for career development these will be limited by the learning capabilities of an individual, and these in turn will be indicated, to some extent, by their educational level when leaving school.

### *Knowledge requirements*

The knowledge requirement is not usually a major problem as the educational system of most countries is well organised, well understood and the achievements made in the examination system are transparent to most employers. It is a fact that very few trainee controllers fail a course because of lack of factual knowledge.

Thus the employer must identify which educational level is required of a recruit and then plan a training programme which he or she is capable of undergoing.

### *Skill abilities*

Since skill abilities are rarely tested at school this must be done by the organisation itself. Although initial skill abilities are useful, the aim of the tests should be to assess *trainability* for achieving the final skill performance level of the programme.

The major problem in recent years has been assessing the potential of a candidate to acquire the necessary skills of a controller. Numerous studies have been made and several in depth analyses have resulted in paper and pencil tests followed by skill tests which were thought to be appropriate to the job of a controller. Unfortunately most of the skill tests were made by assessing a range of aptitudes in isolation from each other and thus not allowing for the interaction which occurs when a controller actually carries out his/her job.

In view of this complex situation, and with success rates often low as 50% or less, it has been suggested that a simpler approach might be to accept a high drop out rate and just train plenty of candidates for the actual job. Besides being costly such an approach creates much personal (and family) unhappiness whilst putting a great strain on the resources of the training centre.

Better results are now being obtained (Haglund, Backman, Berndt, 1994), by utilising dynamic skills testing, perhaps in the form of simplified controller practical exercises from the early training phase. However, it is essential to make the exercises independent of previous expertise in the ATC field as their main aim is to test for trainability.

The FAA have found (Broach, Brecht-Clark, 1993) that they can use this simplified approach by designing a mini - course which can be run over a few weeks but will identify those candidates with the necessary potential for learning knowledge and practical skills.

*Recruitment specifications*

Thus when drawing up recruitment specifications the elements which will need to be considered are:

1. What is the job? What balance is needed between the requirements of knowledge, skills and attitudes?

2. What jobs are available in the future? And which ones are realistically possible? Which ones will the employer expect to be filled by the present trainee controllers?

3. What educational qualifications are required and what personal characteristics are needed?

Each of these elements will make an impact on the training phase but it is often difficult to separate custom from actual need.

Thus selection tests and interviews will need to assess a candidate with respect to characteristics such as educational abilities, mental skills, motor skills, personal characteristics, quality of speaking the national language, knowledge and use of English language, stress tolerance and social experience (e.g. Military service).

The testing and interviews are usually conducted by teams consisting of a representative from the personnel department, the air traffic control general directorate, the training department/school/institution, the operational units and maybe an industrial psychologist.

With so many interests involved it is essential that the group is committed to the selection criteria used, and all staff in subsequent phases accept the challenge of successfully progressing the recruits.

**Conclusion**

Before standards can be maintained they must be carefully evaluated. This can be achieved through rigorous verification and validation procedures. The process of checking and adapting must apply through all stages of the controllers progress from selection through to full performance capability.

An external input to the procedures can help to improve the process but care must be taken to balance the degree of external expertise with the specific requirements of the jobs being evaluated.

**References**

Baldwin, R. (1991) 'Training requirements for automated ATC'. In J.A.Wise, V.D.Hopkin and M.C.Smith (Eds), *Automation and Systems Issues in Air Traffic Control*. NATO ASI Series F, Vol. 73, (pp 469-479). Berlin: Springer- Verlag.

Baldwin, R. (1993) 'The interaction of stages in validating and verifying ATC training'. In J.A.Wise, V.D.Hopkin and P. Stager (Eds.), *Verification and Validation of Complex Systems*. NATO ASI Series F, Vol. 110, (pp 651-657), Berlin: Springer- Verlag.

Broach, D., Brecht-Clark, J. (1993) 'Validation of the Federal Aviation Administration Air Traffic Control Specialist pre-training screen', *Air Traffic Control Quarterly*, 1, pp.115-133.

Davies, J.L. (1993, June) 'The development and the use of performance indicators within Higher Education Institutions: A conceptualisation of the issues', in *The Development of Performance Indicators for Higher Education*, edited by H.R. Kells, OECD, Paris.

Haglund, R., Backman, B., Berndt, B., (1994), *Recruitment, Selection and Training of Air Traffic Controller Students,* Luftfartsverket, Series of reports by the Swedish Civil Aviation Administration, Department of Air Navigation Services, Stockholm, Sweden.

Hopkin, V.D. (1991), 'Closing Remarks', In J.A.Wise, V.D. Hopkin and M.C. Smith (Eds.), *Automation and Systems Issues in Air Traffic Control.* NATO ASI Series F, Vol. 73, (pp553-559). Berlin: Springer-Verlag.

International Civil Aviation Organisation (ICAO). Annex 1 to the Convention on International Civil Aviation, International Standards and Recommended Practices - Personnel Licensing. And see ICAO document AN-WP/6630AN of 22/11/91

ICAO. Doc 4444-RAC/501/12, 'Procedures for Air Navigation Services (PANS): Rules of the Air and Air Traffic Services'.

ICAO Circular, 241-AN/145, Human Factors Digest No. 8 (Human Factors in Air Traffic Control).

International Organisation for Standardisation (ISO). The 9000 series apply to various requirements. In Europe they are referred to as EN 29000 and in the U.K. as BS 5750.

Nash, T. (1992) LOFT - *Where Is It Going?,* Civil Aviation Training, Vol.3, Issue 1.

# 13 Teaching for visualizing in air traffic control

*Anne R. Isaac*

**Introduction**

Although imagery, and its practical application, visualization, was discussed in the eighteen hundreds (Galton, 1879), it was not until the latter half of the nineteenth century that imagery was studied as a psychological phenomenon.

In an early attempt to describe the formation of images, Galton (1879) published an article in which he alikened their formation to 'composite photographs on the brain, of many impressions from the sense of sight'. In further research Galton (1883) discussed the mode of visual presentations in different people and suggested that the visualizing faculty could be developed by education. He also claimed there were natural differences in the visualizing ability across races as evidenced by reports from the South African Bushman and Eskimos.

The Eskimos had been reported to map vast areas of country which they apparently mapped in their heads. One such report was of a chart drawn from memory of the coastline from Pond's Bay (latitude 73°N) to Fort Churchill (latitude 58°44′N) which stretched for 960 nautical miles. Galton concluded:

> A visual image is the most perfect form of mental representation wherever the shape, position and relations of objects in space are concerned (p. 78)

It would clearly be an advantage to understand more of this phenomenon in order to help those professionals in aviation who spend much of their time using these visualization skills to complete their tasks. This chapter will attempt to describe the nature and function of visualization and how these skills can be used in the teaching and training of air traffic controllers.

## The nature and function of visualization

Although the nature and function of visualization has been hotly debated for the last one hundred years, recent evidence has suggested a common neural focus of visualization and perception (Farah, 1985, Farah and Smith, 1983, Isaac, 1990).

The experimental evidence supporting this hypothesis was described by Farah:

> The ability of images to affect the quality of perceptual representations implies a common locus of processing for imagery and perception, and the finding that this interaction depends on an integral combination of the shapes and positions of the images and stimuli implies that there is a common neural locus (p.102).

These experimental results have been subsequently supported by Marks (1984), Isaac (1990) and Isaac and Marks (1994). Further research to date has used the model of image generation proposed by Marks (1986). Marks described the image as a quasi-perceptual experience occurring in consciousness, which had a psychophysiological component and was finally interpreted or understood in the verbal semantic system. Marks (1986) described the generation of, and conscious access to, visual images in the following terms:

> Images are generated and accessed in a tri-modular system which consists of an 'image-compiling system' which computes and composes the image from elements of memory, a 'long-term memory file' containing elements of the visual appearance of objects, and an 'image-readout' which provides for conscious monitoring of images (p.156).

These findings have been verified and expanded by Isaac (1990) who concluded that subjects reported differing degrees of vividness and ease of image generation which favoured those classed as high imagers.

From a theoretical stand point many researchers have formulated models of behaviour but few have focused primarily on the nature of the input or the process leading to the generation of specific cognitive strategies. It is also evident from previous writing and research regarding skill acquisition (Welford 1960) that there is a lack of acknowledgment for the different role of visual imagery in skill learning. The following model is offered to help illustrate the importance of visual imagery in such cognitive skill learning.

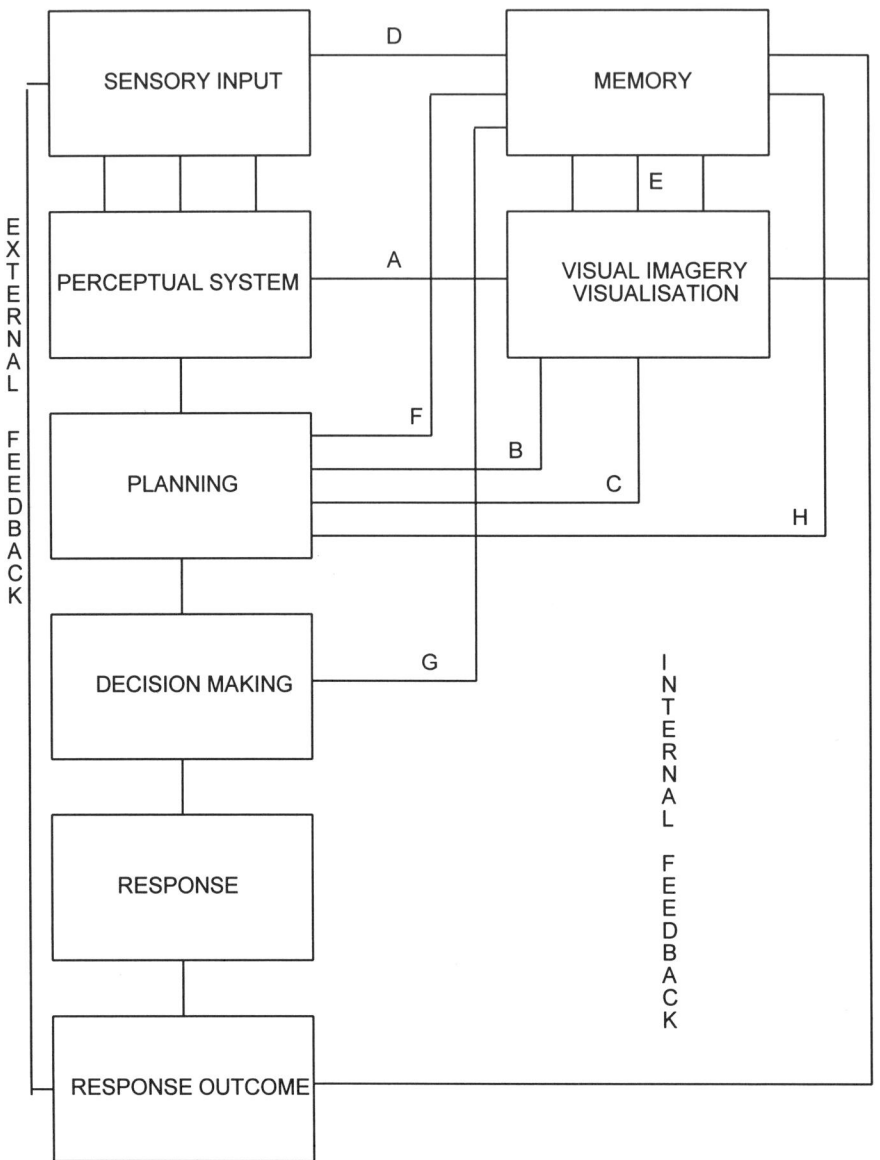

**Figure 13.1 Imagery and visualization as a PROACTIVE system**

This model illustrates the input of visual imagery and visualization to the planning and decision making in cognition. It is suggested that imagery can be used by the subject from the time information enters the sensory system, to its transformation into a response. Imagery can be either single or multimodal (visual, auditory, etc) and parallels the perceptual input (A) and is used at this level and beyond. It can input at the planning stage (B) as a proactive system, and the feedback from this (C) is suggested as the system used by skilled subjects. Visualization, it is suggested, includes either pathways D or E without further input into the system.

Pathways F, G and H signify the part played in planning in a direct way by memory. This may be the result of memory for actual procedures or airline characteristics which may not include imagery requiring judgements of space and time, illustrated by pathways B and C.

With particular reference to previous research and this model the chapter will continue to address the significance of visualization in Air Traffic Control.

## Visualization in air traffic control

Many of the skills found in air traffic control (ATC) and flying have common elements; indeed many air traffic controllers have flying experience during training and pilots are also educated in aspects of air traffic control.

Except near airports controllers do not see aircraft. They must rely on indirect information provided before the flight, sensed by ground-based installations, transponded from aircraft, computed from collated data, or spoken by aircrew or other controllers. This information then has to be stored, sustained and presented to both controllers or pilots in an accessible form for use.

Air traffic control keeps aircraft safely separated within a common region of airspace. Separation is maintained strategically by planning the traffic flow before and during flights, and tactically by instructing the pilots of specific aircraft or to change to a different heading, speed or height. With the exception of spoken messages from pilots and ATC's, information about the aircraft under control is sensed automatically, for example by radar. This information has to be converted into the main channels of human sensing, vision and hearing, and presented at a pace, in a form, and at a level of detail matched to human limitations.

Air Traffic Controllers sometimes worry about what they call 'losing the picture'. Sometimes it is the meaning of the perceived information rather than the information itself that is apparently lost. Rebuilding a picture lost in this way can be a long, slow process involving the transfer of information from short-term memory to long-term memory, (Whitfield, 1979). The controller who takes over an operating position from a colleague requires quite a long time to build up a picture of the traffic.

> Once he has constructed it, he relies heavily on it for controlling traffic and feels vulnerable if circumstances suggest that this carefully constructed picture may vanish, disappear or become meaningless (Hopkin, 1982, p.156).

More recently a review of air traffic services training programmes in Australia (Clark, Sharp, Johnson, Lyon, Traubuann and Spurgeon, 1987) suggested that skills common to ATC included:

> visualization of air traffic in three-dimensions. The building of a 3-dimensional picture without the aid of radar. This picture is vital in service and control operations and includes ability to transpose two-dimensional map information into a three-dimensional air space visualization (p.37).

It was also suggested by Sperandio (1977) that as air space was three-dimensional, air traffic controllers who detected and resolved traffic problems needed a mental image of this space that was also three-dimensional.

In terms of the use of imagery in the skills of ATC, experimental studies using psychophysical measures have illustrated the influence of eye fixation of imagery ability. 'Imaging subjects fixate their eyes on the parts of the display screen that would contain the most salient parts of the imaged picture' (Farah, 1985, p.93)

Further investigation concerning eye movement and scan path consistency (Marks, 1983) has provided strong support for the notion that imagery has a somatic component which compliments the sensory component.

The implication of this work in ATC can be found in these and other results published by the author (Isaac, 1994). These results confirm that air traffic control personnel not only report very high imagery but also understand and use imagery extensively in both radar and non-radar situations. Finally this research also highlighted the fact that the competencies of air traffic controllers, as reported by supervisors, is correlated to self-reported imagery.

Although this previous research indicates a robust finding regarding the correlation between the skills of visualization and the task found in air traffic control; how can these visualization skills be identified and taught.

**Selection and training**

In order to appreciate the complexities of this problem we should return to the proposed model. Refer to Figure 1 of this chapter.

As was discussed earlier the main inputs in the system due to imagery were the pathways D and E and therefore it would be useful to elicit whether prospective ATC personnel had the ability to think in visual terms and indeed whether they could create and use these images. There are several questionnaires which are based on self-report visual and imagery abilities which have been used in ATC selection in New Zealand.

Secondly the pathways B and C illustrate the use of visualization in the planning and, by implication, the decision making in the ATC environment. In terms of these propositions there would certainly be an advantage in using this knowledge in the training of ATC personnel.

Firstly the type of syllabi should be reviewed in order to ascertain whether each stage or area of learning is conducive to the use of imagery and visualization. For instance, it is known that procedural control is likely to use the skills of imagery more than radar, that primary radar is more demanding of visualization than secondary radar and that approach is more demanding than tower control. With this knowledge the training of ATC personnel should perhaps be more carefully timetabled. In New Zealand the trainees follow a syllabi which tries to encourage and enhance the use of visualization as the training progresses. With this premise the following progression is followed:

- Introduction to ATC with special reference to flying skills - this includes playing 'blip driver' in the radar simulator;
- Introduction to radar - using the radar simulator without labels to start followed by full label display;
- Radar rating;
- Introduction to procedural control;
- Aerodrome training;
- Approach training;

- Rating in the field for approach aerodrome.

This timetable enables the controller to progressively use imagery and visualization in the tasks demanded.

As the introduction of technology increases in the ATC environment the fundamental skills will also change and this not only has implications both in selection but also in the competencies required by the work. Visualization is a valuable and often neglected skill which needs to be trained and enhanced just as all other competencies found in this aviation environment.

But what of the training? How can we enhance the pathways labelled D and E in the skill learning model?

If the previous research in this area is to be adopted then there are certain variables which should be considered in the training environment.

- As has already been mentioned, selection for personnel who have natural tendencies in imagery and visualization would be an advantage.
- The skill of visualization should be introduced to the ab initio controllers from the start of their training. This could be a formal presentation within either skill learning in the technical sense or as part of the human factors syllabus.
- The trainees should have as much practical application of this competency as possible. This could include self report exercises using imagery in a generic way as well as in the aviation specific environment.
- The trainees should be encouraged to talk through various traffic scenarios. They should be encouraged to 'see' the traffic in a three-dimensional environment. They should also be encouraged to 'show' others with whom they are training where the traffic is located and where it will be in a given time frame. The parameters of time, speed, distance and space can all be included in these exercises.

There is considerable evidence that the use of imagery is progressive. Therefore the following points should be considered.

- The trainees should start with the development of their images
  - they should be clear, vivid and controllable.
  - the images they produce should be very large to start with.
  - they should then progress to moving these images when and where required.

- they should then develop more than one image and in more than one dimension

The trainees are usually encouraged to talk through their planned decisions in the simulation scenarios. There are several things which can enhance the use of imagery at this stage.

When the trainee makes a questionable decision or in some cases no decision, ask them exactly what they were thinking. Where did they 'see' their aircraft and where would the aircraft 'be' having issued this instruction. Check that they include, position, time and space values in this response.

It is difficult to obtain descriptions of how controllers solve problems, but one method is to ask the controllers to verbalise the problem concurrently or retrospectively. There are, as Hopkin (1982) reports, 'aspects of air traffic control which are essentially spatial and visual and which do not lend themselves to complete description in words' (p.42).

- It has often been reported that when a trainee stops chattering about all their decisions, or makes decisions before verbalizing it with the trainer, they have 'got the picture'.
- It is easy to ascertain when a trainee has got the picture. If you ask them - they will tell you. This response often varies from
  - no picture
  - vague picture
  - static but uncontrolled
  - clear and static
  - moving
  - the full picture

It must not be forgotten that trainees will all have different methods which they prefer in dealing with the tasks in ATC. Before starting any practical exercise it is important that you give the trainees sufficient time to organize their preferred mode of operation. Often those trainees who take more time to start such exercises turn out to have the clearest picture and as a result produce the safest most orderly and expeditious flow of traffic - I believe this is the tenet of Air Traffic Control.

## References

Clark, N., Sharp, C., Johnson, B., Lyon, J.D., Trautmann, K., & Spurgeon, P., (1987) 'Review of Air Traffic Services training programme'. Unpublished report submitted by Nicolas Clark: Ottawa, Canada.

Farah, M.J. & Smith. A.F., (1983) 'Perceptual interference and facilitation with auditory imagery'. *Perception and Psychophysics 33*, 475-478

Farah, M.J., (1985) 'Psychophysical evidence for a shared representation medium for mental images and percepts'. *Journal of Experimental Psychology: General 114*, 91-103

Galton, F., (1879) 'Sychometric experiments'. *Brain, 2*. 149-162

Galton, F., (1883) *Inquiries into Human Faculty and its Development* London: MacMillan.

Hopkin, D.V., (1982) 'Human factors in air traffic control'. *NATO Advisory Group for Aerospace Research and Development.* (Agardograph No. 275). London: Technical Editing and Reproduction Ltd.

Isaac, A.R., & Marks. D.F., (1994) 'Individual differences in imagery experience: Developmental changes and specialization'. *British Journal of Psychology* 85, 479-500.

Isaac, A.R., (1990) *The Role of Imagery in Movement - It's Nature and Function.* Unpublished PhD thesis Otago University.

Isaac, A.R., (1994) 'Imagery ability and air traffic control personnel'. *Aviation Space and Environmental Medicine 65*, (3) 96-99.

Marks, D.F., (1983) 'Mental imagery and consciousness: A theoretical review'. In A.A. Sheikh (Ed) *Imagery*: *Current Theory, Research and Application* New York: Wiley.

Marks, D.F., (1984) 'The new structural approach to image formation, Psychophysiology and Psychopathology'. *Journal of Mental Imagery* 8, 95-104.

Marks, D.F., (1986) *Theories of Image Formation* New York: Brandon House.

Sperandio, J.C., (1977) 'From the plane-space to the air mobile space: Experimental comparison between two displays of spatio-temporal information'. *Psychological Abstracts* 58, 884.

Welford, A.T., (1960) 'The measurement of sensory-motor performance: Survey and re-appraisal of twelve years progress'. *Ergonomics 3*, 189-230.

Whitfield, D., (1979) A preliminary study of the Air Traffic Controller's 'Picture'. *Journal of the Canadian Air Traffic Controllers' Association 11*, 19-28.

# Human factors instruction-aviation medicine

# 14 Teaching - aviation medicine

*Robin Griffiths*

## Introduction

Aviation human factors training and aviation medicine training have enjoyed an unusual symbiosis since the beginning of aviation's lengthening history. In many cases the collaboration of psychologists, doctors and others in related specialities has led to a great synergy, with a growing understanding of the other's complex area of expertise and respect for their professional skills. On the other hand, the relationship has sometimes been marred and significantly harmed by professional jealousies and sins of trespass committed by one speciality into the realms of the other. This chapter aims to show how aviation medicine and human factors can achieve that synergy that enables the best possible level of training to be achieved at whichever level it is projected.

## Aviation medicine in context

Aviation medicine training is often provided for pilots as part of a human factors training course to meet pilot licensing training requirements. Many countries now include human factors or human performance training as a key element of pilot training, being as vital a basic an aviation science as meteorology or aerodynamics. There is an element of aviation physiology and medicine in all such courses, usually intended to help the student to understand the nature of the interface between the human organism and the aviation environment. Altitude physiology training to ensure proper recognition and management of hypoxia incidents has been a long standing requirement for many professional pilots. More recently this has been incorporated into wider human factors curricula including perceptual aspects of fight and the effects of fitness or illness on pilot performance and risk of pilot incapacitation.

Aviation medicine training may sometimes form part of a wider human factors training syllabus, either as a key component of the curriculum or an option for special interest groups. On the other hand, human factors education is a critical core topic in any aviation medicine training course taught at any level. Human factors courses usually include a significant element of aviation medicine and aviation physiology in their syllabus. The choice of delivery for instruction will be determined largely by the nature of the course, the characteristics of its audience, and the availability of appropriately qualified and experienced instructors.

Aviation medicine should be differentiated from its related subjects of aviation physiology, occupational medicine, ergonomics, flight nursing or aeromedical evacuation, and aviation psychology.

Aviation physiology syllabus structures will be familiar to most readers, centering on the physiology of exposure the aviation environment. This has been conventionally confined to flight, with the bulk of topics arising from altitude physiology, thermoregulation/survival, perception, and acceleration physiology. The more accepted protocols now include the wider environment, including circadian dysrhythmia, fatigue, ageing, pilot incapacitation and radiation. They also include other aviation personnel to a greater degree, such as air traffic controllers, cabin crew, ground engineering and traffic staff, and rescue personnel.

Aviation is an unusual and particularly demanding work environment, whether the individual is in paid employment or simply flying for pleasure. The general principles of occupational medicine, a recognized speciality in many countries of the work, equally apply to pilots working in the aviation environment. These will include hazards such as noise, radiation, toxic chemicals, vibration and organizational psychology.

A number of students in postgraduate aviation medicine courses are involved in the transport of sick or injured passenger patients by air. These roles require an appropriate level of understanding of the effects of exposure to aviation related stresses such as heat/cold stress, hypoxia, reduced ambient pressure, noise vibration, and potentially time zone changes.

The type of training will usually be provided at the level appropriate to the academic level and needs of the student. For example, flight attendants are usually taught sufficient aviation physiology for them to understand the physiological effects of reduced cabin pressure that may cause medical problems for passengers in flight, and as a prelude to the use of oxygen equipment. A significant number of cabin crew come from a health sciences or nursing background, and this may create real difficulties when trying to establish a common ground for a foundation of basic knowledge when other students lack such skills. A certain minimum competency base is required to deal with medical emergencies in flight and with the management of invalid passengers; this need has become more acute with the provision of more sophisticated medical equipment on board long haul aircraft. For example, Qantas now carry automatic defibrillators on their Boeing 747 series aircraft, and staff are trained to use these in the case of a presumed cardiac arrest. Many of these para-clinical responsibilities are through proxies; the provision of sophisticated drugs and medical equipment on board aircraft for use by medically qualified passengers requires some degree of informed supervision of their use by cabin staff.

The boundaries are often very hazy and the overlaps between the various subjects are numerous. The secret formula for achieving those standards of excellence in providing aviation medicine training lie in exploiting those relationships and overlaps to reinforce their linkages of association and causality.

Very often, the perspective will vary according to the interest and experience of the teacher and the purpose for teaching the subject. For example, spatial disorientation may be a focus for vestibular neurophysiology for an aviation physiologist, but for an aviation human factors trainer the why and how may be less important than the what, in this case being the effect on pilot performance and flight safety. An aviation medicine doctor may on the other hand be interested in how physical or mental pathology, or toxicological insults, affect the physiological parameters and the response of the human organism. Depending on the audience, all of these will be important to a varying degree to each student.

## The audience

Teaching aviation medicine will inevitably be tailored to the specific needs of its student audience. Too often teaching aviation medicine as a speciality to non-specialists has failed, not because the teacher doesn't have a good grasp of the subject, but rather because the teacher is unable to cross the divide to the lay audience. The inappropriate use of unexplained technical terms, jargon and abbreviations will quickly lose the attention, goodwill and comprehension of an audience.

The audiences tend to be differentiated into a number of reasonably distinguishable groups. Medical and human factors professionals tend to have a key interest in understanding the topic as a whole often before developing their special interests and research into narrower fields in the area. There are also those who, from a variety of backgrounds, take aviation medicine/physiology as an 'interest only' course, for a variety of reasons.

Aviation professionals will often be in training to meet pilot licence or training establishment training requirements and the objectives will be clearly indicated by their application of aviation medicine to their training environment. Particularly where there is a Civil Aviation Authority qualifying examination or internal examination by the training establishment, the objectives are focused on preparing students for the examination. This is not always helpful as students may tend to rote learn rather than attempt to build an understanding of topics that may help them some time in their future flying career.

The approach of many military organizations to aviation medicine and physiology training may provide a better model. Military aviators are commonly required to attend periodic refresher training following a comprehensive basic training course at the ab initio level. NATO advice recommends more frequent and extensive training for fast jet rather than transport and helicopter crews, although the justification for this may be debated. Regular refresher training is also a feature of hypoxia training for air transport crews. Air traffic controllers are sometimes provided with aviation medicine and physiology training. There would appear to be a strong justification for widening the availability of this to air traffic controllers. The air traffic controller is often unaware of the physiological and medical implications of an in-flight depressurisation or hypoxia incident. Formal training may improve the management of such incidents. The training may usefully be extended from altitude physiology to clinical topics such as pilot incapacitation, and prevention and management of spatial disorientation/visual misperceptions.

## The curriculum

There is no such thing as a 'typical' curriculum, as the syllabus and emphasis will be determined by the needs of the audience. The focus on making linkages between topics presented and its relationship to their potential applications in the aviation activities of students will drive an objectives based curriculum. However, common themes can be drawn from the range of topics that may be taught. A number of subject headings may be derived that will require at least some superficial coverage in order to place aviation medicine as a topic area in some sort of context and order.

The broad headings are as follows:

1   Relevant anatomy and physiology

2   Altitude physiology

3   Biodynamics

4   Environmental sciences

5   Perceptual sciences

6   The human factors/medical interface

7   Pilot incapacitation and medical certification

8   Clinical medicine in the fitness to fly category

9   Occupational medicine

10   Environmental health

11   Special operations: air ambulances, high altitude, etc.

Relevant anatomy and physiology sciences must be taught at an appropriate level. For example, medical practitioners in a postgraduate medical course still require a revision of undergraduate anatomy and physiology. In addition, depending on the subject matter, they may require a new approach and greater level of detail than that normally taught in order to understand the specialist aviation medicine topic area. For example, an understanding of altitude physiology or biodynamics at a medical specialist level requires a very detailed underpinning of cardiorespiratory physiology in both cases. In many cases, at an undergraduate level the basic biological sciences can be relatively focused and abbreviated if the audience shows adequate precourse competency in the area.

Problems tend to arise for distance taught courses where it is much more difficult to evaluate the adequacy of precourse experience and understanding as teaching proceeds. For many extramural courses, it has to be assumed that students have no biological sciences background and provision made for this before the commencement of the course proper. This can be provided by inclusion of a foundation biological sciences reader in the first module of the course. If available a course in basic biological sciences, with exemptions for those suitably qualified, can be specified as a pre-requisite for any aviation medicine paper.

Altitude physiology embraces a variety of topics, all of them sharing a common focus on the effects of reduced ambient and partial pressures of oxygen and nitrogen. The discussion of hypoxia is usually linked to the nature and effects of hyperventilation, sometimes causally linked with hypoxia. The reduced effects of ambient pressure are usually discussed only in the context of decompression illness, effects on gases in body cavities, and pulmonary barotrauma with arterial gas embolism. However, the discussions may be extended with more sophisticated audiences to the nature of diving related dysbarism and 'mountain sickness'. Altitude physiology training is often a statutory requirement for air crews engaged in air transport operations above 10,000 feet pressure altitude. This may tend to place some constraints on the syllabus as students often feel obligated to focus on those aspects they know will be examined.

Biodynamics embraces the sciences of both long term acceleration and short to medium term accelerations such as occur in impact and ejection escape. The biodynamic sciences are extremely complex requiring a good knowledge of physiology and physics. Depending on the depth to which the subject is taught, the biodynamics training curriculum tends to be focused on practical applications, such as improving g-tolerance or G-LOC avoidance measures. Acceleration physiology is generally only taught as far as it is required to permit an understanding of how g tolerance may be reduced or increased, and how g protection measures work. The avoidance of such factors and measures are central to the prevention of pilot incapacitation due to long term acceleration.

The focus on g protection measures in order to improve g tolerance for fast jet military crews as an air combat manoeuvring (ACM) enhancement tool often extends the training requirements. For example, training is often given in the correct way to perform the Anti-G Straining Manoeuvre (AGSM). This may be based on films and classroom training, practised in dual flight. However, some military organizations, notably the USAF train and screen their fast jet crews in the more controlled high g environment of a centrifuge. This permits students to practise their AGSM performance, and demonstrate its effectiveness in improving g tolerance to themselves. It also provides an opportunity for teaching staff to monitor performance and provide feedback to the student on errors in performing the AGSM. This is particularly effective when video records are available. The centrifuge g profile test not only provides an excellent practical training and performance assessment tool, it also does permit screening of crews. For example, some pilots who meet the fast jet medical standards will have major difficulties with g tolerance. This is particularly of concern on some instances where otherwise healthy individuals demonstrate cardiac abnormalities in a high g environment. The significance of some electrocardiograph (ECG) changes may not be clear, but high g related cardiac events on the centrifuge that may reduce the effectiveness of the heart as a pump raise concern about fitness to engage in ACM flight.

Environmental sciences deal with those factors in the aviation environment that affect human performance and health. In particular, these include as a subset altitude physiology and biodynamics as particular relevance to aviation. Additional topics include the thermal environment, noise, vibration, and radiation. These should be differentiated from those effects that aviation might have on the local environment and ecological stability. The topic is particularly important because of the reduction in pilot performance and flight safety that might arise from such environmental factors. The ability to control the environment local to pilots and other aviation workers now means that there is a significant potential to improve safety through environmental control designed to enhance pilot performance. The effect of those environmental factors that adversely affect the longer term health and well-being of pilots is also of serious concern. For example the effect of solar ultraviolet light and blue light in the cockpit to cause health problems such as cataracts should be recognized and dealt with promptly. These environmental factors affecting pilot performance may not necessarily fall into the usual categorization of the causes of hazards into physical, chemical or biological groups. For example factors such as psychological stress, fatigue or circadian dysrhythmia may have major effects on pilot performance with much greater variability, and the attendant problems of measurement and assessment.

Perceptual sciences dealing with the visual and orientation systems in particular are of special significance in the aviation setting. The structure and function of the eye are an essential prelude to discussion of the avoidance of collisions or serious visual illusions. The effect of acceleration or low grade hypoxia on visual performance under marginal visual performance conditions can address ways in which solutions may be found.

On the other hand, while spatial disorientation is better understood once the basic principles of vestibular physiology are communicated, there is less opportunity to utilize this as a preventative measure. The reasons for this are complex; the role of the vestibular and proprioceptive systems in spatial orientation are less clear than for visual illusions. The vestibular system for example is less clearly involved in the orientation of pilots as a discrete function in flight, being primarily a perceptual control for eye movements and postural righting reflexes. The integration of a variety of sensory inputs and the way this affects the development of spatial disorientation is best illustrated by the 'giant phenomenon'. The various inputs may be involved in a variety of orientational functions so that postural reflexes and conscious attempts to maintain orientation by pilots are mutually incompatible. The teaching of spatial disorientation has objectives that are not perhaps as clear as they may at first appear. The way in which the semi-circular canals and otoliths contribute to the classical illusions of 'pitch up', 'graveyard spiral' and 'the leans' does not provide an inventory of ways in which spatial disorientation may be avoided. Such classical illusions are rare, and contribute to only a small proportion of aircraft accidents where spatial disorientation is the principal cause. In the majority of such accidents, a disproportionate number of which are fatal, the cause was a non-specific loss of situational awareness rather than the evolution of a specific classical illusion. The teaching objective is therefore to distrust perceptual information in favour of instrument data, and recognize the limitations or inapplicability of the vestibular system to orientation in flight.

The human factors/medical interface is difficult to define and the controversy over whose specialist knowledge is paramount is often irreconcilable. This in particular occurs where there are physiological bases for decrements in human performance of a psychological nature. Spatial disorientation fatigue and vision are common boundary areas. The common interests in these subjects can be handled positively but often are dealt with badly. The vital nature of such subjects to aviation safety means that this grey area is ignored at the teacher's peril. Medical and psychology specialists have both a great deal to offer and may present quite different, but complementary perspectives, to the same subject, to the students' benefit. Overlaps and pragmatic difficulties in programming lectures may sometimes mean that there is an element of repetition that students find irksome, but this is preferable to gaps in the curriculum because topics are not considered to be in one area or the other. The interface should present opportunities to teach better and with a broader base, rather than a challenge or problem to be overcome.

Pilot incapacitation risk and medical certification standards are central to the routine medical examinations of air crew. Despite this, these concepts are often poorly understood by pilots and doctors alike. The effects of sudden or progressive dysfunction in various bodily systems on the risk of pilot incapacitation must be clearly understood. The nature of pilot incapacitation must be clearly defined in operational rather than clinical terms, as these are more useful to pilots when developing concepts of the avoidance of illness likely to cause acute incapacitation.

This approach is of much greater utility when developing pilot incapacitation training programmes. It also makes quite explicit the limitations of routine medical examinations as a screening tool in preventing acute incapacitation, and the responsibilities of air crew to self monitor for premonitory changes or symptoms. The commonest cause of pilot incapacitation is acute gastro-intestinal upset, due either to food poisoning or viral gastro-enteritis. This and other common causes of in-flight incapacitation are not likely to be detected at routine medical examinations and are not preventable except by appropriate pilot response to any 'warning signs'. The inability of practicable screening tests such as resting ECGs to detect 'silent' (meaning symptomless) coronary artery disease requires attention to changes in health or performance by prompt access to medical advice. Despite this, 25% of cases of sudden death due to coronary artery disease occur in pilots with no previous symptoms. The recent death of a British Airways captain while taking in- flight rest is good example.

Clinical medicine in the fitness to fly category is similar to the above, but rather than relating to sudden incapacitation risk is designed to assess the ability of the pilot to perform the tasks required for flying. This in particular focuses on the capabilities to see and hear adequately, but the functional aspects of many body systems may play a vital role in flying activities. The level of functional capability and its effect on human performance are more precisely defined than sudden incapacitation risk. The visual acuity and colour perception capability required for pilots are still the subject for considerable debate. The majority of visual and colour perception tests performed in the course of routine medical examinations are screening tests, designed to pick up those individuals who require more detailed assessments rather than being functional thresholds in their own right.

Occupational medicine is a crucial aspect of aviation medicine. The principles of health promotion and protection for people at work extend to every aspect of aviation medicine practice. The cockpit or flight deck are the place of work for many pilots, and even private pilots are in effect 'working' while flying even for recreation. The basic tenets of occupational health are that the work or the working environment should not harm the worker, and that the health status or other characteristics should not adversely affect the performance of work tasks. These principles are well developed in aviation medicine. Other participants in the aviation industry are more clearly engaged in some sort of occupation. For example, cabin attendants, air traffic controllers, airline traffic staff and baggage handlers are all engaged in occupations with recognized occupational health hazards. The hazards for cabin attendants are in particular burns and traumatic injuries sustained while preparing food in flight, lifting baggage or pushing trolleys. Less obvious hazards include the potential exposure to harmful doses of radiation by the foetus where cabin crew are permitted to continue flying duties while pregnant. Traffic staff and baggage handlers suffer a disproportionate number of back injuries from lifting heavy cases often in constrained or awkward postures. The exposure of air traffic controllers to occupational stress has been well recognized and perhaps even over-emphasized. However, they also suffer from many of the potential health problems associated with prolonged use of visual display units, such as ergonomic disorders and visual strain.

Environmental health issues are particularly associated with the effect of the aviation industry on the local environment closely surrounding airports. These especially include the duration timing and intensity of noise due to large jet aircraft during take off and climb out phases. The potential for environmental and atmospheric pollution by jet and piston engine exhaust emissions are a significant concern. For those whose responsibilities include advice to airport authorities concerning the health aspects of their enterprise, these may be important topics.

Special Operations: There are particular topics that will be taught in response to the special circumstances in which they are involved in aviation. This will usually relate to their involvement in air transport operations where passenger considerations become prominent. Topics of particular relevance to this area include the factors that determine passenger cabin safety, and travel health. Passenger cabin safety factors include the operation and design of flights and aircraft to permit safe emergency evacuation, the prevention of effects of in-flight fires, and the safe design of aircraft structures to minimize the potential for injuries to passengers.

Travel health will cover a broad range of subjects from the fitness of passengers with recognized medical problems to fly, the prevention and management of in-flight medical emergencies, and the threat to travellers' health from a vast range of tropical diseases. The carriage of invalid passengers by air and the use of aircraft as ambulances may be a speciality in its own right for those whose work involves this; a number of aviation medicine practitioners are anaesthetists and intensive care specialists who work with air ambulance services.

Military aviation medicine has been the most active practice area in aviation medicine since 1914 (Ernsting and King, 1988). The recognition of many environmental and operational factors that reduced pilot performance took place in the First World War. These included the effects of flying in cloud and high g flying in aerial combat. The first episode of GILOC considered by many to be a modern phenomenon associated with highly manoeuvrable aircraft occurred in 1918 in a Sopwith Triplane at 4 1/2 g. The Second World War saw many other developments in aviation medicine that were regarded as essential for maximum pilot performance. These included the development of reliable oxygen equipment that would operate in a high g environment for fighters. Other equipment had to meet the needs of the many unpressurized aircraft such as transport aircraft and bombers that flew at high altitude for prolonged periods of time with large numbers of crew and passengers. The increased speed and manoeuvrability also drove the development of g pants and anti g straining manoeuvres. There was also an increasing problem of escape at high velocity, which led to the development of the ejection seats. Often these developments were being pursued by both friendly and enemy forces, sometimes with considerable common ground between the two separate research programmes, and in others remarkably different ways of finding alternative solutions to the same problem. The wars in Korea, Vietnam and the Cold War maintained the pace of aviation medicine research and development. The needs of the high altitude nuclear deterrent aircraft and photo-reconnaissance 'spy planes' for special protection in terms of cabin pressurization and personal protection in the event of breach or failure of cabin pressurization led the way in high altitude research, until the development of Concorde.

The first balloonists were often qualified doctors or physiologists such as Paul Bert and later Haldane for whom flight was a means to perform research into the nature of the atmosphere and respiration. Aviation medicine, which is as old as aviation itself, really came into its own with the development of medical fitness standards for air crew in the First World War, and these standards became applied to civilian air crew in the following decade (DeHart, 1985). Bauer in the USA was the first to formalize any medical standards for civil air crews using those developed in the preceding Great War. These were later adopted by ICAO, and application to air crews around the world became effectively universal. This has been in part been driven by the military but also by the work of dedicated aviation medicine specialists working with the respective civil aviation authorities of each country and the aviation medicine research and teaching establishments.

**The medium**

The medium for teaching will be determined by the needs of students and the availability of the appropriate technology. The needs of many students to gain access to training while still in their normal place of work has led to a burgeoning of distance teaching courses in the subject. However, many courses are still based on the orthodox classroom approach, where students are taught face to face.

The practical nature of aviation medicine and related topics will inevitably impose a requirement for a certain amount of live student participation and personal experience of aviation related activities. The availability of special teaching material is often enhanced by research establishments who are able to replicate a number of the environmental stressors in aviation. The use of centrifuges, decompression chambers and climatic chambers for personal experience based training is very effective as a measure to reinforce the material first taught in theory. There are many aspects of aviation which are best taught by personal exposure, such as aircraft simulation, the cockpit environment and complex operations such as airlines and the military.

There have been a number of courses offered in aviation medicine, based on an attendance classroom and personal experience teaching medium. This is often preferable for short courses and those which demand high levels of personal participation or experience. In many cases, aviation medicine training courses may serve other purposes such as the fitting of specialized flying equipment or routine medical examinations. The advantages of such courses is that they are relatively dense in terms of student contact time, and permit a larger number of concepts to be explored and taught in short space of time. The attendance structure course also facilitates the arrangement of visits and personal experience training such as the simulation of hypoxia, either in a decompression chamber or oxygen dilution chamber. Students also have the benefit of learning from the experiences of each other and from informal contact time with teaching staff. The disadvantage is that if the course extends beyond a few days, students may find the costs of training increase in terms of absence from work or home. In countries where the training establishments are far away from many students or where students have to travel overseas for training, the costs of training and the likelihood that there will be ready access to training is markedly reduced.

The result has been that many courses are now distance taught. These may use a variety of media that are available. The correspondence based course which relies solely on written materials may be very limiting to students if there is no access to a local tutor and opportunities for personal experience. The personal experience drawbacks can be overcome by ensuring that students have ready access to the tutor, by phone fax or E-mail. The basic correspondence course is usually supplemented by live personal experience based work at a residential school or practicum session. These may be single or multiple, and the relative contribution to the course material may be quite high (Rayman, 1993).

Many lectures may be given in audiotape or video form, or by simultaneous broadcast, using University networks or public TV channels. These provide the student with educational material, facts images and concepts that may add to, replace, or supplement material in written form. The provision of alternative teaching materials in non-written media may be chosen because the medium is more appropriate to the teaching objectives. For example, didactic 'lecture' form teaching may be given in the form of audio and videocassettes because a truly interactive medium is not required, except that students and teachers alike may follow up the 'lecture' with a series of questions.

In addition to written and other didactic teaching material, there is a considerable need for interactive work by students and teachers, that does not necessarily imply that personal attendance is required. For example, some courses are heavily based on teleconferencing, either audio only or audio and video based. These enable students truly at a distance to interact in a tutorial or lecture setting while in different countries or continents. More recent initiatives (Autunano, 1993) have seen the use of computer technology based training such as computer based/aided training, expert systems, embedded training, E-mail and simulators for structured self directed learning by students. This may be supplemented by learning through the acquisition of information from databases such as CD roms, digital video interactive, and hypermedia.

## Considerations in teaching aviation medicine

The teaching of aviation medicine requires a number of key competencies:

1. Good communication skills.

2. A general grasp of aviation medicine, physiology and human performance.

3. A special interest and enthusiasm for the subject generally and in certain areas.

4. An ability to build empathy with the students, understanding their needs and wants from a training syllabus.

5. Credibility to be able to speak with authority on aviation related matters.

6. The credibility issues has often been addressed by using only medical and human factors staff who have a flying qualification. This certainly helps with the ability to empathize and project but should not be considered an absolute prerequisite.

Good access to library and other database resources is obviously essential, but very few libraries carry the full range of material needed for a comprehensive knowledge of all subjects that may be required. As a result many teachers find they need to have access to a research facility that can obtain and provide teaching materials that may be required. In addition, staff at these centres will usually be abreast of recent developments and future plans that may not be yet in the textbooks and journals.

The breadth of the subjects required means that there will be a wide range of lecturer skills and teaching resource materials required to cover the subject comprehensively. The degree to which this can be devolved to a number of staff will depend on the local availability of skills and experience among teaching staff. As always, a love of the subject and good research and teaching skills can permit staff who do not have the specialized aspects of subject as their major career focus to nonetheless provide effective and well received training.

## References

Autunano M.J. (1993) 'Use of advanced technology in distance education'. *Aviation Space & Environmental Medicine*, 64 (9) 876.

DeHart R.L. (1985) *Fundamentals of Aerospace Medicine*, Lea & Febiger, Philadelphia.

Ernsting J. & King P., (1988) *Aviation Medicine* 2nd Edn, Butterworths London.

Rayman (1993) Personal Communication.

# Human factors instruction- some specific applications

# 15 Training accident investigators for the human factors investigation

*Dmitri V. Zotov*

## Introduction

Human factors are involved in about 70% of all air accidents. It is almost universally recognized by the authorities responsible for accident investigation that, if we are to make a significant improvement in present accident rates, we will have to investigate the human factors involved more effectively than has been the case in the past. Investigators need to be trained to identify human failures just as well as they now identify mechanical malfunctions. In designing training to this end, there are two principal considerations:

1. What knowledge do investigators need to identify human factors effectively?

2. How should this knowledge be presented?

*The provision of training*

It might be a good idea to start by considering the function of formal training in the overall scheme of an investigator's training. Training in this very practical art is essentially an apprenticeship. The trainee starts by accompanying an experienced investigator, and learns by observation. Over a period of time he will participate in progressively more complex investigations, taking on more of the load, until he is capable of undertaking the lead role himself. The International Society of Air Safety Investigators has established, as basic criteria for admission as a Member, minima of five years experience and participation in the investigation of ten accidents. This seems to me, from experience both as trainee and trainer, to be a reasonable level to be reached before the investigator can be considered fully competent.

Organizations vary in the way in which they present their formal training. Some prefer, say, one two-week course each year; others start with a long introductory course of perhaps a couple of months duration. Either way, formal instruction is unlikely to comprise more than 5% of the total training. We must therefore keep in mind that formal training is an adjunct to practical instruction, rather than being complete in itself.

While such training produces competent investigators, there may also be a need to address recurrent training. There is an ever-increasing body of knowledge in some fields, for example systems (fly-by wire and 'glass cockpits') and structures (such as composites and dynamic gust response). Human factors is, of course, such a field. At present, keeping up to date is generally left to the individual, particularly through the medium of the Journal of the International Society of Air Safety Investigators. While not decrying this approach, accident investigators tend to be very busy investigating accidents. Like the woodsman who was so busy chopping down trees he had no time to sharpen his axe, investigators may have neither the time nor the energy to study new developments. Taking time out for an updating course may be the solution, provided that the course is purpose-designed, covering only new material and its application. We must not tell investigators what they already know, or we shall lose their attention through boredom. From experience, two weeks seems to be about the maximum time for which organizations can spare staff for such courses. If the material is strictly limited to what is essential, this should be adequate for an annual or biennial update.

Separate from the question of recurrent training is the provision of human factors training for experienced investigators who learnt their craft before the importance of human factors was appreciated. You may meet entrenched resistance when trying to put across the need for human factors to such investigators - this is discussed later - but apart from dealing with this, they will benefit from the full course that you would provide for novice trainees. For all their expertise elsewhere, they are novices in this field.

Generally, formal training for accident investigators has been provided by external agencies, such as the University of Southern California and Cranfield Institute of Technology. There is a sound reason for this: the time taken to set up a course, to teach it, and to keep it up to date is more or less independent of the number of students. To train investigators in-house can only be cost-effective for very large organizations, such as the United States Air Force. Moreover, in a rapidly developing field such as human factors, an investigative agency may have neither the sources of information nor the time to keep sufficiently abreast of developments. And universities, in particular, have resources for, and expertise in teaching - something sadly lacking in some of the in-house courses the author has experienced.

However, a word of caution in staffing the course. Accident investigators need to be very experienced in aviation, in part so that they have credibility within the aviation community. In exactly the same way, the training that you provide needs credibility. It is equally essential that the training be controlled, and generally presented, by experienced investigators. By all means call in doctors, ergonomists and psychologists to lecture in their particular fields, but this should be the jam in the sandwich, not the bread and butter.

## What the investigator needs to know

It would be tempting to think that, as pilots are involved in accidents, and investigators are generally pilots, it would suffice to put investigators through the same human factors training that pilots now receive. While such training is part of the picture, without modification it would be both too much and too little.

Consider, for example, crew resource management (CRM), now widely accepted as a tool for minimizing vulnerability to error, and for coping with the unexpected. The pilot needs to know what CRM is and how it can help him; further, he needs training (perhaps by Line Oriented Flight Training) in its practical application. The end product, from the pilot's point of view, is the ability to use CRM to avoid or avert accident situations.

The investigator must also know what CRM is, but needs also a deeper knowledge of why it is necessary, since he may have to recommend its introduction to others who may need convincing. He has less need to practice its practical application. However, the real difference is that the investigator must be able to recognize when the absence of CRM was a causal factor in an accident.

To train the investigator in CRM we must not only demonstrate the practical need for it and how it may be achieved, but also examine the theoretical background. Then we look at accidents which show the absence of CRM: a functioning Cockpit Voice Recorder is nice to have, but not essential; we might also look for failure by the monitoring pilot to detect errors, and a lot can be learned from ATC tapes.

So, while we should certainly expose the investigator to the human factors considerations in which we train pilots, that training needs to be considerably modified to be of best value to the investigator.

It would be a reasonable assumption, now and for many years to come, that investigators have had little human factors training during their flying careers, other than aviation medicine. They are, of necessity, people of wide aviation experience, and their flying training will have pre-dated the introduction of human factors into the pilot training syllabus. Where the investigator has primarily an engineering background it is even less likely that he will have had any formal human factors training.

But in addition to human factors for pilots, the accident investigator needs knowledge which a pilot would find esoteric. Some of this is needed during the field investigation: an investigator must know how to elicit information from witnesses, and why witnesses err in good faith; he must be able to evaluate witness information and draw inferences from it; and he must become familiar with body language, since he will be lied to by experts.

Another such area of knowledge is pathology, sufficient at least to understand what the pathologist is telling him, and to realize the limitations of that information.

Leading on from pathology is crashworthiness and survivability - why did the victims die? It is the investigator's job to make recommendations to minimize the effects of accidents, as well as to avoid them, and so he must be familiar with impact kinematics, aircraft structures and their response to impact, restraint and protective systems, optimum design of the airfield environment, fire and evacuation.

The investigation of collisions and airmisses is almost invariably an investigation into the human factors behind them - limitations of vision, design of Air Traffic Service systems, design of cockpits, and workloads.

This brings us to the area of corporate and management failures - Professor Reason's 'latent failures' which are behind many major disasters. The investigator needs to be familiar with the Helmreich (1990) and Reason (1990) concepts of the influence of factors beyond the cockpit.

> In 1989, a Fokker F28 commuter jet airliner attempted to take off from Dryden, Ontario, with thick snow on the wings. The aircraft got airborne, but failed to climb out of ground effect, struck trees and caught fire. The crew were aware that it had been snowing during their stopover in Dryden, and the real question for the investigators was, how

could a very experienced pilot (24 000 hours) make such a faulty decision to attempt the take-off? Dr R.L. Helmreich was appointed to assist the Commission of Inquiry with the human factors investigation. He considered the 'environments' within which the crew operated: the crew itself, and its communications with the outside world; the physical environment, including the aircraft with its distinctive characteristics, and the meteorological conditions; the organizational environment, for example the support or lack of it provided by the airline; and the regulatory environment, provided by the Department of Transport by regulations, surveillance and other monitoring.

Helmreich visualized this series of environments as concentric spheres of influence, each affecting those inside. With this crew-centred model, he was able to show how deficiencies in the outer environments combined to produce pressures on the crew. While no one deficiency, of itself, was likely to have caused the accident, the sum total resulted in pressures such that the crew decided to take off without, apparently, considering the effect of snow on the aircraft's performance.

Professor Reason studied a series of major disasters, including Chernobyl and Bhopal. He formed a view of accident causation, at least in a highly regulated industry such as airline operations, in which accidents are the result of systems failure. The active errors made by the crew at the sharp end are the end-product of latent failures which result from faulty decisions within the organization concerned, often long before the accident. Reason uses the analogy of pathogens waiting within the body to cause a disease when the right conditions occur. He suggests looking for precursor events, and failure of the feedback loops which should have alerted the organization to the deficiencies, enabling corrective action prior to an accident.

The investigator will usually start by investigating deficient actions by the crew, and be led back to the factors in the surrounding environments which potentiated those actions, before seeking the defects in the organizational systems which permitted them. He therefore needs to be familiar with both concepts.

Table 1 is presented as a guide to course designers. It is reasonably comprehensive, but no claim is made as to completeness. The horizontal divisions indicate suggested break points, so that the course can be subdivided into a number of elements, each requiring about two weeks of full time instruction, if this approach is preferred.

**Table 15.1 Elements of Human Factors training for air accident investigators**

| | |
|---|---|
| **FIELD INVESTIGATION** | |
| Witnesses | Interviewing techniques |
| | Deficiencies |
| | Analysis of information |
| | Body Language |
| | |
| Pathology | Injuries and their implications |
| | Disaster Victim Identification |
| **CRASHWORTHINESS AND SURVIVABILITY** | |
| Impact Kinematics | |
| Structural Response | |
| | |
| Restraint and protection | Harnesses |
| | Clothing |
| | Helmets |
| | Impact Absorption |
| | |
| Fire | Minimization |
| | Suppression |
| | Evacuation |
| | Smokehoods |
| | |
| Aerodromes | Environment |
| | Rescue Fire Services |
| **THE HUMAN** | |
| The Body | Functions |
| | Food and oxygen |
| | Alcohol |
| | Medication |
| | Stress |
| | Sleep, Dysrhythmia and Fatigue |
| Ergonomics | Fitting the pilot to the cockpit |

| | |
|---|---|
| **THE MIND** | |
| Perception | The Somatogravic Illusion |
| | Visual Illusions |
| | The Black Hole |
| | |
| Human Error | Information Processing |
| | Error Taxonomy |
| | |
| Flicker Vertigo | |
| **ORGANIZATION** | |
| Crew Resource Management | |
| Airmisses and Collisions | |
| Engineering accidents | |
| External Factors | The Helmreich Model |
| | The Reason Model |

**Training the investigator**

I was waiting to meet a colleague, in a provincial airport, before going to the scene of an accident.

> 'There he is', said my wife - quite rightly.
> 'How did you know?' I asked, for she had never met him.
> 'Well', she replied, 'He *looks* like an Inspector of Air Accidents'.

Now I am unsure that looks have much to do with the selection of accident investigators, but there is no doubt that they are different from the average student, or the average aviator, for that matter. Consider the qualifications that are required even before starting to learn the craft: A wide aviation background, minima of an Air Transport Pilot Licence and 3000 hours as pilot in command are commonly required for pilots. Engineers are usually required to be at least a Chartered Engineer with flying experience. A military background is often preferred, since there is no better training in commanding the large numbers of personnel and highly expensive resources that may be needed on an accident site.

It follows, then that accident investigators are not young: they already have one, and sometimes two, successful careers behind them.

In imparting knowledge to them, therefore, you will need to adopt a different approach from that which might be successful with undergraduates or young pilots. An interactive lecturing style is unlikely to be effective, especially where this is designed to show gaps in the class's knowledge and so lead to the next topic. The students may indeed be ignorant, but they do not like to be shown to be ignorant, especially in front of their contemporaries. They look to you to fill in the gaps in their knowledge, not to demonstrate your own superiority.

The importance of this can hardly be overemphasized. I once saw a most distinguished lecturer so antagonize a class in this way that they asked for him to be withdrawn from lecturing to the course. I doubt that the class absorbed much of what he said.

You are dealing with people with a lifetime of practical experience, who are used to positions of considerable authority. Treat them as intelligent equals: be careful not to 'talk down' to them. Successful lecturers in this environment use a style where information is presented directly, with as many illustrations from real accidents as possible.

Keep in mind the age of your students: they may have relatively poor short-term memory recall, and therefore need to reinforce lectures by reading. Supplement your lectures by comprehensive printed notes, which will act as a reference and aide-memoire in years to come.

Minimize the number of references you quote. Dozens of references and footnotes will merely irritate your students: they have neither the time nor the facilities to follow them up. Keep your references to those things they will find useful - standard texts, detailed explanations too long to go in your notes, and so on. To the greatest extent possible, your notes should be self-contained.

An alternative to conventional lecture-based courses is extramural study. Senior people may not take too kindly to sitting for long periods in class. On the other hand, they will be well used to learning on their own, having usually gained their professional qualifications in this way. I have found extramural courses to be gratifyingly successful. While it is difficult to include much 'hands on' training in such a course, other than by on-campus seminars, this is not really a handicap: the necessary 'hands on' training will be obtained during the 95% of training that is on the job.

## Overcoming resistance to human factors investigation

As recently as 1990, a major investigating authority was teaching its new inspectors that it was better not to discuss human factors, because they could not be 'proved'. Aviation psychology has been described as 'piling speculation on hypothesis'. Particularly if you are dealing with experienced investigators, you are likely to encounter considerable resistance to psychology and sociology, which are regarded as 'soft' sciences, incapable of producing the precise results provided by engineering and physics. Be prepared for this, and be ready to show the uncertainty that an investigator may encounter when dealing with physical evidence.

Some physical evidence is ephemeral (eg icing) or can be established only within wide bands (metal fatigue); meteorology may offer little substantiating evidence (local and temporary windshear). But these uncertain factors produce very real effects, and of course cannot be ignored. Likewise with operations investigation: a witness estimate of '1000 feet' may in reality represent anywhere between 500 and 2000 feet, depending on circumstances. But 'fuzzy' evidence, whether physical or human factors, is none-the-less evidence, and should not be discarded just because there is an element of uncertainty about it. Taken in conjunction with other evidence, it may provide a valuable insight into the circumstances of the accident. (O'Hare, 1990).

Conversely, some human factors evidence can be very clear-cut - for example, reaction times in given circumstances, or the certainty of illusions such as the somatogravic effect.

We might then persuade the horse to partake of the water by reviewing accidents in which human factors have played a part, starting with those where there is clear-cut physical evidence. An accident such as the 'wrong runway' landing at Gatwick (Air Accident Investigation Branch Report No AAR 2/89) might be a good starting point:

> The aircraft was returning from overseas, and would be making a night landing. The crew were aware that the parallel runway was closed for maintenance, and the secondary parallel runway (to the left of the main runway as the crew approached) was in use. They saw two parallel sets of lights, that to the left having a green centreline and no edge lighting. The radar approach had aligned the aircraft with the right set of lights. The copilot queried which runway they were approaching, and the captain, thinking that this was a prompt, realigned the aircraft with the left-hand set. In fact, the left-hand set was the taxiway, the right-hand

lights were for the secondary runway, and the main runway lights were off.

Heavy braking and reverse thrust were required during the landing roll, but the aircraft stopped short of another aircraft which was on the taxiway at the time. This latter aircraft tried to turn off onto the grass when its pilot realized what was happening, but became bogged and was unable to clear the taxiway completely.

It transpired that the captain of the landing aircraft originally thought he was correctly aligned (as he was) but when prompted by the copilot he thought both runways must be lit. The secondary runway was normally used as a taxiway when the main runway was in use, and when so used it had taxiway lighting. Neither pilot knew that when it was used as a runway, the secondary runway had ICAO standard lighting.

Because the crew were alive to describe both what they had seen and their thought processes, it was possible to make a positive analysis of this accident. Illustrations in the report showing what the crew saw indicate how easy it was for them to be deceived, the taxiway lighting having features very similar to runway lighting. This accident illustrates a number of human factors in an entirely convincing fashion

With real world examples to grasp, the investigator is more likely to be receptive to a general overview of human factors.

To be convincing, such an overview would have to go beyond a bald presentation of results. For example, I was recently told by a very experienced investigator that he could not accept that a pilot could misread a three-pointer altimeter by 1000 feet: it was only misreading by 10 000 feet that caused accidents, so only turbine-powered aircraft needed digital altimeters. If such an attitude is to be overcome, it will be necessary to produce chapter and verse - in this case, of course, Dr Rolfe's work at Farnborough in the 1960s:

> From the early days of flight, barometric altimeters had used a pointer presentation. At first a single pointer was enough; as greater precision was required for night and instrument flying, a second smaller pointer was used to indicate thousands of feet, the larger pointer showing hundreds. When aircraft began flying above 20 000 feet a third, small 'tens of thousands' pointer was added.
>
> In the 1960s two airliners flew into the ground under control, each having reported at ten thousand feet. Clearly, the crews had misread their altimeters. RAE Farnborough were tasked with finding out why

this should be, and how to correct it. The result is the digital presentation used today on all large airliners, and the problem was overcome.

However, in the course of his investigation, Dr Rolfe discovered that not only was the ten thousand pointer susceptible to misreading, but that the thousand foot pointer was even more likely to be misread. (Rolfe, 1963).

Now misreading by 1000 feet while flying visually may not usually be very important (though it could lead to infringement of controlled airspace) but now that many light aircraft are being flown under IFR (particularly light twins being flown on scheduled services since the deregulation of airlines) the consequences of misreading by 1000 feet may be just as serious as misreading by 10 000 feet used to be. There have been documented cases of aircraft flying into the ground about 1000 feet below their reported height. Rather than the facile explanation that the pilot was trying to mislead the controller by false reporting, and was trying to fly visually below cloud, it is far more likely that, just as with the airliners in the 1960s, the pilot had misread his 3 pointer altimeter.

Then one could present a management-related accident with clear physical evidence - the windowless BAC 111 (AAIB Report No AAR **1/92**) suggests itself (inadequate staffing, perceived time pressure, supervisory deficiencies, poor lighting, badly organized stores), leading to a more general discussion of corporate factors:

> As the aircraft climbed towards 20 000 feet the left windscreen blew out. The commander was sucked halfway out the windscreen aperture, but was restrained by the cabin crew while the copilot flew the aircraft to a safe landing.
>
> The windscreen had been replaced before flight. Cabin pressure had overcome the securing bolts, 84 of which (out of a total of 90) were of less than the specified diameter.
>
> Maintenance was usually performed at night. The shift was short-staffed, and the available engineers were involved in a higher priority task. Although the aircraft was not required next day, the engineering manager was aware that the next shift was also short-staffed, so he decided to change the windscreen himself. Finding the part numbers for the replacement bolts would have been a time-consuming task, the

manager selected replacement bolts by matching them with those he removed.

There were only a few bolts of this size in the stores, so he sought more in another cabinet in a poorly lit area. He identified what he thought were identical bolts by feel, the light being insufficient to read the faded drawer labels. These bolts were, in fact, slightly thinner.

When the manager torqued the bolts, the feel as the torquedriver slipped met his expectations. What was actually happening was that the threads were catching only in the locking portion of the anchor nuts, and slipping in these when torqued up.

There were cues that could have shown that incorrect bolts were fitted: the bolt heads were smaller than the countersunk area in which they were fitted; a few of the original bolts were refitted, but the difference in feel when these were torqued up was not detected. Next night the manager changed another windscreen using different bolts, but he rationalized this by deciding that the aircraft were at different modification states.

There was no duplicate inspection, nor was there required to be.

At the policy level the Leeds/Bradford overrun (AAIB Report No **2/87**) would be illuminating - the aircraft was operated entirely within the certification boundaries, which brings into question the whole certification process.

**Instructing and testing**

Accident investigation is a very practical subject. Your students will grasp what you are telling them better if you avoid abstraction as far as possible. Use the many examples from real accident investigations: valuable lessons can be learnt by re-examining past investigations where human factors have been ignored or down-played. Naturally, when we are discussing engineering phenomena like metal fatigue, we use physical examples that the students can see and touch. Past accident reports are the human factors equivalent, and are even better if they can be supported by the actual evidence gained at the time.

When the theoretical aspects have been presented, follow up with a fair sprinkling of 'How I dunnit' reviews of investigations, by the Investigator in Charge. These can cover the methods of investigation in much more detail than is available in formal reports - the preliminary hypotheses, the wrong turnings, the insight that pointed the way to the final conclusion.

Wide though the field is, human factors comprises only a fraction of the knowledge that an investigator needs; from metallurgy to meteorology, aerodynamics to aviation law. The range is far too great for any individual to master. What is necessary is that he has been exposed to such knowledge, sufficiently to recognize factors when he sees them; and knows where to look for detailed information, and whom to ask.

It follows that there is no merit in the students learning facts per se; a fortiori there is no merit in conventional examinations. Besides, in the real world of accident investigation, the work is 'open book', and there are no significant time constraints. We are trying to educate our students to work effectively in this real world. They are sufficiently intelligent and experienced to recognize this for themselves. What we seek to impart are principles of investigation, so that, when the time comes, the investigator will be able to apply the knowledge that is available.

With extramural courses we can both test the students' understanding, and at the same time provide the opportunity for learning in a controlled environment, by setting assignments. We are not concerned here with lists of facts, or writing polished essays: we want the students to analyze situations using the information we have provided. (By all means ask them to list things, as a way of guiding their thoughts in the right direction, but keep in mind that the list is a means, not an end).

A successful method is to provide the students with pertinent information from real investigations, and have the students analyze these in the light of what they have been studying. For example, having studied workload and information processing, give them the data to analyze from an accident in which the pilot became overloaded.

By suitable choice of scenario you can also require the students to do the sort of research that would be needed in real life. A cabin fire accident in an F27, for example, would require them to locate an F27, or the Manuals, or someone who has flown one, in order to discover the difficulties in operating the exits, and sources of fuel and ignition, in the particular circumstances.

With an internal course, time constraints may make realistic assignments more difficult to devise. If you ask more limited questions, they may be of more limited value in getting students thinking along the right lines. A better way is to take advantage of having the students together to introduce them to the collegiate approach which is a feature of real investigation. By having a group working on a problem, apportioning the work among themselves and synthesizing the individual efforts to produce a final result, a surprisingly large assignment can be tackled in a relatively short time. To the objection that this does not allow individual grading of students, the rejoinder is 'so what?' We are not trying to select investigators - that has been done already - nor is there any point in ranking them in order of merit. We are simply trying to make them more effective in their work, and group assignments have proved very effective in doing so.

As much benefit can be gained from the individual critique of assignments, as from writing them. Here the tutor must be prepared to spend considerable time on each student's work. This will vary between assignments and between students (the more able students usually requiring less time) but a band of two to three hours per paper would not be out of the ordinary. You will be astonished at the variety of well thought out responses that even an apparently simple question will provoke, and there is seldom much advantage in having a 'staff solution' prepared in advance.

To bring the course to a satisfying conclusion, you could set your students to evaluating a major human factors accident. With New Zealand students, the obvious subject is a re-examination of the Air New Zealand accident on Mount Erebus in Antarctica. Not only was this a major disaster by any standards, but also the investigation and subsequent Royal Commission continues to be controversial to this day. The assignment requires them to use almost all they have learnt, from investigation management and witness credibility, through crew resource management and limitations of vision, to organizational aspects, and the underlying philosophy of different concepts of accidents. A lot of reading and revision is required, and for extramural students the assignment takes at least a month, but feedback from the students indicates that it is well worth while.

**Summary**

When instructing investigators in human factors investigation, we are seeking to inculcate methods of investigation rather than to teach facts. We do not expect the investigator to master such a large field; instead, we expose him to knowledge so that he can recognize phenomena when he meets them, and knows when and how to seek further information.

Our students are generally mature, experienced and successful. They require a different approach to instruction from that which may be appropriate with younger students.

Examinations are an unsatisfactory teaching tool, because the real-world tasks of the investigator are 'open book' and not subject to significant time constraint. Assignments and group work, dealing with realistic material, are much better able to reinforce the application of methods of investigation. This is what we are seeking to implant.

**References**

Air Accident Investigation Branch Report No AAR 2/87. Lockheed Tristar G-BBAI - Leeds/Bradford Airport, 27 May 1985.

Air Accident Investigation Branch Report No AAR 1/92. BAC 111 G-BJRT - Didcot, Oxfordshire, 10 June 1990.

Air Accident Investigation Branch Report No AAR 2/89. BAC 111 G-AYWB - Gatwick Airport, 12 Apr 1988.

Helmreich, R.L. (1990). *Human Factors Aspects of the Air Ontario Crash at Dryden, Ontario.* Analysis and Recommendations to the Commission of Inquiry into the Air Ontario Crash at Dryden, Ontario. NASA/University of Texas Aerospace Crew Research Project.

O'Hare, D. (1990). 'Human factors in aircraft accident investigation'. *Journal of the International Society of Air Safety Investigators*, April 1990. ISASI, Sterling, VA.

Reason, J. (1990). *Human Error*. Cambridge University Press, Cambridge.

Rolfe, J. (1963). 'An appraisal of digital displays with particular reference to altimeter design'. *Ergonomics*, 8(4), 425-434.

# 16 Human factors in Chinese civil aviation training

*Liu Hanhui*

**Introduction**

Since 1976, the average accident rate of the world's commercial transportation jet aircraft fleet has remained at 3 per million departures. Because the size of civil aviation is rapidly extending, the absolute number of accidents does, in fact, increase. Today's modern aircraft are substantially more expensive than their predecessors and carry substantially greater numbers of passengers. The consequences of accident are therefore far greater reaching and far more disastrous, and the aim of the world's aviation industry, from the airline to the manufacturer to the administrative agency, is to endeavour to find ways to improve flight safety. The Civil Aviation Administration of China (CAAC), since its foundation, has always adhered to the principle of 'Safety and Prevention First'.

Statistics show that in modern aviation, 'human factors' are the primary cause of accident. About two-thirds of all modern accident cases have been found to have been caused by flight crew errors and the remaining one-third incidents were related by instances of air traffic controller errors, mechanical faults traced back to negligence on the part of maintenance engineers and others. Therefore, experts estimate that 80 - 90% of accidents in modern aviation have been caused by human factors and this is reflected by the data of accidents/incidents in China which shows almost the same tendency.

According to ICAO, human factors is a concept defining people in their living and working environment; about their relationship with hardware, software, and the general environment around them together with their relationship with other people. In an aviation context, how these inter-relationships are dealt with will determine whether an aeronautical professional will pilot a flight safely or unsafely. To deal with all these relationships properly, an aeronautical professional must possess a particular quality, particular skills and knowledge, and particular personality characteristics.

Generally, flying operations are complicated, requiring rapidity and precision, hence this 'operational skill' can only be obtained and retained through extensive training. The 'knowledge' factor is more complicated. Modern aeronautical knowledge is a huge ocean. What is more, this knowledge is renewed quickly and continuously. To acquire the vast knowledge requires a fundamental, elementary knowledge base, and to apply knowledge to practice relates to the individuals own ability for inference. It is therefore necessary to have a systematic education for the knowledge factor.

'Personality' characteristics relate to aspects such as attitude, psychological quality, responsibility, professional ethics and so on. Programme to change some aspects of crew members personality over several weeks via cockpit resource management training, was tried with little success. In fact, an individuals personality characteristics are moulded from pupillage by the long term effects of family, society, school, etc. The development of attitude and aero-professional ethics must begin at the ab initio training school, be enforced by the enterprise culture environment and be further re-inforced by on the job training.

These three criteria, skill, knowledge and personality characteristics are integrally linked together, forming a whole which determines the individuals professional capability. A pilot who is good in basic operating skills but is lacking in professional knowledge, may be deficient in areas requiring judgement and decision making. It could be difficult for him to execute a safe flight. On the other hand, an individual capable of talking significantly on flight theories and having a vast expanse of knowledge, but who is poor in operating skill will not make a good pilot either. An individual who has adequate skill and knowledge but lacks the appropriate attitude and psychological quality may be seized with panic in case of emergency, may not go-around when missing an approach due to vain glory or might not cooperate harmoniously with other crew members because of an uncommunicative and eccentric disposition. These individuals will certainly not make good pilots in terms of flight safety. Therefore, with respect to the training of skill, knowledge and personality, trainers should not attend to one thing alone and lose sight of the others. Knowledge will allow the skill factor to be guided by theory, skill will compliment the knowledge by being rooted in practice, and suitable personality traits will not only help the individual to fully grasp the skill and knowledge components, but will also insure that potential skill and knowledge is made full use.

In essence, training a class of aeronautical professionals is in itself a type of systematic engineering. A comprehensive education system should be founded for each class of professional: pilot, controller, mechanic etc. Extending this argument (longitudinally), ab initio training, on the job training and the enterprise culture environment in these systems should form a continuous instruction service. Furthermore, (laterally), the training of skill, knowledge and personality characteristics should be combined optimally in such a system.

In China, the *ab initio* training of the majority of pilots, controllers and mechanics is achieved in distinct colleges such as the Civil Aviation Flight College for pilot training, and the Civil Aviation Institute of China for air traffic controllers and mechanics. In these colleges basic 'stick and rudder' skills, systematically taught aeronautical knowledge together with elementary scientific knowledge, and some aspects of personality such as attitude, professional ethics, discipline, collectivity, and teamwork, are properly combined together. Although the dilemma of how to optimally combine this type of training still needs to be studied in more detail, our experience shows that results from this type of training are indicatively very positive. Since a comprehensive foundation has been laid, and a thorough grounding in basic skills acquired, junior professionals from these types of colleges and training institutions will achieve faster advancement through the airline hierarchical infrastructure and upward career path than those who have not had the benefit of training at such institutions.

Recently, people's attention is focused on 'human factors' by statistics of accidents; education and training are regarded seriously by international aviation industry. In aviation-developed countries, not only are licenses more strictly controlled and simulators more developed, but there are also many short term curricula in which the training of skills, knowledge, and attitude are properly combined, such as 'cockpit resource management' (CRM) and 'Human factors courses'. Those curricula have been widely adopted by airlines. The effects on flight safety are very positive.

But perhaps due to over emphasizing short term effects, civil aviation training usually concentrates on operating skills in the past. This mode originated from the professional training tradition of old industrial countries. Originally, to training workers of production line, an operation was broken into several skill factors, each skill factor then was learned and practiced. Once a worker learned the operation skills of his post and passed the examination, then the training was over. The efficiency of this type of training is high in deed. This method was used for the training of aviation professionals. Even for pilot training, it is usual to divide a flight into several procedures; again a procedure may be divided into several sub procedures. Several skill factors were drawn from those procedures or sub procedures. The primary goal of training was to teach those skill factors and make trainee be able to operate aircraft. The instruction of knowledge served the needs of skill training exactly. For example, if it is necessary for the pilot to calculate in flight, then only the formulas for the calculation were given. Understanding of those formulas were not required, hence ignored.

This type of training is still useful today. It could be used not only for teaching junior member of staff, but also for senior professionals, including pilots in skill training.

On the other hand, this mode could not satisfy the needs of today's civil aviation. In sharp contrast to early aircraft with the human eye as the only instrument on board, the modern airplane is a very complex and highly automated large system which is an agglomeration of almost all scientific achievements. For example, many tasks performed by pilots before, have been taken over by automatic systems now. Pilots acts as a monitor and manager more and more. Under normal conditions, the workload of pilots is reduced by automation. But everything has two sides. Automation and computerization bring in new workloads such as key board input in which it is easy to make a mistake. What is more, once a system fails, or special circumstance arises for which there is no program in the software, then pilots face a more difficult situation. When the aircraft was controlled by hand, it was easy to determine how a problem situation developed. It was relatively much more simple for pilots to judge and make decisions. During automatic flight things are totally different; pilots may find abnormal situations arise suddenly. In order to make what's happened clear it a complicated task for pilots analyze, it is even more difficult to make judgements and decisions. One's ability to analyze and judge depends on one's knowledge and the structure of the knowledge in the brain. The systems of modern aircraft are very complicated requiring a great deal of knowledge preparation to avoid making mistakes when sudden events occur. The statistics of flight accidents of modern transportation jet fleet show that as high as 50% of 'human factors' incidents are due to error in judgement or decision. That is, modern aircraft with high performance and automation put into operation reduced physical workload but raised the requirement for a higher knowledge level and ability in analysis and judgement for aero professionals. The traditional education mode centred on skill training must be reformed otherwise civil aviation education will not keep up with the rapidly developing aeronautical techniques. According to some authors, only 25% of ability needed by pilot was obtained via traditional training. Recently, in developed nations an education system which carries out a more comprehensive capability training was deliberated. Persons with breadth of vision already realize that aviation education is a very complicated matter, and that strengthening knowledge education may be the right way to change the accident rate.

The Civil Aviation in China keeps developing very fast. Ten years ago our fleet only had small and old aircraft, but today we have all kind of the most advanced airplanes in the world, so knowledge education is particularly important for us. Not only knowledge regarding new techniques, automation, and computerization, but also human factors knowledge itself should be addressed in our refresher training or CRM courses.

Recently it was revealed that highly developed competence in a defined area is the product of the inter-play between knowledge structure and processing abilities. Making judgements and decisions is a process of interrogating and solving problems. The nature of the organization of domain related knowledge determines the quality, completeness and coherence of the internal representation of problem, which in turn determines the efficiency of further thinking. Hence, when talking about the education for pilot's not only the knowledge's and skills that are needed should be addressed, but also how to organize them should be studied.

There are several ways to organize knowledge. In the 'Knowledge Process Hierarchy Model' given by G.J.F. Hunt (Hunt, 1993), the most important pilot accomplishments were grouped under six heads: performance management, systems management, navigation management, command, flight standard and flight operations. Each group may be taught by well known courses, for example performance management accomplishment by aerodynamics, aircraft performance, aircraft stability and control, and systems management knowledge by aero engine, aircraft systems and avionics. In this way, the domain related knowledge elements are organized according to their internal logical relationship.

Another way often used is to organize knowledge's and skills according to actual flying procedure. This is particularly useful for emergent events, such as engine out landing, and encountering wind shear.

These kinds of procedurally organized subjects are easy to learn and convenient to use. In cases of emergency they can be output very quickly. So this way of knowledge organization is widely adopted. Since its time efficiency is high, in some nations this form of procedural is the main format used.

But the knowledge elements in such a procedural organization are collected from different domains of science. Internal logical relation is weak between those elements. When such packaged knowledge was learned, the result would be that pilots knew the hows, but not the whys. During special events that were different from those learnt in this procedural training pilots may not be able to infer correctly for judgements and decisions from knowledge so learnt.

On the other hand, in the formal manner of organization although knowledge elements are not connected directly with real flight procedure, they are taught systematically with scientific logical relations. So in this way one learns not only knowledge itself but also how to infer with those knowledge's. For modern aviation, both ways of organizing knowledge are useful. People should not attend to one thing and lose sight of another. The important matter that should be carefully considered is how to schedule the instructions of those two forms of knowledge's.

In China it is suggested that for *ab initio* training in civil aviation colleges a systematic aeronautical knowledge education should be carried out afterwards as part of on job training or refreshing courses. It is usually recommended to use packaged knowledge in a procedurally organized form. The former will lay a good foundation for one's professional proficiency to develop. The latter would satisfy job's requirement quickly, making the efficiency of training very high. Of course, one should not divide the two absolutely. It is possible to include some procedurally organized training in the systematically scientific courses. It is also needed to make procedurally organised training as logical as possible. In some cases it may be necessary to give our senior professional systematic supplementary education on certain domain knowledge.

Team efficiency is the central point of human factors training. Good individual quality in skill, knowledge, and personality lays down a solid foundation for high team efficiency only. Its reality needs good teamwork. Since teamwork concerns how people deal with the relationship between them. It depends on people's culture background to a high degree. Because their long history and Eastern culture background, Chinese have their strengths and weaknesses. For good teamwork the CAAC adopts actively the human factors training courses such as CRM and LOFT that is widely used by Western countries but chooses the focal points according to its own condition that may be different from Western's.

China is a developing country, Civil Aviation of China is a developing enterprise. Although CAAC has long tradition of thinking highly of human factors, the acceptance of modern concept and method adopted by world's civil aviation industry may be only beginning. Like our industry we believe that the human factors training in China will catch up very soon.

**References**

Hunt, G.J.F. (1993) 'The verification of pilot abilities as a basis for validating flight crew competency'. In John A. Wise, V. David Hopkins and Paul Stager (Eds.), *Verification and Validation of Complex Systems:Human Factor Issues*. Berlin: Springer-Verlag.

# 17 Assessing human factors in primary aviation

*Stanley R. Trollip*

**Introduction**

In this chapter, I deal with the issue of assessment - that is, how to check that your students have acquired the required human factors knowledge and skills that you have been teaching them.

This assessment allows you to accomplish the important instructional goal of providing feedback to your students so they can improve their human factors behaviour. This is done both by relating your students' performance to the human factors principles associated with safe flying, and by providing the basis for linking the students' performance with relevant behaviour. That is, you should link deficiencies in human factors performance with the behaviours or attitudes that caused them. For example, if you notice that a student is frequently late for lessons or has not prepared adequately, you should point this out. But you should not stop there. You should explore with the student the underlying cause for this behaviour. It may be stress, fatigue, or poor workload management. Whatever it is, it is important that the student learns that lapses in human factors behaviour are a result of certain behaviours or attitudes which can be improved or corrected.

Assessment, or evaluation, can take place both formally and informally in the same way as instruction can. You can provide formal written tests and examinations in your ground school instruction, as well as informally ask students questions orally whenever you are with them. You can do the same with human factors skills and attitudes. You can set formal evaluations during a specific flight period, and you can informally watch how your students perform during every flight. Combining both formal and informal evaluation is ideal for human factors evaluation because the practice of human factors is continuous. It is not good enough for your students to perform well only in formal assessment situations when they know you are observing. They must exhibit these skills and attitudes at all times.

I start this chapter with a discussion of what aspects of human factors to assess. Later I discuss how to conduct the assessment.

## What to assess

One of the goals of good human factors assessment is its integration into instruction. The important word is 'integration'. That is, human factors assessment should be made part of instruction in as seamless a way as possible. What is wanted are pilots who fly safely, rather than pilots who can merely recite facts about human factors. Thus a major part of the assessment of pilots' human factors capabilities is determining how safely they fly.

This can be accomplished on an ongoing basis by the flight instructor during every flight. That is, the instructor should be constantly aware of human factors issues, even while teaching the pilot the technical aspects of flying. By integrating human factors instruction and assessment into the technical instruction, it highlights the fact that human factors issues underlie all aspects of flying. Human factors is not a distinct and separate subject. It is an approach to flying or, perhaps, even a philosophy of flying.

A good human factors approach to flying requires the pilot to know facts, have information, exhibit skills, and have the attitude and discipline to use them. It also requires that the pilot is able to relate each of these to components of safe flying. Consequently, as instructors, we must assess all of these.

### *Knowledge*

Knowledge is the basis of human factors. The skills and discipline of human factors depend on knowing what can affect your ability as a pilot, when this may happen, and what the effects are. In addition, you also need to know how to prevent, cope, or compensate for these effects. The first step in assessing human factors, then, is knowing what knowledge to assess.

There are a number of topics in a human factors syllabus that act as background or as advance organizers for learning. Often, there is no need to test these directly. For example, there is no need to test your students on whether they know the accident statistics for the last ten years, or whether they know the Software—Hardware—Environment—Liveware (SHEL) or information processing models. These topics are helpful in putting a framework around human factors, but are not intrinsically important to being able to function in a proper human factors manner.

Similarly, there are also details of information that are 'nice to know', but which do not enhance a pilot's ability to perform in a manner consistent with human factors principles. For example, it is nice to know that there is a greater density of cones than rods in the center of the retina, but it is not necessary to be able to remember this detail in order to understand the role of central and peripheral vision.

What we want to assess, therefore, is knowledge that is necessary to have in order to be able to function well from a human factors perspective. Sometimes, we can assume that a pilot knows something from the way he or she uses human factors skills. Other times, we have to ask the pilot direct questions relating to the knowledge.

*Information*

Knowledge about human factors is important, but not the only thing that a pilot needs to know. A pilot also has to have current information about the circumstances of the flight, such as the weather forecast, details of the destination airport, and so on. Similar to the situation with knowledge, it is sometimes obvious from the action he or she is taking that the student has this information. At other times, you will have to ask for the information directly.

*Skills*

In addition to knowing the underlying knowledge, it is important that a pilot has and uses the appropriate set of skills to fly in a manner consistent with human factors principles. The presence or absence of these skills is usually the best indicator that a pilot is basing his or her performance on human factors principles. From an operational perspective, these skills are what we most want to see.

*Attitudes*

The final issue we want to assess in our students is the attitude they have towards human factors. That is, it is important not only that students have the knowledge and skills pertaining to the various issues in human factors, but also that they have the right attitude. This means that your students have to believe in human factors and take steps to integrate it constantly into their everyday flying lives.

## How to assess human factors knowledge

Assessment of human factors knowledge can be done either formally or informally. Any formal test is, by its nature, obvious and even obtrusive. This cannot be helped. If you have to get to what your students know about a topic, you may have to give them a formal test. On the other hand, you can also learn a lot about what your students know by asking them questions informally outside of the formal classroom, during pre-flight briefings, flights, or post-flight debriefings.

*Formal testing of knowledge*

One of the ways of checking whether your students have the required knowledge is to give them written tests. Typically this happens as part of formal groundschool instruction. Your goal in giving such tests is to find out just what your students know. Therefore, it is important to write the questions in such a way as to minimize guessing, because if it is easy to guess a correct answer you will never have confidence that the test results are really indicative of what the students know.

In this chapter, I am not going to give a lesson on how to plan and prepare good written tests. More than likely, you already have most of these skills.

*Informal testing of knowledge*

Informal testing of knowledge occurs when you ask students questions orally. This can happen in class, during preparatory ground instruction or a pre-flight briefing, during a flight, or even outside the confines of the airport, at a bar or social gathering. For the most part, informal testing usually comprises open-ended questions. You evaluate your student as you listen to the response. Typical of such informal questions are:

If you lose an engine a few seconds after take-off, what is the sequence of things you would do?

or

You look tired this morning, how is that likely to affect your pre-flight planning? And your flying?

or

You are planning to fly to Fleming Field in South St. Paul. How long and wide is the runway? Is there any slope? Do you expect to suffer any visual illusions flying into it?

In each of these cases, you have to evaluate the student's response against what you know of the subject, and should provide insightful feedback right away.

This informal testing can be difficult to do well, because it requires careful preparation on your behalf. Without the preparation, the questioning is likely to be haphazard, or you may forget to do it at all. This type of informal questioning about human factors, however, is the cornerstone of ensuring that human factors is integrated into your instruction. It brings human factors issue into all aspects of flight. Of course, it also provides you with ongoing assessment of the student's progress.

## How to assess human factors information

As I mentioned before, information is an essential part of flying in a manner consistent with human factors principles. Wherever possible, you should try to use the skills that the student is displaying as an indicator of the fact that he or she has the appropriate information. For example, if the student has checked the slope and dimensions of the destination runway, you may want to assume that he or she knows the associated landing illusions. You must remember, however, that you are making an assumption here.

If you cannot make such an assumption, or if you are uncomfortable about the assumption, you can always ask a direct question, such as 'What is the slope of the destination runway?' Either way, you have to feel confident that the student has acquired the necessary information.

## Assessing human factors skills

It is important to remember that many human factors skills are not observable in the same way as those of handling the aircraft. In order to get to these skills, you often have to look at your students' performance in a different way, sometimes having to be active yourself in ensuring that the skill is observable.

A human factors skill is typically the application of knowledge and information to a real situation. For example, with respect to landing illusions, the associated skills are doing the research to find out the potential illusions at unfamiliar airports and landing there safely. In order to assess these skills, you would periodically ask the student about the details of runways at a destination airport, and what illusions would likely occur there. You would also observe the student's performance in landing at these unfamiliar airports.

Similarly, you could ask the student what they had done to prepare for the current flight. You would expect a list of actions, including having got a good night's sleep, having eaten a nutritious meal, having visualized and planned the manoeuvres to be flown, and so on. This type of question helps link prior behaviours to performance and highlights the need for being thoughtful about flying long before it is time to fly.

Another area that is important for you to assess are the skills of judgement and decision making. One way of doing this is to observe your student handle different, unexpected situations. Typically these would be made-up scenarios that you provide, such as engine failures, precautionary landings, or fuel emergencies. Or you could ask questions such as 'If you had just enough fuel to fly from Minneapolis to Chicago, Meigs Field, with legal reserves, what increase in headwind would cause you to divert to another airport en route? Which airport would you divert to?' In addition to assessing the student's performance associated with the situation, you can also ask probing questions, such as: 'What were the alternative solutions you considered?' or 'What were the risks associated with each of your alternatives?' or 'Why did you choose that particular approach to solving the problem?'

If the student has not got ready answers for these questions, it is likely that various alternative solutions were not consciously explored. Again, the more aware the student is of the requirements of good decision making, the more thorough the process is likely to be.

I have mentioned on several occasions that human factors must be integrated into your instruction and assessment. By asking questions like

*Designing Instruction for Human Factors Training in Aviation*

the ones above, you can accomplish this. Your student would naturally start associating issues such as visual illusions with landing, or generating options and assigning risk to decision making and judgement. From your perspective, this approach enables you to ensure that good human factors principles are always present, and not just during an assessment flight.

As with testing human factors knowledge, preparing to assess human factors skills will require you to do some preparation. You will need to look at each lesson you have, each manoeuvre that the student will fly, and develop means for getting at the underlying human factors skills. Although this may be difficult at first, you will get the hang of it and the assessment will also become integrated into your instruction. Later in the chapter, I provide you with a lot of help in doing this.

**Assessing human factors attitudes**

The final type of assessment that you want to do is of the students' attitudes. There is no way to do this other than by observation. It is not good enough to ask students what their attitudes are, because few people will answer that their attitudes are deficient. You have to observe them perform and behave on a day-to-day basis to obtain a good idea of their real attitudes.

What you want to look for is evidence that the student is interested in flying safely the whole time. This attitude manifests itself in a number of ways that you can monitor. First, there must be discipline. This means that the student does not cut corners in flight preparation or in the execution of flight manoeuvres and procedures. Second, the student should demonstrate an awareness of vulnerability; that things do go wrong from time to time. Evidence of this attitude is usually found in good contingency planning and anticipation of possible problems. It can be seen in the exercise of good judgement. Third, the student should have high standards. This can be observed when the students are always trying to improve their skills.

Assessing your students' attitudes can be difficult. I believe that your experience and instincts will give you a good indication. If you sense that a student's attitude is not what you would want, make sure that you raise the issue and discuss it openly and constructively.

## Practical guides to assessment

In this section I provide you with a series of guides or checklists for determining how proficient a student is with respect to human factors. In each checklist I deal with the observable indicators of knowledge, skills, and attitudes and show you how to get at the information you want. Where knowledge or information is not directly observable or assumable, I suggest what sorts of questions you may want to ask.

The checklists deal with typical human factors topics covered in a primary aviation curriculum, such as eyes, the body, and so on. A few checklists represent broader topics, such as workload management and decision making. I have made any necessary notations about the use of each checklist immediately after the checklist.

Each checklist is divided into three sections. The first (labelled 'Knowledge') deals with the knowledge and information that the student has about the topic. The second (labelled 'Skills') is a list of observable indicators (or behaviours) that provide information about the student's skills in the area. The third (labelled 'Attitude') deals with how you can estimate the student's attitude towards the topic.

*Stress*

I start with how to assess how a student handles stress. I use this as my first example because it is not readily apparent how one would assess a person's ability to deal with it. The topic of stress also raises other issues that are important, such as the need for human factors skills to be used outside of the flying environment as well as in it. For example, a person's ability to fly safely can be affected by his or her current level of chronic stress. As you know, chronic stress has its roots in how we live our everyday lives. So, if we are to deal with chronic stress, we have to deal with issues not related to flying.

Another comment is important. We realize that most of the time in flight instruction we can only simulate the stresses a pilot would feel if threatened by a real emergency. Although we can never be sure how someone will react in a real emergency, I believe that if the student exhibits the correct skills in a simulated situation, he or she is reasonably likely to bring the same skills to bear in a real emergency.

In the checklist below (figure 17.1), for each item that the student answers or performs satisfactorily, check the box marked **S** (for satisfactory performance). If performance is not what you think it should be, check the box marked **I** (needs improvement). It is always helpful to provide feedback to the student, so space is provided on the checklist to write any comments you may have. I urge you to write positive comments as well as critical ones. That is, if the student does something well, praise is in order.

*Discussion*

It will be helpful for you if I lay out the process I went through to create this checklist. Anytime you are assessing someone, you can only reach your conclusions on the basis of what you see and what you hear. I call these observable indicators because they are visible (or audible), in contrast to what is inside a person's head, which is invisible. I use these observable indicators as windows into what is going on inside the person's head. For example, if you are interested in assessing a student's attitude about a topic, you would not get very reliable results if you merely asked the student. Rather, you have to observe how the student behaves and performs over time. Thus, if a student's ongoing behaviours are good, I assume that the appropriate attitude is in place.

In the specific case of stress, from a human factors perspective, we are interested in the student's ability to deal with it effectively. We cannot just ask the student if they are doing so because most students would answer 'Yes' irrespective of how well they were dealing with it. In reality, stress is insidious, and your students may not even recognize that they were stressed until the situation became extreme. So, how do we go about assessing the ability to deal with stress?

We believe that some factual knowledge is needed about stress because without it, it is unlikely that a student will be able to handle it when it appears. Consequently, you should ask students the types of questions listed under Knowledge Indicators in the figure. These questions can be asked formally or informally in ground school or in preflight briefings. If you notice that a student is stressed, you should also ask questions to find out whether he or she is aware of it. You would not do this by asking directly 'Are you stressed?' Rather, you would ask questions that would get to the same conclusion, such as a sequence like 'What are common indicators of chronic stress?', 'How are you doing with respect to these indicators?', and so on.

During flight, acute stress is the one most likely to occur, usually caused by anxiety about what is being done at the moment, such as stalls, simulated engine failures, and so on. You can observe whether your students are dealing with this properly by watching what they do during the manoeuvre.

For example, if they are gripping the yoke tightly with white knuckles showing, they are not dealing with it. However, if they prepare for the manoeuvre by taking a few deep breaths beforehand or holding the controls with finger tips, this is evidence that they realize what is happening and are taking steps to minimize the effects. Another symptom of acute stress in the cockpit is fixation. That is, students lose their ability to have a complete scan of the instruments and the outside world. So, if this full scan is present, it is an indicator that the student is dealing with any acute stress.

These coping mechanisms are the appropriate skills to deal with acute stress, so we assume that if they are present the student knows how to handle acute stress. We list the appropriate skills under Skill Indicators.

The most difficult aspect to assess is the student's attitude. As I mentioned earlier, asking what the student's attitude is rarely gives you accurate information. What student would tell you that he or she had a bad attitude? It is also not very reliable to ask a student to deal with stress in a given manoeuvre. One-time performance only indicates that the student has the necessary skills, but not necessarily the right attitude. Having the right attitude implies that the student conscientiously applies his or her knowledge and skills whenever necessary, and not just in times of being tested. So assessment of attitude usually means observing whether your students exhibit their skills at all times. In the case of stress, the best ongoing indicator of a good attitude, is how the student deals with chronic stress; the stresses brought about by lifestyle. If your student routinely arrives early for lessons and is well prepared, this is likely to be a good indicator that the student is handling chronic stress well, because chronic stress usually causes people to be rushed, late, and unprepared. In the Attitude Indicators section of the figure, we list the behaviours you can observe that are likely to indicate the presence of a good attitude. Note that both refer to the need for constant behaviour over time.

One other comment is in order. Acute stress is something that can happen during any flight, and chronic stress can occur anytime during a person's life. So, in order to assess it, you must be looking for these observable signs whenever you are with the student, both in the aeroplane and on the ground. What this means for you is that you have to maintain a high level of awareness about your students at all times.

# Designing Instruction for Human Factors Training in Aviation

| Topic: Stress | S | I | Comments |
|---|---|---|---|
| **Knowledge indicators**: Question the student re: | | | |
| Differences between acute, chronic, and traumatic stress. | | | |
| Recognizing different types of stress. | | | |
| The effects of these types of stress. | | | |
| Dealing with the different types of stress. | | | |
| Recognizing stress in oneself. | | | |
| | | | |
| **Skill indicators**: Observe that the student, in situations of acute stress: | | | |
| Gets self under control (eg. breathes, relaxes grip on yoke, verbalizes procedures, etc.). | | | |
| Completes a total scan of instruments and external references. | | | |
| | | | |
| **Attitude indicators**: Observe that the student: | | | |
| Prepares and organizes for *every* lesson (eg. reads lesson plan, has thought through the current lesson, etc.). | | | |
| Organizes his or her *everyday* personal schedule to eliminate rushing. | | | |

**Figure 17.1 Evaluation checklist for stress**

You may copy this and any of the other checklists to help your assessment of human factors issues.

*Workload management*

The second difficult area is workload management, which is so crucial to safe flying. As with stress, we want to be able to assess a student's capabilities in this area by observing what they do rather than merely by asking what they should do. It will be necessary, however, to ask questions to establish what is going on in the student's mind. For example, at any time during the flight, the student should have sets of goals, such as diverting around a thunderstorm or re-establishing radio contact with ATC if it has been lost. The only way to find out what these goals are is to ask. Similarly, it is often impossible to observe if the student has planned ahead, so asking pertinent questions is appropriate.

Under 'Knowledge Indicators' in figure 17.2, you can find the types of questions you may ask to help you assess how well the student is performing in the area of workload management.

There are also observable behaviours that will give you an idea of how the student is coping. These are listed under Skills Indicators and include such items as information gathering, task delegation, use of available resources, as well as keeping in control when things go awry. Of course, if the student is well organized, you may never have the opportunity to observe the student slow down in order to calm down and get perspective.

As with skills, the strongest indicators associated with having a good attitude with respect to workload management are *consistent* execution of the appropriate skills. That is, it is not good enough to manage workload appropriately just in a test ride. The student should do so at all times.

| Topic: Workload Management | S | I | Comments |
|---|---|---|---|
| **Knowledge indicators**: Question the student re: | | | |
| Establishing goals (eg. avoiding thunderstorms). | | | |
| How the time available affects their ability to consider options. | | | |
| When it is appropriate to deviate from SOPs. | | | |
| The necessity for deviation from procedures if the situation occurs. | | | |
| Briefing crew on the plan of action to meet current goals. | | | |
| Who can be used as 'crew' and when. | | | |
| Planning ahead. | | | |
| | | | |
| **Skill indicators**: Observe that the student: | | | |
| Determines certain information ahead of when it is needed (eg. fuel level, required altitude, weather, surface, landing surface conditions). | | | |
| Organizes and prioritizes work. | | | |
| Use all available resources. | | | |
| In multi-crew situations, delegates tasks and follows up on them. | | | |
| Follows procedures, but allows for deviation when the situation requires. | | | |
| Consciously slows things down when things are getting out of hand. | | | |
| | | | |
| **Attitude indicators**: Observe that the student: | | | |
| Consistently demonstrates the above behaviours in all situations. | | | |
| Is always prepared and organized. | | | |

**Figure 17.2 Evaluation checklist for workload management**

*Situational awareness*

A third difficult area to assess is situational awareness; the ability of a pilot to keep abreast of what the current situation of the aeroplane is, as well as predicting what future ones will be.

There is no theoretical knowledge about situational awareness, so the only questions to ask concern the information inside the student's head (figure 17.3). This is information that you need to know to assess what the student knows about the current situation. To assess a student's forward planning, you can ask 'what-if' questions, such as 'What if the weather goes down at the destination airport?' or 'Where would you land if you lost your engine now?' or 'How would you deal with an electrical failure on an ILS?' The answers to these questions would give you an insight into the student's awareness of the flight.

The appropriate skills dealing with situational awareness are listed under 'Skill Indicators' in figure 17.3. The observable behaviours deal with the monitoring of all available information and making adjustments to deal with changes. As before, consistent application of the skills is the best indicator of a good attitude towards situational awareness.

| Topic: Situational Awareness | S | I | Comments |
|---|---|---|---|
| **Knowledge indicators**: Question the student re: | | | |
| What the current situation of the flight is. | | | |
| The consequences of all decisions. | | | |
| The impact of 'new' information on the current situation. | | | |
| Hypothetical situations. | | | |
| **Skill indicators**: Observe that the student: | | | |
| Monitors all sources of information (eg. environment, weather, cockpit instruments, self etc.). | | | |
| Adjusts to 'new' conditions (eg. Changes in altitude, speed, direction, etc.). | | | |
| **Attitude indicators**: Observe that the student: | | | |
| Is consistent in demonstrating the above behaviours in all situations (including non-aviation situations). | | | |

**Figure 17.3 Evaluation checklist for situational awareness**

## Designing Instruction for Human Factors Training in Aviation

*Decision making and judgement*

A fourth area of human factors that needs evaluating is decision making and judgement. This is a difficult area because it is so difficult to formalize. In the same way as the previous topics, in order to evaluate a student's performance, we need to get inside his or her head to discover what they are thinking about a particular situation, as well as finding out whether they know some basic information about decision making and judgement. We do this by asking the types of questions listed under 'Knowledge Indicators' in figure 17.4. The questions about the current situation must be asked in the cockpit, while those dealing with knowledge of the process can be asked on the ground.

The observable behaviours that indicate a grasp of the skills associated with decision making and judgement are also listed, as are those that will give you insights into whether the student has a good attitude towards making good decisions. As before, the latter is assessed by observing the consistency with which the student applies the skills.

| Topic: Decision making and Judgement | S | I | Comments |
|---|---|---|---|
| **Knowledge indicators**: Question the student re: | | | |
| What the current problem or issue is. | | | |
| What the current objectives are. | | | |
| What the current priorities are. | | | |
| What the planned course of action is. | | | |
| What the necessary information is to make decisions on the current circumstances. | | | |
| What the external factors are affecting good decision making and judgement (eg. peer pressure, commercial pressure, etc.). | | | |
| What the internal or personal factors are affecting good decision making and judgement (eg. fatigue, stress, etc.). | | | |
| | | | |
| **Skill indicators**: Observe that the student: | | | |
| Plans ahead (eg. route, extra fuel, alternates, etc.). | | | |
| Sets priorities. | | | |
| Checks variables (eg. Weather reports, forecasts, etc.). | | | |
| Uses information to make decisions. | | | |
| Takes on more responsibility for making decisions as training advances. | | | |
| Self evaluates. This may need prompting. | | | |
| | | | |
| **Attitude indicators**: Observe that the student: | | | |
| Resists peer or commercial pressures. | | | |
| Plans, prepares, and organizes ahead of time. | | | |
| Maintains situational awareness. | | | |

**Figure 17.4 Evaluation checklist for decision making and judgement**

*Designing Instruction for Human Factors Training in Aviation*

*Background information*

For the remainder of the chapter, I provide the assessment checklists for the more straightforward of the human factors topics, such as background information, the brain, the body, the eyes, the ears, cockpit resource management, and good flying practices.

Figure 17.5 illustrates a checklist that deals with the background information concerning human factors. As you can see, I do not think that there is any knowledge from this section that warrants asking questions about. With respect to observable skills, I believe that if the student comes prepared to fly and plans each flight thoroughly, these are indicators that he or she understands the basic principles of human factors. Similarly, if the student demonstrates these skills consistently, this is a good indicator of having a good attitude towards human factors.

| Topic: Background Information | S | I | Comments |
|---|---|---|---|
| **Knowledge indicators**: Question the student re: | | | |
| N/A | | | |
| | | | |
| **Skill indicators**: Observe that the student: | | | |
| Comes prepared for the lesson or flight. | | | |
| Plans ahead during the flight. | | | |
| Questions unclear topics or instructions. | | | |
| | | | |
| **Attitude indicators**: Observe that the student: | | | |
| Is always prepared for a lesson or flight. | | | |
| Consistently plans ahead during the flight. | | | |

**Figure 17.5 Evaluation checklist for background information**

*The brain*

Although the brain is central to everything we do in flying, your assessment of what your students know about its role in human factors can be quite limited. This is largely due to the fact that your evaluations of all other human factors areas deal with the brain indirectly. Figure 17.6 contains the brief checklist for the brain. It is self explanatory.

| Topic: The Brain | S | I | Comments |
|---|---|---|---|
| **Knowledge indicators**: Question the student re: | | | |
| The role of the brain in gathering information. | | | |
| The differences between short-term and long-term memory. | | | |
| | | | |
| **Skill indicators**: Observe that the student: | | | |
| Pays attention to all aspects of the flight. | | | |
| Deals with potential expectancy problems by confirming or corroborating information received | | | |
| | | | |
| **Attitude indicators**: Observe that the student: | | | |
| Is always prepared for a lesson or flight. | | | |
| Consistently plans ahead during the flight. | | | |

**Figure 17.6 Evaluation checklist for the brain**

*The body*

In contrast to the brain, there is a lot of factual information that the student should know about the body. The types of questions about basic knowledge are shown in figure 17.7 under 'Knowledge Indicators'. There are also few questions that help you understand what is currently happening to the student.

During a flight, one of the few observable skill indicators is whether the student adequately deals with the potential for hypoxia. Again, attitude can be assessed by observing how the student treats his or her body in everyday life. Abusing alcohol, eating badly, missing good sleep, and so on, are all indicators that the student does not have a good attitude to the human factors issues related to the body. Other indicators are that the student prepares for flights where the temperatures will be extreme.

| Topic: The Body | S | I | Comments |
|---|---|---|---|
| **Knowledge indicators**: Question the student re: | | | |
| Issues concerning medication and self-medication. | | | |
| The effects of alcohol. | | | |
| The effects of drugs. | | | |
| The effects of smoking. | | | |
| When hypoxia occurs and how it affects the body and brain. | | | |
| The effects of the different types of fatigue. | | | |
| The importance of good nutrition. | | | |
| How temperature extremes affect performance. | | | |
| What he or she has eaten recently. | | | |
| Whether they are fatigued. | | | |
| | | | |
| **Skill indicators**: Observe that the student: | | | |
| Takes steps to avoid becoming hypoxic. | | | |
| Dresses appropriately. | | | |
| | | | |
| **Attitude indicators**: Observe that the student: | | | |
| Consistently treats his or her body well with respect to medication, alcohol, drugs, smoking, fatigue, and nutrition. | | | |
| Prepares adequately for adverse environmental conditions, such as heat and cold. | | | |

**Figure 17.7 Evaluation checklist for the body**

*The eyes*

The eyes play a big role in flying, and there are many human factors associated with them.

As with most topics, you will have to ask questions to ensure that the student has the basic knowledge relating to the eyes. You will also have to ask questions to find out what the student is currently thinking. Under 'Knowledge Indicators' in figure 17.8, the first two questions get at the current information, while the remainder check basic knowledge.

*Assessing Human Factors in Primary Aviation*

There are a lot of observable human factors skills associated with the eyes. These are listed in figure 17.11 under 'Skill Indicators'. As you would imagine, most of these relate to look out and visual illusions. Attitude to the human factors of the eyes can be assessed by ongoing behaviours. If the student needs to wear corrective lenses, these should be worn at all times, as should sunglasses in bright sunlight. Finally, the student should be constantly aware of and dealing with potential visual illusions.

| Topic: The Eyes | S | I | Comments |
|---|---|---|---|
| **Knowledge indicators**: Question the student re: | | | |
| Possible illusions where they're going to land. | | | |
| Possible motion illusions. | | | |
| The effects of air quality on vision. | | | |
| The effects of obscuration on vision. | | | |
| The effects of blood stream contents on vision. | | | |
| The effects of fatigue on scanning. | | | |
| Visual expectancy. | | | |
| | | | |
| **Skill indicators**: Observe that the student: | | | |
| Looks out (scans for traffic, fixes on a point to deal with empty field myopia). | | | |
| Uses maps, charts, people etc to identify illusions. | | | |
| Visually assess meteorological factors to identify illusions. | | | |
| Visually assess landing surface to identify illusions. | | | |
| Lands safely in presence of illusions. | | | |
| Identifies possible motion illusions. | | | |
| Adjusts lights at night to take accommodation into account. | | | |
| | | | |
| **Attitude indicators**: Observe that the student: | | | |
| Deals with visual problems, such as accommodation and adaptation, by wearing corrective lenses that won't fall off in turbulence. | | | |
| Uses sunglasses. | | | |
| Consistently is aware of and adapts to illusions. | | | |

**Figure 17.8 Evaluation checklist for the eyes**

*The ears*

You should assess whether the student understands and has knowledge concerning the role of the ear in orientation and the importance of hearing and hearback (figure 17.9). You can also ask the student questions about the likelihood of disorientation for any manoeuvre or what they heard in a communication.

The skills involved are avoiding things that may induce disorientation, such as picking something off the floor while in a turn, minimizing the risk of aural expectation by ensuring that the information is correct, and by reading back information to ensure accuracy. In addition to using the consistent application of skills as an indicator of a good attitude, you can also observe whether the student takes precautionary steps to minimize hearing loss, both in the cockpit and out.

| Topic: The Ears | S | I | Comments |
|---|---|---|---|
| **Knowledge indicators**: Question the student re: | | | |
| The role of the ear in orientation and disorientation. | | | |
| The importance of hearing and hearback. | | | |
| Susceptibility to disorientation in the current flight situation. | | | |
| The details of any communication. | | | |
| | | | |
| **Skill indicators**: Observe that the student: | | | |
| Takes actions to avoid becoming disoriented. | | | |
| Deals with potential expectancy problems by confirming or corroborating information received | | | |
| Reads back all important information. | | | |
| | | | |
| **Attitude indicators**: Observe that the student: | | | |
| Consistently applies the skills above. | | | |
| Takes steps to prevent hearing loss. | | | |

**Figure 17.9 Evaluation checklist for the ears**

*Cockpit resource management*

Although most people think of cockpit resource management as applying only to situations in which there is more than one person in the cockpit, I think it applies to every flight because of the need even of a single pilot to manage resources. Obviously, some of the items in the checklist in figure 17.10 apply only to multi-person crews, but many apply to all flights (which I have marked with an *).

The knowledge requirements for cockpit resource management are simple, but, as you can see, there are numerous skills that play a role. A student's attitude in this area is assessed largely by observing his or her openness to self-improvement, by assertiveness, and by the consistent application of the appropriate skills both in the cockpit and on the ground.

| Topic: Cockpit Resource Management | S | I | Comments |
|---|---|---|---|
| **Knowledge indicators**: Question the student re: | | | |
| *What is considered crew? (For example, Instructor, passengers, flight attendants, maintenance personnel, etc.) | | | |
| *The effects of communication on team building. | | | |
| **Skill indicators**: Observe that the student: | | | |
| *Helps others to deal with stress. | | | |
| *Uses all available resources. | | | |
| *Takes initiative. | | | |
| *Listens actively. | | | |
| *Consults others. | | | |
| *Speaks up. | | | |
| *Uses appropriate communication style for the situation. | | | |
| Verbalizes future actions. | | | |
| Shares information and briefs others. | | | |
| Uses positive reinforcement. | | | |
| *Self-evaluates (admits mistakes). | | | |
| **Attitude indicators**: Observe that the student: | | | |
| *Is open to suggestion. | | | |
| *Speaks up when appropriate. | | | |
| *Consistently applies the skills above. | | | |
| *Self-evaluates with respect to CRM skills. | | | |

**Figure 17.10 Evaluation checklist for cockpit resource management**

*Good flying practices*

The final area you want to assess is good flying practices. These capture the overall approach that the student brings to flying. As you would expect this is skill-based and attitude-based, so there are no items under 'Knowledge Indicators'. There is a number of skills that you would expect to observe throughout all flights. And, as before, the attitude of the student can be evaluated by the presence or absence of certain actions. These are all listed in figure 17.11.

| Topic: Good Flying Practices | S | I | Comments |
|---|---|---|---|
| **Knowledge indicators**: Question the student re: | | | |
| N/A | | | |
| | | | |
| **Skill indicators**: Observe that the student: | | | |
| Follows SOPs and procedures. | | | |
| Sets a good example. | | | |
| Sets high standards for self. | | | |
| Maintains currency. | | | |
| Flies within current proficiency level. | | | |
| Self-evaluates. | | | |
| | | | |
| **Attitude indicators**: Observe that the student: | | | |
| Consistently follows procedures. | | | |
| Promptly amends or updates manuals and publications. | | | |
| Uses current information (eg. Maps, charts, GPS database, etc.). | | | |
| Continuously learns and improves. | | | |
| Maintains currency. | | | |

**Figure 17.11 Evaluation checklist for good flying practices Self-assessment**

One final word on assessment: As I have said before, one of the skills that a flight instructor should impart is that of self-assessment. That is, a pilot must not only learn how to fly in a way compatible with human factors principles, but should also be able to evaluate his or her own performance. This is important because for most of a pilot's career, he or she the only critic available. To accomplish this, you should frequently ask the student to evaluate his or her own performance after a manoeuvre. You would then critique both the performance on the manoeuvre and the quality of the self-evaluation.

## Conclusion

The assessment of human factors knowledge, skills, and attitudes is possible to do provided you are aware of the need to do it and have prepared for it properly. In the beginning, it may be best for you to have an evaluation sheet that lists issues like those just described in the sections above. For example, figure 17.3 is an example evaluation form for an exercise on turns. Note that it contains only human factors issues that pertain to turns. General issues would be on a separate General Human Factors Evaluation Form.

It is also useful to remember that since human factors are always with us, whether we are flying or not, you can assess your students even when they are away from the airport. Opportunities abound to observe how people are aware of the factors that affect them. For example, if you notice that a student does not listen to other people when in a discussion or argument, you can use this to alert you to watch for the same behaviour in the cockpit. If a student is habitually late for class or is ill-prepared for class, you can use this to check whether the same behaviour occurs before a flight. If you know that a student is highly stressed for some reason, you can observe how this affects everyday performance, and so on.

In each case, the student's behaviour away from flying gives you insights into what may happen in flight. It also gives you a good opportunity to provide further instruction or remediation.

The evaluation of human factors is still in its infancy. There is very little information available on how to do it well. However, a couple of things will help. First, it is unlikely that a person will be different when flying than what they are away from it. So what you observe in a person in everyday life most probably is a good indicator of what they will be as a pilot.

Second, if you are yourself aware of human factors issues, your instincts about your students' abilities is likely to be good. I think the use of checklist for evaluation is very helpful, but you should also pay attention to your professional instincts.

A word of caution: You should regard the tables above and the discussion in this chapter as providing guidelines for your assessment, rather than being the final word on how to do it. human factors assessment is something new, and there is still a lot to be understood on how to do it properly. You should incorporate your own thoughts and insights into the process, and should discuss the issues with your colleagues.

Human factors affects everyone the whole time. As we try to help people learn about these things, we also need to try to evaluate how successful they are being. This evaluation can then be fed back to them as a basis for further learning and insights. And it can also be useful to you for examining how you are facilitating your students to learn about themselves. Assessment of human factors is not easy, but it must be done.

# Author index

Alexander, P.A., 22, 26
Anderson T.A., 36, 43, 104, 112
Anderson, John R., 102, 103
Atkinson, R.C., 31, 43, 44
Autunano M.J., 251, 253
Azbell, J.W., 30, 44
Backman, B., 223, 225
Baldwin, R., 206, 216, 224
Barnes, R.M., 119, 126
Bassok, M., 134, 138, 157
Baudhuin, E.S., 131, 132, 155
Bedard, J., 135, 155
Bellezza, F.S., 22, 26
Bent, J., 119, 126
Berndt, B., 223, 225
Biggs, J.B., 22, 26, 90, 93
Bjork, R.A., 131, 135, 139, 156
Bloom, B.S., 21, 26
Boff, K.R., 174, 203
Brecht-Clark, J., 223, 224
Briggs, L.J., 21, 26
Broach, D., 223, 224
Brown, J.S., 112, 137, 155
Bruner, S.J., 5, 15

Bunderson, C.V., 30, 38, 43
Burton, R.R., 112
Cannon, J.R., 135, 138, 153, 160
Cannon-Bowers, J.A., 149, 155
Caro, P.W., 61, 91
Cavagnol, R.M., 104, 112
Chaiklin, S., 135, 155
Chambers, W.S., 82, 93
Chapanis, A., 134, 156
Chi, M.T.H., 20, 26, 130, 135, 139, 155, 156, 160
Clark, N., 230, 234
Collins, A., 137, 155
Converse, S.A., 149, 155
Cormier, S.M., 131, 155, 156
Crook, C., 10, 15
Crosthwaite, R.G.B., 92
Dahl, O-J., 95, 103
Davies, J.L., 209, 224
Degani, A., 147, 156
DeHart R.L., 250, 253
Downs, S., 151, 156
Duguid, P., 137, 155
Eisele, J.E., 82, 93

Elshout, J.J., 22, 27
Englehart, M.D., 21, 26
Entwistle, N., 22, 23, 26
Ernsting J., 249, 253
Fairweather, P.G., 35, 43, 104, 112, 113
Farah, M.J., 227, 230, 234
Farr, M.J.,130, 135, 156
Feltovich, P.J., 20, 26
Fischer, G., 112
Fitts, P.M., 173, 203
Fleishman, E.A., 83, 91
Flexman, R.E., 61, 91
Flores, C.F., 136, 160
Foushee, H.C., 130, 144, 156, 158
Fowlkes, J.E., 61, 92
Fransson, A., 23, 26
Frederico, P., 156
Furst, E.J., 21, 26
Gagné, R.M., 9, 15, 21, 26, 91, 102, 103
Galton, F., 226, 234
Garland, D.J., 174, 204
Garvey, W.D., 173, 204
Gelman, R., 131, 156
Gibbons, A. S., 30, 32, 35, 36, 38, 43, 44, 104, 112, 113
Gick, M.L., 131. 156
Glaser, R., 9, 15, 20, 24, 26, 27, 130, 131, 134, 135, 138, 156, 157
Goldberg, Adele, 95, 103
Greeno, J.G., 131, 135, 156
Gronlund, N.E., 12, 15
Hackman, J.R., 140, 157
Haglund, R., 223, 225
Hagman, J.D., 131, 155, 156
Hammerton, M., 131, 157
Hays, R.T., 62, 82, 83, 91
Heller, F., 180, 204

Helmreich, R.L., 128, 130, 143, 156, 158, 160, 260, 261, 263, 271
Hill, W.H., 21, 26
Holyoak, K.J., 131, 156
Hopkin, D.V., 230, 233, 234
Hopkin, V.D., 174, 183, 204, 216, 224, 225
Hunt, G.J.F., 7, 10, 15, 16, 129, 157, 164, 170, 276, 278
Hunt, L.M., 15, 16, 17, 24, 27, 164, 170
Isaac, A.R., 227, 230, 234
Jacobs R.S., 61, 91
Jacobs, J.W., 82, 83, 91, 93,
Jansweijer, W., 22, 27
Jensen, R.S., 117, 126
Jensen, R.S., 80, 91, 93
Johnson, B., 230, 234
Johnson, W.B., 174, 204
Johnston, A.N., 128, 129, 131, 136, 143, 144, 146, 155, 157, 158
Jones, M.K., 36, 44
Jordan, N., 173, 204
Judy, J.E., 22, 26
Kaempf, G. A., 153, 159
Kanki, B.G., 128, 130, 143, 158, 160
Karim, M., 104, 113
Kearsley, G.P., 30, 38, 43
Kennedy, R.S., 61, 92
King P., 249, 253
King R.V., 104, 113
King, J.H., 129, 158
Klahr, D., 22, 27
Knirk, F.G., 131, 132, 135, 149, 159
Kolb, D.A., 135, 144, 158
Koonce, J.M., 83, 92
Kozulin, A., 155, 158

Kraemer, R.A., 80, 92
Krathwohl, D. R., 21, 26
Kuo, G., 104, 113
Larkin, J., 20, 27
Lauber, J.K., 144, 158
Lave, J., 132, 135, 136, 137, 155, 158, 159
Lederer, 117, 126
Li, Z., 36, 44
Lin, Y., 23, 27
Lincoln, J.E., 174, 203
Lines, 104, 112
Linn, R.L., 12, 15
Lintern, G., 61, 80-82, 83, 92, 93, 159
Lyon, J.D., 230, 234
Macfarlane, R., 92
Marks, D.F., 227, 230, 234
Mauk, R., 82, 93
Mauriño, D., 128
McCormick, E.J., 3, 16
McDermott, J., 20, 27
McKeachie, W., 23, 27
Merrill, M.D., 16, 21, 27, 36, 44, 102, 103, 104, 112
Miller, A., 145, 159
Montague, W.E., 22, 27, 131, 132, 135, 149, 159
Myrhaug, B., 95, 103
Nash, T., 215, 225
Naveh-Benjamin, M., 23, 27
Newall, A.A., 16
Nolan, M.D., 61, 92
North, A.A., 7, 16
Nygaard, K., 95, 103
O'Neal, A.F., 35, 43, 104, 113
O'Neil, H.F., 131, 159
O'Hare, D., 265, 271
Olsen, J.B., 30, 38, 43
Ortega, K.A., 135, 159

Osgood, C.E., 131, 159
Pariès, J., 163, 170
Parker, D.L., 61, 92
Pearson, M., 144, 159
Perry, P., 151, 156
Phelan, P., 78, 92
Phillips, D.C. 135, 159
Pines, A.L., 17, 27
Povenmire, H.K., 61, 92
Pressien, B.Z., 155, 158
Prince, C., 82, 83, 91
Prince, C., 82, 91
Purcell, J.A., 135, 138, 153, 160
Quaintance, M.K., 83, 91
Ramsden, P., 22, 23, 26
Rayman, 251, 253
Reason, J., 260, 263, 271
Redding, R.E., 135, 138-140, 153, 159, 160
Reigeluth, C.M., 92
Reimann, P., 135, 160
Resnick, L.B., 135, 139, 156, 160
Robertson, J., 38, 43
Robson, David, 95, 103
Rogers, D.H., 104, 113
Rolfe, J., 131, 160, 267, 271
Roscoe, S. N., 7, 16, 61, 69, 80, 82, 91, 92, 93
Ross, M.J., 61, 93
Ryder, J.M., 135, 138, 139, 153, 160
Salas, E., 82, 83, 91, 140, 143, 149, 155, 160
Sanders, M.S., 3, 16
Schneider, W., 134, 138, 160
Schnitz, J.E., 30, 44
Schön, D.A., 255, 260
Seamster, T.L., 135, 138, 153, 159, 160
Sharp, C., 230, 234

Shelton, M., 34, 44
Shepherd, W.T., 174, 204
Sheppard, D.J., 61, 82, 92, 93
Shuell, T. J., 17, 27
Siegler, R.S., 22, 27
Simon, C.W., 134, 160
Simon, D.P., 20, 27
Simon, H.A., 16, 20, 27
Singer, M.J., 62, 82, 91
Smith, D., 144, 159
Smith. A.F., 227, 234
Sperandio, J.C., 230, 235
Spring, C., 23, 27
Spurgeon, P., 230, 234
Stager, P., 174, 204
Stark, E.A., 62, 82, 93
Steele, G.L., 95, 103
Stolurow, L.M., 31, 36, 42, 44
Stroustrup, Bjarne, 95, 103
Suppes, P. 31, 44
Swezey, R.W., 140, 143, 160
Tannenbaum, S.I., 149, 155
Taylor, F.V.,173, 204
Tennyson, R.D., 102, 103
Telfer, R., 90, 93, 119, 120, 126, 129, 160

Thomley, K.E., 82, 93
Thorndike, E.L.,.131, 160
Trautmann, K., 230, 234
Trollip, S.R., 104, 113117, 126
Waki, R., 104, 113
Welford, A.T., 228, 234
Wendon, A, 25, 27
Wenger H., 136, 137, 159
Wertsch, J.V., 155, 160
West, L.H.T., 17, 27
Westra, D.P., 82, 93
Whitfield, D., 230, 234
Wielinga, B.J., 22, 27
Wiener E.L., 128, 130, 143, 147, 156, 158, 160
Wightman, D.C., 80, 81,82, 93
Williams Jnr, A. C., 61, 91
Williges, B.H.,61, 91
Wilson, T., 119, 126
Winograd, T., 136, 160
Wise, J.A., 174, 204
Wittrock, M.C., 22, 27
Yates, K.E., 61, 92
Zhang, J., 36, 44

# Subject index

*ab initio* 4, 13, 60, 61, 82, 105, 126, 129, 137, 144, 146, 162, 164, 166, 167, 169, 232, 242, 272-274, 277
accident 39, 78, 80, 118, 124, 127, 196, 200, 201, 203, 246, 257-272, 274, 281
    rates 70, 257, 272, 276
    investigators 80, 257-260, 262, 263
Advanced Qualification Program (AQP) 49, 129, 156
air traffic control 3, 8, 160, 173-195, 197, 199-205, 214, 224-227, 229-235
    air traffic controllers 8, 179, 183, 189, 229, 230, 231, 234, 240, 242, 248
aircraft manufacturers 8, 47-49, 117
airlines 8, 11, 50, 78, 79, 105, 108, 110, 117-119, 120-122, 124-126, 153, 162, 163, 164-167, 169, 170, 211, 229, 248, 250, 260, 261, 266, 267, 272, 274
appraisal 17, 18, 21, 234, 271
apprenticeship 32-35, 137, 257
    cognitive 33
assessment 11, 13-15, 18, 28, 33, 51, 55, 87, 90, 101, 113, 117, 123-125, 135, 169, 184, 192, 203, 206, 209, 211, 212, 216, 245, 248, 279, 280, 282, 283, 285, 286, 288, 289, 295, 301-303
attitudes 10, 13, 68, 82, 83, 130, 145, 168, 188, 191, 193, 203, 216, 222, 223, 266, 273, 274, 279, 280, 282, 285-302
authority 9, 97, 205, 252, 264
    aviation 68, 69, 71, 265
    Civil Aviation Authority 119, 126, 164, 242
    command 9
    inspectors 61

New Zealand Qualifications Authority 87
automation 90, 128, 150, 181, 183, 195, 211, 216, 224, 225, 275, 276

certification 35-37, 41, 42, 52-55, 57, 106, 131, 174, 176, 179, 190, 204, 243, 247, 268
checklist 84, 111, 125, 197, 199, 286, 287, 289, 291, 292, 294-302
coaching 33, 112, 142, 213, 215
command 9-11, 13, 49, 149, 153, 164, 187, 263, 267, 276
communication 4, 36, 55, 72, 78, 111, 119, 120, 122, 124, 150, 151, 177, 185, 186, 196, 199, 211, 252, 253, 261, 299, 300
competency 7, 13, 15, 16, 61, 76, 86, 157, 164, 169, 232, 241, 244
   analysis 10
   assessment 51
   based 37, 39
   specification 10-12, 14
computer 44, 48, 74, 75, 87, 93, 102, 105-109, 148, 160, 163, 179, 181, 186, 187, 192, 194, 195, 199, 200, 202
   applications 53
   assisted 43, 44
   based administration 30
   based aviation courseware 52
   based curriculum 53
   based instruction 13, 28-31, 50, 57, 58, 105, 112, 113, 168
   based learning 5, 47-49, 56, 217
   based technologies 48
   based testing 16, 170
   based training 16, 48, 58, 94, 104, 109, 119, 168, 215, 251
   equipment 52, 69, 75
   managed instruction 28, 30, 34, 35, 43
   network 42
   phobia 75
crew coordination 4, 157
crew resource management 120, 121, 128, 130, 143, 146, 148, 162, 259, 263, 270
criteria 19, 25, 26, 67, 68, 127, 130, 131, 139, 146, 147, 164, 184, 202, 205, 206, 208, 214, 224, 258, 273
culture 48, 155, 158, 166, 277
   corporate 34, 48, 75, 121, 273, 274

decision making 6, 10, 12, 16, 31, 64, 77, 79, 84, 120, 122, 124, 125, 157, 164, 182, 186, 229, 231, 273, 284-286, 293, 294

education 3-5, 10, 15, 25-27, 29, 41, 43, 44, 57, 59, 62, 74, 76, 87, 90, 103, 112, 113, 117, 120, 121, 126, 155-159, 161, 162, 164-167, 207, 216, 224, 226, 240, 251, 253, 273, 274, 276, 277
evaluation 3, 4, 7, 12, 15, 25, 35, 49, 53, 58, 61, 62, 73, 87, 90, 92, 93, 109, 111, 121, 122, 124-126, 149, 153, 176, 182, 188, 190, 199, 213, 217, 219,

279, 280, 289, 291, 292, 294-303

feedback  18, 24, 38, 39, 52-53, 87, 90, 104, 111-113, 122, 123, 143, 147, 149, 151, 153, 188, 192, 193, 216, 229, 245, 261, 270, 279, 283, 287

human error  127, 128, 176, 181, 189, 196, 197, 200, 263, 271

instruction  3-7, 12-15, 27-32, 34-40, 42-44, 50-52, 58, 61, 62, 64, 66, 76, 78, 81, 83, 85, 87, 93, 95, 101, 103, 105, 107, 108, 111-113, 117, 119, 120, 125, 126, 131, 132, 135, 138, 149, 151, 156, 157, 159, 160, 168, 170, 178, 183, 192, 198, 203, 214, 219, 221, 233, 240, 258, 270, 274, 275, 279, 280, 282, 283, 285, 286, 302

instructional
  conditions 5, 63, 74, 75
  design, 3, 6, 10, 11, 16, 26-29, 47, 49, 50-53, 56, 83, 94, 131, 192
  fidelity 65, 66, 68, 84,
  methods 5, 35, 198
  objectives  6, 12, 24, 25, 29, 43, 53, 56, 100, 101, 125
  psychology 4, 27
  resources 5, 6, 15, 101
  strategies 6, 29, 47, 50, 51, 53-54, 56, 101
  system 6, 15, 47-49, 64
  system design (ISD) 6, 47-50, 52, 56, 159, 160
  templates 53, 56, 57

integration  18, 33, 39, 54, 76, 81, 118, 119, 123, 126, 129, 130, 138, 143, 146, 151, 152, 155, 246, 280

knowledge  4-7, 9, 10, 13-15, 17-27, 29, 30, 32-34, 36, 37, 41, 44, 52, 62, 70, 76, 79, 89, 102, 117, 118, 128-130, 132, 134-139, 141, 151-153, 155-158, 161, 162, 164, 173-177, 179-184, 188, 191-194, 196, 202, 203, 206, 208, 213, 214, 216, 217, 220-224, 231, 241, 244, 246, 252, 257-260, 264, 269, 270, 273-277, 279-282, 284-302
  base 7, 9, 10, 15, 17, 26, 36
  structures  7-10, 21, 22, 135, 137

latent failures 260, 261
learner control 51, 52, 54, 56, 57
learning objectives 50, 51
learning theory  5, 6, 26, 130, 131, 134, 137, 139, 157
lexical loop 30
locus of initiative 36

medicine  35, 161, 162, 170, 234, 239-253, 260
memory  26, 27, 152, 182, 187, 201, 226, 227, 229, 296
  long term 9, 22, 227, 230
  short term 230, 264
  working 22, 23

simulation  37, 43, 52, 53, 57, 59, 61-63, 66, 67, 73-75, 79, 80, 87, 90-107, 109-113, 120, 132,

138, 141, 144, 156, 156, 158, 159, 168, 184, 189, 192, 233, 250, 251
simulator  12, 32, 47, 52, 53, 57, 59, 60, 69, 71-76, 79, 81-88, 90-93, 111, 121, 123-125, 129, 131, 133, 144, 146-148, 151, 155, 162, 163, 168, 212, 215, 217, 219, 220, 231, 251, 274
situated learning  32, 34, 136-140, 153, 159
skill acquisition  60, 63, 64, 67, 80, 82, 83, 90, 101, 102, 228
skill maintenance  60, 63, 64, 67, 83, 90
stress  72, 80, 110, 120, 188, 189, 193, 202, 224, 240, 245 248, 250, 262, 279, 286-290, 294, 300, 302
syllabus  38, 39, 60, 61, 67, 70, 76, 77, 80, 83, 85, 86, 89, 112, 119, 120, 126, 128-130, 133, 140, 196, 231, 232, 240, 243, 244, 252, 260, 280

task analysis  24, 29, 38, 136-140, 152, 153, 155, 159, 160, 183
task fidelity  63, 64, 66,67, 73
trainers  4, 11, 25, 26, 60, 61, 69, 74, 78, 81, 86, 92, 118, 121, 159, 212, 214, 215, 233, 241, 258, 273
  generic  7, 68
  part task  64, 82, 99, 118,
  procedural  66, 69, 133
transaction shells  44, 47, 53-54, 57

work model  38, 39, 43